The Deepest Human Life

THE DEEPEST HUMAN LIFE

An Introduction to Philosophy for Everyone

SCOTT SAMUELSON

THE UNIVERSITY OF CHICAGO PRESS   Chicago and London

The University of Chicago Press, Chicago 60637
The University of Chicago Press, Ltd., London
© 2014 by The University of Chicago
All rights reserved. Published 2014.
Paperback edition 2015
Printed in the United States of America

23 22 21 20 19 18 17 16 15   3 4 5 6 7

ISBN-13: 978-0-226-13038-5 (cloth)
ISBN-13: 978-0-226-27277-1 (paper)
ISBN-13: 978-0-226-13041-5 (e-book)
DOI: 10.7208/chicago/9780226130415.001.0001

Library of Congress Cataloging-in-Publication Data

Samuelson, Scott, author.
    The deepest human life : an introduction to
philosophy for everyone / Scott Samuelson.
        pages cm
    Includes bibliographical references and index.
    ISBN 978-0-226-13038-5 (cloth : alkaline paper)—
ISBN 978-0-226-13041-5 (e-book)   1. Philosophy.
I. Title.
    B74.S26 2014
    100—dc23
                              2013032855

♾ This paper meets the requirements of
ANSI/NISO Z39.48–1992 (Permanence of Paper).

The deepest human life is everywhere, is eternal.

William James

CONTENTS

PRELUDE ON LIGHT POLLUTION
AND THE STARS

We had the sky, up there, all speckled with stars, and we used to lay on our backs and look up at them, and discuss about whether they was made, or only just happened—Jim allowed they was made, but I allowed they happened; I judged it would have took too long to make so many. Jim said the moon could a laid them; well, that look kind of reasonable, so I didn't say nothing against it, because I've seen a frog lay most as many, so of course it could be done. We used to watch the stars that fell too, and see them streak down. Jim allowed they'd got spoiled and was hove out of the nest.

MARK TWAIN

An ever-growing number of people have their view of the sky obstructed by the light pollution of our cities. Some go years without once gawking at the moon or the stars. It's an apt metaphor of our whole human situation. There's a haunting line by Kabir, the mysterious fifteenth-century Indian poet, a kind of mystical Mother Goose: "They squander their birth in isms."[1] He's thinking of the few major religious traditions of his day, but the idea applies even more poignantly to our collection of religions, political affiliations, spiritualities, identities fabricated by marketers, and even theories constructed in philosophy departments. The glow of these beliefs, at their best, can guide us through life. But they often amount to a kind of light pollution. The feeling of possessing knowledge can be the worst enemy of the truth. Beliefs and theories, and the identities associated with them, are as indispensable and fascinating as politics, but they are, from the perspective of true philosophy, at worst impediments and at best starting and stopping points of a much larger journey, which involves going off into the darkness once in a while and taking a good long look at what shines above us.

The story I have to tell is about how, in the words of William James, "the deepest human life is everywhere."[2] The coordinates of a meaningful life—the stars, in my analogy—are there for any of us to see and puzzle out. The questions, stories, and injunctions of the great philosophers aren't the speeches of angels loafing in their celestial abodes. Even the most formidable thinkers speak to us out of lives pretty much like our own, with their daily routines, their little aches and pains and pleasures, and their occasional upheavals. Their feet have no more wings than yours or mine.

This book is my attempt to bring philosophy down from its ethereal theorizing and put it back on the earth where it belongs, among wrestlers and chiropractors, preschool music teachers and undertakers, soldiers and moms, chefs and divorcées, Huck and Jim—you and me, in fact.

*

When I was sixteen years old, I stumbled on Thomas Aquinas's five ways of proving the existence of God. As I read his precise, exulted prose in the Iowa City Public Library, two feelings overwhelmed me: first, the idea of proving God was by far the greatest thing a human being could do; second, I no longer believed in God. Not that I had a clue what Aquinas was saying: I read the proofs with sublime incomprehension. I believed—illogically, wrongly, thrillingly—that to pronounce on the existence of God somehow proved that we were capable of inventing God. I was certain through all my adolescent uncertainty that whatever he was doing was the height of human achievement. I wanted in. Socrates, in the beginning of Plato's *Republic*, tempts his interlocutors into an extended conversation about justice by asking them to collaborate in the founding of a city. Thomas Aquinas, against his intentions, was tempting me into the founding of the universe. Though I hadn't read more than a page of philosophy, though I didn't even understand the page I read, I wanted to be a philosopher.

A little over a decade later, I was finishing a PhD in philosophy at Emory University. The obvious path before me was to drift into a full-time position at a decent institution, work my dissertation into a book, zero in on a specialty, publish some articles and reviews, and lick the necessary wingtips to get tenure. But some sense of destiny (I would have never called it that then) kept me from ever taking such a path seriously. Though I'd proven myself capable of publishing articles and giving papers in the world of philosophy, I rebelled against the prospect of a microspecialty and the bureaucracy of tenure. Moreover, I hadn't gotten into philosophy in order to become a scholar of philosophy, however wonderful and necessary the work of scholarship can be.

When my mother called me from Iowa saying that she'd read in the local classifieds that Kirkwood Community College had a full-time philosophy position open, it seemed a reasonable way to get health insurance. The saying "a job is a job" is particularly poignant for philosophers. Diogenes of Sinope, one of our profession's early practitioners, used to beg money from statues. When asked why, he replied, "In order to get used to being refused." But he didn't have a pregnant wife. And neither my wife nor I really wanted to live in a barrel and relieve ourselves outside, as were Diogenes's customs.

Another decade later, my wife and two kids were sound asleep upstairs, and I was alone in the *selva oscura* (the "dark wood," a phrase from Dante's *Comedy*, which to someone with as little Italian as me initially looks like the "obscure self"), staring at the fire in our stove's belly, reflecting on the question of my destiny: exactly the activity I preach to my students, exactly the activity I'd been avoiding as assiduously as they do. You see, earlier that night, someone at a dinner party had had the gall to ask me, "Are you fulfilling your destiny?" The rude question was partially my fault. I'd brought up the subject of destiny, inspired by my recent perusal of the *Mahabharata*, the gargantuan Sanskrit epic of ancient India (it's about three times as long as the Bible), which narrates the fratricidal war between the Pandavas and the Kauravas. To talk abstractly about destiny may be boring or fascinating, but to be asked if you're fulfilling your destiny has an archer's precision in piercing to the heart of the matter. I'd hemmed and hawed, wiggling out of an honest answer like only someone trained in philosophy can do. But now, before the fire, I had only myself to confront.

My initial morose thoughts were that I should be doing more with my talents. As much as I loved teaching at a community college, it was, after all, a community college. Friends of mine at more prestigious institutions, my family, even some of my students, had all prodded me, with various degrees of subtlety, to work on advancing my academic career: a path my choices in life had essentially made vanish. My dark thoughts wandered—though maybe that's the wrong verb—to a story from the *Mahabharata*, the very story that had provoked the bewildering question of my destiny after I'd told it at the dinner party.

A certain Ekalavya, a member of the most despised outcaste tribe, asks to study archery with the great guru Drona. Arjuna, the hero of the *Bhagavad Gita* (one short chapter of the *Mahabharata*), becomes through Drona's tutelage the greatest archer in the world. But Drona disdainfully turns down Ekalavya, despite his considerable talents because the smelly presence of an outcaste would upset the other students. So, Ekalavya goes off to a secluded place in the woods and carves a little sculpture of Drona, which he sets up as an idol to oversee his solitary practice with bow and arrow.

One day Arjuna is out hunting. His dog runs off into the woods and starts yipping at the outcaste archer, who gets irritated and sends off a volley of arrows so expertly that without causing injury they instantaneously plug the dog's mouth. The dog runs back to his master, who looks in awe at the gagged beast. Arjuna then sulks back to Drona and whines, "You told me you'd make me the greatest archer in the world." "And I have," the teacher responds. Arjuna points dejectedly at his pet, obviously the work of someone greater.

Drona and Arjuna head back to the woods to find out what's going on. They discover and watch in amazement the lone archer practicing with his carved idol of the great teacher. Finally, Drona goes up to him and asks, "Am I your teacher?" The archer bows deeply, honored by the guru's presence, and says, "Of course you are." In India at the time it was customary that teachers weren't paid until after they'd successfully taught their students; but after graduation they could ask for any fee they saw fit. So, the teacher says, "Your abilities prove that you have graduated, and now I ask for my payment." Even more deeply honored, the student says, "Whatever you ask, teacher." To which Drona responds, "I ask for your right thumb."

Ekalavya takes out his knife, unhesitatingly chops off his right thumb, and gives it to the teacher, who then turns to Arjuna and says, "There, now you're the greatest archer in the world."

What's the story of Ekalavya about? A teacher who chooses the elite over the common. A student who offers the teacher a fulfillment of his calling. The possibilities of participating in the highest economy of education. The psychological blockages that prevent such participation. The brutal tragedy caused by the stupid divisions we draw. The story, it seemed, fragmented into two clear images: the possible me and the real me. I'd chosen to teach Ekalavya, but something in me was clinging to the prejudices of Drona.

Suddenly, out of the darkness of my obscure self, moments of the past ten years began flickering: self-forgetful times when I was in the presence of philosophy, not philosophy as a professional activity, but philosophy as it really is: the search for wisdom, a way of life. My mind beamed with faces of soldiers, housewives, plumbers, nurses, future professors, prisoners, sanitation workers, kindergarten teachers, cancer patients; any number of souls whose current or future profession I never knew; real people of all ages and degrees of literacy, hung up on the very questions—the very same questions—that shaped the tradition I'd been inspired to join after reading five proofs of God. If Simone Weil is right that "absolutely unmixed attention is prayer," then I had been in the presence of God during multiple conversations that took place on my classroom's hideous carpet.[3] The stars were beginning to shine.

I used to read Plato's portrayal of Socrates's conversations and lament that they were inconceivable in our age. Now, whenever I read the passage in the *Apology*, where Socrates questions the luminaries of Athens only to conclude that he's the wisest of all, because at least he knows that he knows nothing, I think of my student Jillian, a nurse's aide, who, though she'd never read Plato, reenacted that very story at the hospital where she worked. When I read Epictetus, the eloquent Stoic philosopher of the first century, I think of James Stockdale in the twentieth century, who maintained his sanity and even his happiness while being tortured in a prison camp by means of what he remembered of Epictetus from Philosophy 6: The Problems of Good and Evil with Professor Philip Rhinelander. I can't think of Kant's moral philosophy without recalling a middle-aged mother who asked me with tears in her eyes if Kant was right. For every philosopher I've taught I've found at least one student whose soul faithfully returns an echo. The teacher has learned from his students that the likes of Plato and Kant are more than the root of complex isms.

The typical way of conceiving destiny is that what seems chancy is clandestinely ordered and rational. But it's stranger than that. As my fire glowed, and I glimpsed my life in the sudden light of destiny, randomness and rationality seemed synonymous, just two words stuttering after the same reality, two faces made by the same face.

Certain internal patterns can pour out of us and make sense of time's zigzags and vicissitudes. All those students who'd been situated by chance, a.k.a. destiny, in the rickety desks before my cheap metal podium formed into a momentous set of constellations, if looked at right.

*

What follows is nothing more or less than the practice of the philosophical life—in part, the story of my own journey, not simply in the sense of personal reminiscences, though I do recount a few, but an exploration of a memory shaped in large part by staring at books and talking to companions about the things of the spirit. I relate the stories and ideas of some great philosophers to the lives of myself, my students, and my friends. In a larger sense, this book is about the journey of philosophy itself, an intensely personal journey that has become the journey of human civilization. The chapters proceed both thematically and historically. Thematically, they're organized around four questions built into the structure of the rational animal. What is philosophy? What is happiness? Is knowledge of God possible? And, what is the nature of good and evil? Historically, the chapters leap from mountaintop to mountaintop (the image is Nietzsche's), beginning with the ancients and proceeding across the ages to the present—in its own way, the collective quest of Western culture. I don't ignore the great religious traditions, which are intimately bound up with philosophy. There is, I hope to demonstrate, an underlying pattern to the search for wisdom, even though the quest often leads to fascinatingly different places. I'm inclined to think that the shape of our individual quests is written roughly in the history of civilization and that the entire journey of civilization is more or less encoded in each of us.

Though philosophy sometimes needs a fire and solitude, it's most fully present in dialogue with others, some possessed by a desire for the truth, most adamant about their fragment of it, like the blind folks in the Sufi fable who have each felt one part of the unfamiliar elephant. I've found philosophy, the real thing, even among those who roll their eyes and nod off at their desks. In one of those foundational paradoxes, I'm never more a student of philosophy than when my blazer is smeared with chalk dust.

PART 1 * *What Is Philosophy?*

How—I didn't know any
word for it—how "unlikely"
ELIZABETH BISHOP

"I see, my dear Theaetetus," Socrates says, "that Theodorus had a true insight into your nature when he said that you were a philosopher, for wonder is the feeling of a philosopher, and philosophy begins in wonder."[1] Samuel Taylor Coleridge adds a touch of poetry to the point, "In Wonder all philosophy began: in Wonder it ends: and Admiration fills up the interspace."[2]

"Wonder" is a wondrous word, suggestive of both puzzlement and awe. Pursuing little mysteries—like why a stick appears broken in water, or why the neighbors believe something different about God, or if you see the same colors as everyone else, or why we're always fighting—has shaken up entire lives and entire civilizations. Older students of mine often remark, with a mixture of reverence and disdain, that philosophy reminds them of their little kids' habit of asking why, why, why. The wonderings of childhood, which help civilization to be absorbed and remade, are definitely of a piece with the stern texts of Aristotle and Kant.

My hunch is that even our little intellectual puzzlements flow from a more basic awe. Often this initial awe pertains to the meaningful root of words like "morality," "happiness," "evil," "beauty," "love." We suddenly experience what those words really point to and are compelled to try to understand them. Marguerite Yourcenar has written, "There are souls that make you believe in the soul."[3] There are also beautiful experiences that make you believe in beauty, evil events that make you believe in evil, and a few rare moments that convince you of the reality of happiness. If philosophy isn't to degenerate into pointless bickering, it's important for us to remember and seek out these sacred manifestations.

There's an even deeper awe at—for lack of a better word—*everything*. Let me explain by relating an initial wonderment of my own.

I must have been about ten years old, and was over at my friend's house. Being two grades ahead of me and hence keener on girls, he thought that we should practice our kissing techniques, using pillows as dummy girlfriends. So there I was, face smooshing around in a strange pillow—for all I knew, a butt of one of my friend's jokes. Somewhere in the darkness of the linen, trying to imagine a certain classmate's blonde curls and sea-blue eyes, my consciousness inexplicably broke and spilled into the eeriest experience, stranger even than kissing, where everything felt extremely iffy. Why does anything exist? Why should I have been born? Who am I? What great cosmic mystery led to my making smooching noises into a pillow? By the same logic, why did the sun, which warms our planet so nicely, catch fire? How could there be other minds, full of the same feelings and questions, haunting the people around me? How could there be strangers? How does time move? Why does time move? Why did another of my friends have to get hit by a speeding car, puff like a horrible balloon, and die? It was as if I'd fallen through some wormhole in the pillow and entered into the numinous zone before creation, where God was scratching His head over possible worlds.

Yes, I was filled with intellectual puzzlements. Even though I was long years from reading philosophy, I managed to formulate the problem in the words of the great metaphysicians: Why is there anything rather than nothing? I know, because when I cracked Martin Heidegger's *Introduction to Metaphysics* as a pretentious seventeen-year-old, I was floored to find my deep bafflement so coolly expounded. But the experience involved more than the formulation of intellectual puzzles; it was as if those questions were jolting through my nervous system with supernatural electricity. I felt all the variations on why and how as one big holy creepiness. My hunch is that all the philosophical perplexities of the past three millennia are contained in such experiences, like how the five hundred generations of an oak's leaves are bound up in an acorn, or how the whole universe is present, if the physicists are right, in three minutes worth of exploding matter.

Being one of those timeless times, I don't know how long it lasted or quite why it ended: I probably just needed to take a breath. In any case, I emerged from the pillow, reoriented myself to the tenuous existence of my friend's bedroom, and in my naïveté tried exuberantly to tell my friend, whose lungs had held out no longer than my own, about my time travel to the beginning of everything. I'll always be grateful to him for what he said. His words were the germ of my whole future in philosophy. He shrugged in the nonchalant way of a companion, "Oh yeah, I've felt that before, too."

1 Portrait of You as Odysseus

A Dialogue between two Infants in the womb concerning the state of this world, might handsomely illustrate our ignorance of the next, whereof methinks we yet discourse in Platoes denne, and are but Embryon Philosophers.

SIR THOMAS BROWNE

"What is philosophy?" Dr. Donald Livingston used to ask us graduate students. After a numbing pause, this old southern gentleman in various crinkled hues of white, a bright handkerchief spilling disconcertingly far out of his breast pocket, would then muse in his sonorous drawl, "If a biologist asks, 'What is biology?' he is no longer doing biology. There is no mathematical formula that answers the question, 'What is mathematics?' But when we philosophers wonder what we're doing, we're doing our job." But let's begin with the more burning question for most of my students: What is class participation?

Fearing the silences of the dazed classroom, I used to follow the custom of giving a certain number of "participation points," which could be earned exclusively by asking and answering questions in class. In my first year teaching philosophy at Kirkwood, I had in class a woman about my age who spent each period scrutinizing me in silence from her cheap desk in the rear of the room. As I'd bumble through lectures and discussions, her stony gaze never left me. But no matter how hard I'd try to stare her down after my most riveting question, she never participated.

Maybe because her brow spoke unmistakably of having earned her bread by its sweat, I began to second-guess myself, imagining that she was stewing to herself, "Who does he think he is, lecturing me on life?" or, "Unbelievable they pay him to do this." Sometimes I consoled myself that she wasn't thinking much of anything, that she was simply punching the clock and struggling to understand enough basics to pass and move a rung up the economic ladder.

I teach a lot of students, upward of 125 a semester; so it's hard for me at first to affix names to faces without the advantage of the notes I scribble on my attendance sheet. It wasn't until I passed back the first assignment that it dawned on me that this was Deanne Folkmann, the author of the best paper by a long shot. Though a little rough around the edges, hers was the only essay that demonstrated a nuanced sense of the text, that quoted and reflected on passages we never talked about, that beamed with the unfakeable glow of real thinking. It was not a prelude to a career in philosophy. It was philosophy.

Other than the greatest thing of all, putting a good book in someone's hands, I'm not sure how much I did for her as a teacher that semester. What I had first taken for punching the clock was in fact a monk-like silence. She was taking in whatever bits of knowledge I dispensed and then revisiting Plato, Epictetus, and Kant in order to illuminate her life. She believed, naively and correctly, that Plato, Epictetus, and Kant could be of service. She reminded me of the sunlit world of philosophy, the world that dawned on me when I first held all the wisdom of Thomas Aquinas in my ignorant hands.

I wish I'd kept her papers. Nowadays, as a more experienced teacher, I'd pull her aside and ask her to tell me about herself. Maybe it's just as well our dialogue went on indirectly, though something in me longs to have heard her voice. At least I had the presence of mind to jot down in my journal what she wrote at the end of her final, the sole personal note she ever struck with me, so personal I almost can hear something of her voice's timbre in it:

> I've realized my quest for knowledge will take me away from my job as a factory worker. For many of my coworkers the paycheck is enough. It's been enough for me at times. Not anymore. Knowledge can take me on a journey to places I can't yet imagine. Strange, but philosophy has made my job more bearable, and it's also made it somehow unbearable. Powerful words to live by: "An unexamined life is not worth living."

That's class participation.

*

We often define human beings as the "rational animal," the sole thing on this earth with the capacity to reason. Michel de Montaigne, one of the wiser human beings who ever lived, tells the story of a fox that inched close to a frozen river and then put his ear to the ice—presumably because if a current was audible, the ice would be too thin and treacherous to walk on. Wasn't the fox, Montaigne wonders, performing a kind of deduction? Doesn't the fox's syllogism—if I can hear water, the ice is too thin; I can hear water; therefore, the ice is too thin—prove that foxes are also "rational animals"?[1]

Once I was watching a feisty young cat by the name of Georgiana who had just discovered that she could climb a certain tree to the tiptop. One time, to her delight, the squirrel she was chasing ran up that very tree. The squirrel got to the topmost branch and realized that he could go no farther. Looking down, he saw the cat darting confidently nearer; then he turned and looked down at the ground, perhaps thirty or forty feet below; then he cast one more glance back at Georgiana. Wasn't that squirrel doing some split-second reasoning? After looking back and forth a few more quick times, the squirrel jumped—with an almost hopeless abandon—and plummeted gracelessly toward the ground. Didn't the squirrel *calculate* his best chance of survival? Isn't the squirrel also, then, a rational animal?

Now, maybe our fox and squirrel were simply acting on instinct. But even if we believe, as Montaigne and I do, that they were performing a mental calculation, we can still distinguish human rationality from animal reckoning. Rationality, at least as it was intended by Aristotle when he defined us as the *zoon logikon* (the rational animal), is more than calculation. Our rationality involves a strange looping in our nature. We're capable of revising our very being, of reordering our values, of turning our calculating abilities back on ourselves. This looping is perhaps most dramatic at the level of politics, where we occasionally engage in revolutions. As yet, there's not been a Marxist honeybee who tried to organize his fellow worker bees to overthrow that queen who's always exploiting their labor. Wolves may fight for who should be the alpha of the pack, but it has never occurred to them to organize their packs into a larger unit that would be governed by a majority show of paws. But we do just such things, and not just in times of revolution. We all ask, "Who am I? What am I supposed to be doing with my life?" And the very act of asking transforms us. We sometimes even wonder if life is worth living at all. Hamlet's famous soliloquy is not, after all, the speech of a madman. The squirrel's internal monologue began,

> To die by claw for sure or else to live
> After the fall perhaps: that is my question,

not, "To be or not to be." By the way, the squirrel lived and limped off as Georgiana looked on from the windy heights with indignant disbelief.

The overarching goals of our fellow animals are pretty clear to them: eat, sleep, protect the pack, stretch, et cetera. If and when they "reason," it is to calculate how to attain those goals. We, too, inherit a complex of similar goals; we, too, spend a lot of time figuring out what to eat for dinner. But we also have the ability to question our goals, to change our minds, and to measure how meaningful our lives are against our conceptions. Through tools, images, and words, we extend who we are into a relatively open space that then curves back on itself. We are, so to speak, the philosophical animal.

Admittedly, philosophy is not the only way we participate in our rationality. Another important—fundamental—way in which we turn our unique power onto ourselves occurs in poetry, art, and music. Inspiration aids us in defining a style of human existence. This musical expression of rationality comes to full bloom in religion, which is God's revelation of a way of life, at least according to the religious believer. But it also includes the overlapping practices we now call culture: our way of life—"ours" not because any of us individually thought it out or even, most of the time, consciously assented to it, but simply because we were born into it and it feels natural.

In the fifth century BC, the common funerary custom of the Greeks was to cremate their dead. Not too far away in India, the Callations' practice was to eat theirs. Once, Darius, the great Persian king, gathered representatives of both groups and asked how much money he could give the Greeks to eat their forebears and how much he could give the Callations to set their dearly departed on fire. No amount of money was sufficient for either group. (Is there a price for which you would take even one nibble of your dead uncle's flesh?)

Each, as you might imagine, was deeply offended that the king would even suggest something so contrary to "nature." Herodotus, who reports all this, draws the conclusion that "if one were to offer men to choose out of all the customs in the world such as seemed to them the best, they would examine the whole number, and end by preferring their own."[2]

Yet everyone does discover, like the Greeks and Callations, that there are different kinds of music, different ways of expressing our humanity. When it dawns on us that there are religions other than our own, that peoples of other cultures have formulated startlingly different images, stories, and rituals in which to encapsulate their humanity, we stand on the brink of philosophy. As the philosopher al-Ghazali observed a thousand years ago, "the children of Christians always grew up embracing Christianity, and the children of Jews always grew up adhering to Judaism, and the children of Muslims always grew up following the religion of Islam."[3] As soon as we wonder, "So who's right—if anybody?"—we enter a new stage of our rationality: philosophy.

*

In a recent article for the *New York Times*, the literary critic Stanley Fish claimed that philosophy is "a special, insular form of thought," and that "its propositions have weight and value only in the precincts of its game."[4] He went on to say that philosophical theses like moral absolutism are at best "rhetorical flourishes" that don't make any difference in how we actually live. As a description of most academic philosophy, his characterization is probably right. Whether in graduate seminars or introductory courses, teachers and students of philosophy often play the game of trying to construct a perfect theory. We criticize weaknesses and inconsistencies in inherited views of goodness, beauty, and truth. We try to construct general explanations. We fidget with questions and answers in the smooth spaces of the mind.

But as a description of real philosophy, Fish's definition is wrong. He makes the common mistake of taking one part of philosophy—the intellectual scrutiny of various positions—for the whole of it, which involves the fullest exercise of our rationality: the seeking out of a meaningful life. Philosophy begins and ends in the realm of plumbers and love and aching backs and hangovers and beauty and painted toenails—in short, the world we regularly confront. Yes, philosophy takes a detour through an often disorienting world of reflection. But all ideas under philosophical discussion, in the end, must be judged on their ability to help us live well.

The great historian of ideas Pierre Hadot has demonstrated that the body of ancient philosophy isn't primarily a bunch of theories but rather a set of spiritual exercises intended to get people back to their true selves. For the ancient Greeks and then Romans, philosophy was anything but "a special, insular form of thought." To engage in philosophy was to commit oneself to the improvement it offered. People turned to philosophies like Stoicism and Epicureanism because their lives were plunged into worries, beliefs, and desires that had alienated them from living good lives. They were after the good life, and philosophy was the discipline of hunting it down.

To some degree, the ancient practice of philosophy in modernity was transformed into a theoretical discipline intended to clarify the concepts of science and morality. But that's not the whole story. I believe that philosophy has never lost its character of being a way of life. When the great modern philosophers wrestled with science and morality, as I will try to show in my later chapters, they had very pressing reasons for doing so. In the seventeenth century, Descartes sought out a certain foundation for knowledge in large part because the world was crumbling around him. In the twentieth century, Hans Jonas reconceptualized God and evil in large part because his mother had been killed at Auschwitz. When a student of mine, a mother who'd authorized a surgery for her son that led to his death, asked me in tears if Kant was right that the consequences of an action play no role in determining its moral worth, I realized quite clearly that evaluating Kantian ethics was much more than a game to be played in the insularity of the mind or the classroom.

When everyday life is deeply satisfying, philosophy is indeed the leisurely activity that Stanley Fish describes, simply a pleasurable exercise of our native desire to know. But when everyday life is less than fully satisfying, there will always be people who set out on a quest for meaning. All of a sudden that leisurely desire to know becomes a pressing desire to find the good life. And when the normal course of everyday life offers very little satisfying to our natures, when we regularly feel the dull aches of bad work, empty leisure, and disoriented politics, then philosophy becomes not just the practice of the few but the need of the many. Such was the situation when regional warlords tore apart ancient China. The warring states period, as it was called, gave birth to the Hundred Schools of Thought, the heyday of Chinese philosophy, in which thinkers like Laozi and Confucius tried to envision a better form of human culture. Such was also the situation in ancient Athens after their defeat by the Spartans in the Peloponnesian War, when their society was plagued by zealous believers and moral relativists. The decline of the Athenian hegemony gave birth to Socrates, Diogenes, Plato, Aristotle, Epicurus, and the Stoics, for whom philosophy was the spiritual practice of living well. Such was also the situation in what we call the early modern period, when Europe was torn apart by warring factions of Protestants and Catholics, the very period that gave us the great modern philosophers who envisioned politics, morality, and science not immediately grounded in factious religion. My hunch is that we're now in a similar boat: if not an empire in decline, we're at least a diffuse civilization of conflicting, often less-than-satisfying social roles. If so, we *need* philosophy.

*

There's a very short story that I believe embodies the mystery of philosophy—and the mystery of being human—in the beloved Chinese book the *Zhuangzi*, which narrates the rambling life and teachings of the eponymous Daoist master.

> Master Zhuang and Master Hui were strolling across the bridge over the Hao River. "The minnows have come out and are swimming so leisurely," said Master Zhuang. "This is the joy of fishes."
> "You're not a fish," said Master Hui. "How do you know what the joy of fishes is?"
> "You're not me," said Master Zhuang, "so how do you know that I don't know what the joy of fishes is."
> "I'm not you," said Master Hui, "so I certainly do not know what you do. But you're certainly not a fish, so it is irrefutable that you do not know what the joy of fishes is."
> "Let's go back to where we started," said Master Zhuang. "When you said, 'How do you know what the joy of fishes is?' you asked me

because you already knew that I knew. I know it by strolling over the Hao."[5]

Master Zhuang (Zhuangzi) and Master Hui (Huizi) symbolize, among other things, two different sides of philosophy, each important in its way. Zhuangzi is wise, funny, religious, poetic, calm. Huizi is logical, serious, prosaic, scientific. However, just like in the famous yin-yang diagram, each contains the seed of the other in him.

The parable begins with an observation that expresses a connection between Zhuangzi and the fish darting up to the surface of the water. It has a simple, musical quality to it. It's the kind of remark we're all apt to say in the presence of other animals, for instance at the zoo, where it's hard to resist seeing our inner lives reflected in the playful, sad, lazing animals. His remark represents the spontaneous way we have of relating to life. Huizi disrupts this spontaneity and questions the validity of its implicit reasoning: enter philosophy. Zhuangzi happily follows this new line of thought and doubles down on Huizi's principle: if one animal can't understand another, how can one human understand another? It's a potentially paralyzing conclusion. All of a sudden we are at the absolute opposite point of where we began. Our spontaneous connection to the world seems far away; now we seem to have no connection to anything at all: maybe nothing makes sense. This, too, is a moment of philosophy.

Huizi timidly admits that he can't know what Zhuangzi is thinking, except that if we accept his principle of exclusion he can't be thinking what the fish are thinking. Rather than continue down this dead end, Zhuangzi returns to the initial observation, only this time with a play on words. Huizi's original question could be more literally translated (so I am told) as, "Whence do you know about the happiness of fish?" It could mean several things. First, "How do you know that?" Second, "I don't think you really do know that." Or third, "Where were you when you realized that?" Zhuangzi playfully disregards the second (intended) meaning and answers the first and the third questions: "I know, because I am here; I know right here by the river." According to Guo Xiang's famous commentary, "Well, what things are born into and what they rejoice in—heaven and earth—cannot change this position, and Yin and Yang cannot take back this livelihood. Therefore, it cannot be called strange if one can know what beings born into the water are happy with from what beings born on land rejoice in."[6] Or, as T.S. Eliot says,

> We shall not cease from exploration
> And the end of all our exploring
> Will be to arrive where we started
> And know the place for the first time.[7]

One of my big points in this book is that real philosophy is an odyssey with distinct stages. It begins in a wondrous and often problematic relationship to common life. It goes through a stage of questioning that leads to a blinding skepticism. Insofar as it continues, there's a moment of illumination, which leads to a form of critical theorizing (this is where professional philosophers often take up residence). But its final destiny is to return to common life and "know the place for the first time." This odyssey is open to anybody. If the beliefs we start from are truly worthwhile, then we shall return to them and know them for the first time; if not, then we'll have to seek out beliefs that work better. We can't know until after we've engaged in philosophy—not simply the academic study of, say, Leibniz, but the real work of examining our life with the high beams of consciousness. Either way, we return invigorated with meaning. Those marvelous lines of Deanne's express the ambiguity of our relationship to our life: "Strange, but philosophy has made my job more bearable, and it's also made it somehow unbearable."

*

At the end of Plato's *Republic,* Socrates tells a myth about what happens to us when we die. He claims that a man by the name of Er was slain in battle, and when his compatriots came to deal with the dead ten days later, his body had not decomposed at all. On his funeral pyre Er miraculously came back to life and relayed in detail what the afterlife is really like. Souls go on a beautiful or horrible journey, depending on how they had lived. At the end of a thousand years, they get to select their next life. Many refuse the life of a human, still bitter about the sufferings of their previous life. Ajax, the strongest of the warriors, chooses to become a lion. The soul of Orpheus, the sweetest of the singers, enters the soft down of a swan's body. Ag-amemnon, who was slain by his wife, turns into an eagle.

Last to choose in Er's story is wily Odysseus, who finds and selects a life neglected by the others, the life of a common person; he boasts that even had he chosen first he would have made the exact same selection. Perhaps, after his legendary journey, he'd come to see the truth of Montaigne's observation that "you can attach the whole of moral philosophy to a commonplace private life just as well as to one of richer stuff," or, as Dorothy puts it at the end of the *Wizard of Oz*, "if I ever go looking for my heart's desire again, I won't look any further than my own backyard; because if it isn't there, I never really lost it to begin with."[8]

You may toil, as Deanne did, in a factory (she's now a nurse, by the way); you may be cruising in a lucrative career; you may be an out-of-work father, a single mother, happily married, or desperately single; you may be or have been a rebellious teen, straight-A nerd, or wallflower; you may have a brain injury; you may even be a professor of philosophy; you surely have quirks, hidden hopes and fears, your own bizarre little ways of loving and passing the time, and a thousand and one other snowflake lacings of the basic patterns; and the soul of Odysseus, inspiration to the most engaging poem ever sung, could well have slipped into your body—*your* body—at birth.

So, let me end this chapter by addressing you as Odysseus, the searcher after a fully human life, the great hero of human rationality, whose cleverness with a wooden horse brought an end to the long Trojan War, who on his way back had to avoid giant cannibals, out-fox the Cyclops, and survive the wrath of the god of the sea, all so he could get back home to Ithaca, the city that symbolizes the truth we're seeking. In the poem "Ithaca," the modern Greek poet Constan-tine Cavafy employs marvelous tact in speaking to Odysseus before his momentous journey, neither completely revealing nor completely concealing the whole truth of what's to come.

> When you set out on your journey to Ithaca,
> pray that the road is long,
> full of adventure, full of knowledge.

Cavafy goes on to say that there's no need to fear things like the blood-drinking Lestrygonians or the man-eating Cyclops, because you'll never encounter them "if you do not carry them within your soul." It's a tactful statement, because Cavafy knows that we do carry them in our souls. We're probably going to have to face them.

> Always keep Ithaca on your mind.
> To arrive there is your ultimate goal.
> But do not hurry the voyage at all.
> It is better to let it last for many years;
> and to anchor at the island when you are old,
> rich with all you have gained on the way,
> not expecting that Ithaca will offer you riches.
>
> Ithaca has given you the beautiful voyage.
> Without her you would have never set out on the road.
> She has nothing more to give you.
>
> And if you find her poor, Ithaca has not deceived you.
> Wise as you have become, with so much experience,
> you must already have understood what these Ithacas mean.[9]

What I love most about Cavafy's poem is that exhortation: "Pray that the road is long."

2 Portrait of Philosophy as Socrates

The indomitable honesty, courage, the love of truth which draw Socrates and us to the summit where, if we too may stand for a moment, it is to enjoy the greatest felicity of which we are capable.   VIRGINIA WOOLF

Though there are a few exceptions (there always are), Cicero's claim has a lot of truth in it: "All philosophers think of themselves, and want others to think of them, as followers of Socrates"—despite the diversity of their systems and beliefs, we might add.[1] I put myself in that long line of philosophers who believe Socrates the wisest, most happy, most just man who ever lived. What Mozart is to music, Socrates is to being human.

Born around 470 BC to Sophroniscus, a stonemason, and Phaenarete, a midwife, Socrates referred to his own philosophical practice as a kind of midwifery, whereby he helped other people give birth to their ideas, though he had no "children"—that is, theories—of his own. A proud citizen of Athens, the great democracy of the ancient world, where citizens participated directly in the governance of the city (though, not unlike our own democracy in its initial form, only land-owning males counted as citizens), he served, by all accounts, with great bravery in the Peloponnesian War. He rarely participated in politics directly, though when he did serve on a jury in a famous trial, one where a set of commanders was being framed, he refused to find them guilty, even though it jeopardized his very life. By the time of his death in 399 BC, he had three young children. His wife Xanthippe, supposedly a shrew, was always complaining (with cause) that Socrates brought home no money for the family. When asked why he agreed to marry such a woman, he replied that horse trainers must practice on the most spirited horses. She likely returned the sentiment.

Socrates's happiness was not the kind we're used to, the kind that glimmers and fades with our circumstances and moods. Maybe it would be better to call it joy, though that word is also misleading in suggesting something other than his steadfast tranquility. It's the joy/happiness/wisdom/justice/well-being/blessedness/shalom/ peace-that-passeth-to-the-edge-of-understanding of one who is completely himself, at ease among any kind of person—zealot, child, slave, poet, drunkard, whore, general, even another philosopher—and able to handle himself with finesse in any situation, even with death breathing down his neck. At one point, when he imagines the after-life, he says he'd like to continue living exactly as he is living now. Johann Wolfgang von Goethe, Germany's closest thing to Shakespeare, once remarked that if he could have just one wish he would choose to be a companion of Socrates for a day. The best description I know of his special felicity comes at the pinnacle of Montaigne's *Essays*:

> Nor is there anything more remarkable in Socrates than the fact that in his old age he finds time to take lessons in dancing and playing instruments, and considers it well spent. This same man was once seen standing in a trance, an entire day and night, in the presence of the whole Greek army, overtaken and enraptured by some deep thought . . . He was seen, when courted by a beauty with whom he was in love, to maintain strict chastity when necessary. He was seen, in the battle of Delium, to pick up and save Xenophon, who had been thrown from his horse. He was constantly seen to march to war and walk the ice barefoot, to wear the same gown in winter and in summer, to surpass all his companions in enduring toil, to eat no differently at a feast than ordinarily. He was seen for twenty-seven years to endure with the same countenance hunger, poverty, the indocility of his children, the claws of his wife; and in the end calumny, tyranny, prison, irons, and poison. But if that man was summoned to a drinking bout by the duty of civility, he was also the one who did the best in the whole army. And he never refused to play cobnut with children, or to ride a hobbyhorse with them, and he did so gracefully; for all actions, says philosophy, are equally becoming and honorable in a wise man.[2]

Socrates left behind as many writings as Jesus—none. We know about him solely through the work of his contemporaries, mainly his student Plato, almost all of whose writings are dialogues starring Socrates. We know about Socrates because of Plato. We know about Plato because of Socrates. In the quartet of dialogues that editors title *The Last Days of Socrates*, Plato uses the history of his teacher's trial and execution to portray the structure and significance of philosophy itself. Philosophy, which seems irreligious, is a deeply holy activity. Philosophy, which seems subversive, is authentically patriotic. Most of all, philosophy, which can strike the elders as corrupting the youth, is the decisive activity for making our lives worthwhile.

YOU GOTTA SERVE SOMEBODY

The *Euthyphro*, the first of the quartet, begins with an ordinary conversation between two men in extraordinary circumstances. Socrates and Euthyphro find themselves before the courthouse, each with business to transact. Socrates is registering for an upcoming trial where he must defend himself against the charges of unholiness and corrupting the youth. Euthyphro's reason for being at the courthouse is juicier. He's going to file charges of murder against his own father! It seems that Euthyphro's servant, in a fit of drunken rage, slit the throat of one his father's servants. The father apprehended the murderous servant, tied him up, threw him in a ditch, and sent for the authorities to find out what should be done to him. In the meantime, the bound servant died.

Euthyphro justifies his case with the claim that he's doing the holy thing in prosecuting his father. He cites Zeus himself as his model, for Zeus also prosecuted his father, so to speak, when he put Cronus in chains for having swallowed his children. Cronus, for that matter, also "prosecuted" his father, castrating Uranus and throwing his severed member into the sea. Socrates zeroes in on Euthyphro's claim and, according to the common pattern of the Socratic dialogues, asks his interlocutor to explain the concept that gives meaning and value to what he's doing—in this case, "What is holiness?"

Some argue that it's unfair of Socrates to ask us to define concepts like love, justice, knowledge, or holiness, for we can know the meaning of words without being able to define them. Yet often the only thing standing between us and the good life is a bad idea. It's hardly unfair to ask for clarity about a word when its proper relationship to life is unclear or in dispute, precisely the times when Socrates does ask. Shall we say of Euthyphro that he knows what holiness is, despite his being unable to define in a satisfactory way the idea of holiness? If so, then what about all those Athenians who profess shock at what he's doing in prosecuting his father—do they, too, know the nature of holiness without being able to define it? What about the Athenians who claim that the Socratic practice of philosophy is unholy—do they also know what holiness is? Or would it be wiser to say that, while all parties may have some thread connecting them to holiness, their inability to speak authoritatively about holiness shows that they in fact don't know what holiness is in all its glory; that their confidence in their embedded knowledge of holiness is exaggerated; that it would be much wiser of them to admit they don't really know and proceed to open their minds to the true nature of their calling?

After some provocation, Euthyphro answers Socrates's question. His response comes in two forms: first, holiness is what pleases the gods; and then, the revised version, holiness is what pleases all the gods. The first answer, on examination, proves problematic because the gods seem to disagree just as much as we do—or, if we adopt a monotheistic conception of the divine, that a single holy text commands different, contradictory things. An eye for an eye. Turn the other cheek. God is just. God is merciful. God demands war. God demands peace. Wisdom is the principle thing. In much wisdom is much grief. Wine is the handiwork of Satan. The thirst of the righteous shall be slaked with wine.

Euthyphro's revised answer, that holiness is what pleases all the gods, raises further questions. What do we do with all the cases where they don't agree? Why do we need many gods (or commandments from God) if they're trustworthy only when they agree? How can we discover what they agree on? Socrates doesn't ask these questions. Instead, he stops playing around and asks—what I would nominate for the greatest question of all time—a question around which much of Western philosophy has been organized. Admittedly, the question doesn't seem so mighty when you first come across it: Do the gods approve of an action because it's holy, or is it holy because they approve of it?

*

Let's approach this majestic riddle by asking a slightly simpler question: What's the most sensible religion?

In another poem by Cavafy called "Infidelity," the poet tells of the wedding banquet of Thetis and Peleus, at which Apollo, the god of prophecy, arises and blesses the newlyweds by promising their offspring a long life untouched by calamity. That child turns out to be Achilles; and as he grows up, his mother eyes him with great tenderness, remembering the god's promise. Of course, he eventually goes off to the Trojan War. One day, some old men arrive at his mother's door with the horrible news that Achilles has been slain in battle. Bereft, Thetis tears at her robes and throws her jewelry on the ground. Suddenly she recalls Apollo's promise and asks what the god was doing when they were slaying her son.

> And the old men answered her that Apollo
> himself had gone down to Troy,
> and with the Trojans he had slain Achilles.[3]

In other words, isn't the most sensible religion polytheism?

Put your prejudices on a hold for a minute, and look at the world in all its wideness and weirdness. What conclusions would you draw about the divine? You'd see a place of astonishing beauty and unthinkable horror, a world where geese are gently reflected in a shimmering lake, and also a world where children curl up next to their dead parents after a devastating earthquake. You'd see a world of orderly seasons and disorderly weather, a world that nourishes the crops we plant, then turns around and destroys them as if in a fit of childish rage. You'd see a world where we all feel the promise and sap of being alive, almost as if a god of prophecy had promised us a long, healthy life; and then you'd see countless perfectly lovable people cut down in their prime. A world of grapes alchemizing into wine, love leading to war, and the butchery of battle inspiring our most breathtaking art. Wouldn't it be logical to conclude that there is no unified mind behind this blasted, blooming, bloody universe, and that the forces of the world, the gods, are a mixed bag: generous, beautiful, cruel, angry, calm, treacherous, sweet, opposed, but most of all volatile and mighty?

Interestingly, the epigraph to Cavafy's poem is a remark made by Socrates in Plato's *Republic*, the gist of which is that stories like the one about Apollo's infidelity are totally unacceptable accounts of divinity, which brings us back to Socrates's great question in the *Euthyphro*. Essentially, he's asking if we should worship goodness or power. Is it the power or the rightness of a command that is truly commanding? In this case, is it the fact the gods command us, or is it the goodness of their command that we should find persuasive? Should we be obedient to power or obedient to goodness?

Euthyphro's attempts at a definition of holiness put him squarely in the power camp. Though Socrates doesn't finalize an answer in the dialogue, he seems definitely in the goodness camp. There's a song by Bob Dylan that goes, "You gotta serve somebody: / It might be the devil, or it might be the Lord, / But you're gonna have to serve somebody."[4] That's about right, particularly if by "devil" he means the worship of power, our own or someone else's, and by "the Lord" he means something like goodness, beauty, or truth—something intrinsically valuable that stands outside the self, something whose action in the world is often no stronger than a flower.

I'm perennially shocked at how few students of mine know the story of Abraham and Isaac, a story common to all three Abrahamic faiths—and, for that matter, a Dylan song ("God said to Abraham, 'Kill me a son' / Abe said, 'Man, you must be puttin' me on'"). But ignorance of the story and its traditional interpretation proves useful when I test them as to where they stand on the power-versus-goodness question. Imagine, I say, that God comes to you in whatever form you would find most convincing—a burning bush, a talking whirlwind, a face of unsurpassable beauty—and commands that you are to kill the person you love the most: son, daughter, spouse, parent, or friend. Further imagine that God informs you that you're being tested. What should you do?

An eloquent answer to this question came from a student named Cheryl, whose little boy, because of day-care issues, sometimes had to attend my class and would color quietly in the corner. She wrote on an exam, "If God asked me to kill my son, first I'd question if the voice was God. Then I'd tell the voice to go fuck itself." She was saying with greater simplicity and oomph the very thing that Immanuel Kant said two hundred years earlier in *The Contest of the Faculties*:

If God should really speak to man, man could still never know that it was God speaking. It is quite impossible for man to apprehend the infinite by his senses, distinguish it from sensible beings, and recognize it as such. But in some cases man can be sure the voice he hears is not God's. For if the voice commands him to do something contrary to moral law, then no matter how majestic the apparition may be, and no matter how it may seem to surpass the whole of nature, he must consider it an illusion.[5]

He adds in a footnote, "Abraham should have answered the alleged divine voices by saying, 'that I should not kill my good son is clear to me; but that you, who appear to me, be God, that is not at all clear and can also never become clear.'" Cheryl and Kant are in the goodness camp.

Abraham is in the power camp (though in the tale of the destruction of Sodom, where he challenges the justice of God's wrath, he switches to the goodness camp). He takes Isaac to the mountain in order to kill him and prove himself a faithful servant of God. The majesty of God, from Whom all things flow, takes precedence over our attachment to anything in His creation. Traditional interpretations of the story laud Abraham for his faithfulness, for passing what must be the hardest test of all, the willingness to give up your own child. Christians, for an obvious reason, make a lot out of this.

But couldn't it be that Abraham fails the test? If God is seeing if Abraham will stick to his deepest sense of right and wrong, even in the face of utter majesty and power, then he fails abysmally. Surely there must be some obscure midrash that regards the suffering of Abraham's line as punishment for his failure to stand by the most fundamental goodness of who we are. Or maybe Abraham *is* punished in the story, for he must live the rest of his days with the broken trust, if not outright rage, in his beloved son's gaze.

In our age of terror in the name of religion and torture in the name of civilization, Abraham's test is hardly out of date. But the problem is not just a religious one. Atheists, too, must decide who or what they're gonna serve. Simone Weil says, "An atheist may be simply one whose faith and love are concentrated on the impersonal aspects of God."[6] A wise atheist might say, "A theist may be simply one whose sense of justice or power requires a face." It's now popular to draw the great dividing line between believers and atheists, but I hold to this Socratic line between people who worship goodness and people who worship power, one that bisects the atheists-believers line and cuts both groups in two. To use the characters of our age, it makes more sense to lump together the power-worshippers Adolf Hitler and Osama bin Laden and the goodness-worshippers Martin Luther King Jr. and Mikhail Gorbachev, than to lump Osama with King based on their shared belief in God and to lump Hitler with Gorbachev because of their secularism.

Socrates and Euthyphro don't come to an understanding of holiness. Socrates leans one way, Euthyphro the other, but, if anything, we're further than ever from a satisfactory answer at the end of the dialogue. Frustrated by Socrates's pointed questions, Euthyphro claims "to have somewhere to go" and runs off. Socrates calls after him, "You're going off and dashing me from that great hope which I entertained; that I could learn from you what was holy and what not and quickly have done with Meletus's prosecution by demonstrating to him that I have now become wise in religion thanks to Euthyphro, and no longer improvise and innovate in ignorance of it—and moreover that I could live a better life for the rest of my days."[7] Euthyphro was originally at the courthouse to file charges against his father. Now he has some pressing engagement elsewhere. Could it be that this inconclusive dialogue changed his mind and his life? Doubtful—but you never know.

ORACLES AND DEMONS

Oracles were consulted in ancient times by all walks of society with the kinds of questions that never go away. Am I going to be caught as an adulterer? Will I split up with my boyfriend? Will so-and-so survive the illness? Will I ever pay back my debts? Suetonius, in his *Life of Nero*, tells how the emperor asked the Delphic oracle, "When am I going to die?" The answer came back, "Let him fear the seventy-three years." Nero, just thirty, was relieved, figuring that he still had more than half his life to live, and dove back into his dissolute lifestyle. Meanwhile, Galba, soon to be the next emperor of Rome, was assembling his army—Galba, who was seventy-three years old. A few weeks later Nero, with the help of his secretary, killed himself.[8]

Chaerophon, toward the end of the fifth century BC, famously went to the temple at Delphi, where "know thyself" was inscribed in the forecourt, to ask the oracle if his friend Socrates was the wisest of all. The answer came back, "No one is wiser." When Socrates got wind of the god's pronouncement, he was puzzled. How could he be the wisest when he's completely devoid of wisdom? He set out to prove Apollo and his priestess wrong (as if to bear out the charge of unholiness that was eventually leveled against him). His strategy was simple: find one person with even a little bit of positive wisdom, which would clearly beat him whose wisdom level was at zero. As the story goes, Socrates wandered around Athens questioning its citizens—politicians, poets, craftsmen—about the special truths they claimed to possess and eventually came to the conclusion that the god had spoken the truth (as if to disprove the charge of unholiness against him). Socrates really was the wisest of all. He did have a little bit of positive wisdom: the priceless knowledge that he knew nothing. Everyone else claimed to have knowledge when in fact they did not, putting them in the hole wisdom-wise.

Socrates tells this parable—it's found in Plato's *Apology*, the second of our quartet—by way of properly introducing himself at his trial in 399 BC. Like all good parables, it seems easygoing at first, but its meaning soon drops off like a coastal shelf. What does it mean to have wisdom? How is his knowledge of his ignorance a kind of wisdom? How can it be that poets don't know about poetry, that politicians don't know about politics, that craftsmen don't know about their respective crafts? Is Socrates humble or prideful, holy or unholy, honest or dissembling? Maybe philosophy is unholy and corrupting, as Socrates's accusers allege, if all it does is undermine the pillars of the community? It took a student who had never read Plato to answer these questions and bring home to me the real meaning of the parable.

*

Because teaching the same back-breaking load of five classes per semester can become spirit numbing, I like to teach as many different kinds of courses as I can. So I found myself in biomedical ethics, a night class filled mostly with nursing students, lab techs, a few souls with dreams of being doctors, me, and Jillian Kramer, a nurse's aide at the University of Iowa Hospitals and Clinics. Unimaginatively I stuck to the standard topics: informed consent, euthanasia, abortion, genetic engineering, and the major ethical theories.

One of our most lively discussions was sparked when I casually asked the drooping class, "What is a hospital for, anyway?" I dispatched the expected answers as they came out. "To heal people." But what about those who have a terminal case? "To ease people's pain." But what about those whose pain can't be eased? "To help people whose pain can be eased." What about those who don't want their pain eased? "To help sick people who want to be helped." Is there no obligation to healthy people? And so on. I wanted to loosen up their minds for an essay I had just assigned by Stanley Hauerwas on the Christian vision of the hospital's mission. Though Jillian was bright, serious, and open-minded, academic philosophy wasn't her thing. But our discussion sparked something in her, and she asked me if she could write on the purpose of hospitals.

A couple of weeks later, as students were handing in their papers and filing out, I pulled her aside and asked how the project had gone. Our conversation in class, she explained, had perplexed her; at first she thought my question silly, but after the discussion, she realized that she didn't have a very clear idea of the overarching point of a hospital, which struck her as odd. To help her formulate a thesis, she lit on the idea of asking everyone and anyone at the hospital about the institution's true purpose: doctors, nurses, patients, administrators. What she found perplexed her. When they could come up with an answer at all, they gave the same pat answers as the students in class, which she was able to prove inadequate. The best answer, she said, was given by some doctor, who, after having his first couple attempts shot down by a nurse's aide, said, "Maybe we're supposed to do all of the above." But she soon figured out that, too, was inadequate. How are they to know when to cure, when to ease pain, when to help patients transition back to normalcy? Should they always give patients what they want? Should they always give them what they need? How do you know when to do one rather than the other? What's their most important mission of all? Why were they there?

The problem, Jillian recognized, is that the hospital can subordinate its whole purpose to mending broken people. Too often pregnant women are treated like they're sick, mourners are dealt with like they're psychological cases, folks clearly dying are pointlessly "fixed."

If the hospital is merely a mechanical body shop, then we live in a less than fully human world. "Imagine," she said, "doctors who'd spent decades studying and practicing medicine, who had never much thought of why they were really doing it!" Imagine, I thought, poets, politicians, and craftsmen not knowing fully the ultimate point of their respective crafts.

Many of her coworkers, she figured, did good jobs—just going on their feel for what they ought to be doing. (After Socrates discovers that the poets can't explain their poems, he concludes, "I decided that it was not wisdom that enabled them to write their poetry, but a kind of instinct or inspiration.")[9] But she wondered if they wouldn't be better off opening their minds to the full truth of it. ("If," Socrates says, "I tell you that to let no day pass without discussing goodness and all the other subjects about which you hear me talking and examining both myself and others is really the very best thing that a man can do, and that life without this sort of examination is not worth living, you will be even less inclined to believe me.")[10] She had to get going and handed her paper to a rapt professor.

I sat down and read her essay then and there. She wrote of how Hauerwas, the theologian I had assigned, helped her to see the problem more clearly. People who are sick grow alienated from those around them: their pain exiles them from the human community. The closest she could come to formulating the goal of a hospital was: to be there for people. To be there when they're sick. To be there when they're dying. To be there for the families who just lost loved ones. To aid people when you could, and when they wanted. But most of all to be there for them, human to human. To be there especially when they're suffering and to help them, as far as possible, to transition from the lonely realms of pain to the regular world again.

She thought that the nurses were the best at this, even if they couldn't articulate it. First, they spend most of their time caring for the individual patients as human beings, trying to make them feel at home—or at least not so far from home. Second, because they spend such time with the patients, and because they observe firsthand how various treatments work, she thought that they tend to know better than the doctors which treatments work best and which are dead ends. The point of medicine is care. Doctors are there, she marvelously concluded, to help the nurses. But doctors, she feared, overrate their wisdom based on how much they know about science. (Socrates on the craftsmen: "On the strength of their technical proficiency they claimed a perfect understanding of every other subject, however important; and I felt that this error eclipsed their positive wisdom.")[11]

Jillian admitted at the end that she didn't feel complete confidence in her conclusions: they were simply the best way she had of putting what she felt deep down. She concluded by saying that her inquiry had opened her to the significance of what she did. She was more inclined to value the work she'd always intuitively known was valuable. Had she read Plato's *Phaedo*, she might have called her conclusions about the hospital "beliefs worth risking."[12]

*

In my freshman year at Grinnell College, I read the *Apology* in Humanities 101, and my class got into a discussion of Socrates's claim that "the unexamined life is not worth living." The expression, to me, formed my inchoate sense of philosophy's value into a lightning bolt of meaning. But not everyone shared my sense of its numinousness. During the discussion, a classmate challenged the idea by bringing up an image miraculously emblazoned on all our minds ever since the second grade: the photo in the *Guinness World Records* book of the two heaviest twins wearing cowboy hats and riding matching Honda motorcycles. The glib student said something to the effect of, "Those guys don't look like philosophers to me, but they seem to be having a really good time on their bikes. Are you telling me their lives aren't worth living?" In other words, can't people live worthwhile lives without philosophy? Can't ignorance, at least sometimes, be bliss?

In the *Phaedo*, just an hour before his death, Socrates says, "Philosophy is nothing but the preparation for death and dying."[13] ("No way to recruit majors," my former professor Johanna Meehan used to say.) Among other things, this statement means that philosophers must confront the fact of their deaths and, by implication, the fact of their lives; for life and death are stages of one underlying cycle. After having been pulled from the car teetering on the cliff, we're apt to think things like, "What have I been doing with my life? Why am I wasting my time on this job? Why have I allowed my relationship with my father to fall into such disrepair? Why haven't I unleashed what I've always felt to be best about me?" Even if, when we're pulled safely from the plummeting vehicle, we come to the realization that we're lucky in our job and relationships, we still return to them with a newfound sense of their meaning, at least as long as death is fresh in our minds. Doing good is meaningless if it's done robotically, if it's done without a commitment to its being good, if it's done without—examination.

Here's the truth, straight from that nurse's aide Walt Whitman: "You are to die—let others tell you what they please, I cannot prevaricate, / I am exact and merciless, but I love you—there is no escape for you."[14] But when we live our lives actively ignoring that most solid of all inductive conclusions, we accept bad substitutes for happiness and holiness, justice and love. The confrontation of the fact of death, the serious appraisal of what we're doing, living in relationship to what's meaningful—that's "the examined life." Don't displace the discussion on an image of overweight twins. You, too, have been photographed with a nice smile. But if the doctor tells you tomorrow that you have only a year to live, will your response be, "Well, I've always known I was going to die, and I've been spending my time well, zooming around with my brother"? Or something else?

Socrates is trying to jump-start the examination process that comes usually only from a confrontation with death. In one of the many great paradoxes associated with Socrates, the man who claims not to understand holiness is closest to being holy. We are following our calling, our divine mission, when we open ourselves up to our calling.

*

Couldn't Meletus, Anytus, or Lycon—Socrates's accusers—have argued that the examined life doesn't open us up to what is truly meaningful, that it in fact does the opposite? The concepts of holiness, justice, love, and happiness have been worked on and perfected for generations, and society blessedly passes these concepts down to the young. To examine these concepts is to open the door to worse influences, to our own self-aggrandizement, to old mistakes, to tyranny. Jillian spoke with a certain defiance in her paper when it came to the powerful claims of very smart doctors and important administrators; and it's no great feat to interpret Socrates's ironic tone as contemptuous.

To make matters worse, Socrates claims to be guided by a *daimo-*

nion, his own little god, a kind of guardian angel. Though the root word "daimon"—demon—acquired its devilish connotation much later as Christians tried to puzzle out exactly what the polytheists were worshipping, we still might say that when people claim to be guided by their own god it's almost always a demon. Once you have opened your mind, what's to stop such little demonic powers from whispering, "Why shouldn't you—who's better suited than any of these idiots—rule single-handedly?" What could be more corrupting? What could be more unholy? Various associates of Socrates could have been named in support of such an argument: for instance, Alcibiades, the playboy of Athens, who at one point knocked the penises off the sacred hermae and then, rather than stand trial for his act of impiety, joined forces with the Spartans against the Athenians; or Critias, Plato's uncle, who became a member of the hated Thirty Tyrants, the pro-Spartan oligarchy installed after Athens's humiliating defeat. Are these the true products of philosophy, blithely following their little "gods"?

It's paradoxical that this most rational of human beings lets himself be guided by a mysterious oracle he hears in his head. This guardian "demon," according to Socrates, speaks a language composed of only one word: "no." Whenever Socrates is about to do something bad or enter into something terrible, his guardian demon says no. Many have interpreted this as the voice of conscience, which seems right but not very illuminating. My own guess about it is that the divine sign is closer to our concept of a calling.

"How am I to live?" Often, perhaps, what keeps us from hearing a clear answer to that imperial question is the cacophony of beliefs and ideas in our minds. We've been told we're supposed to do this, we suspect we're supposed to do that, the people around us expect yet another thing out of us. Maybe if we were to examine these beliefs fully, to the point of really realizing our ignorance about them, we'd find a silence in ourselves in which we'd be able to hear something genuine. Or, as in the case of Socrates, at least be able to figure out what we're not supposed to be doing. "The daimon of Socrates," his great interpreter Michel de Montaigne says, "was perhaps a certain impulse of the will that came to him without awaiting the advice of his reason. In a well-purified soul such as his, prepared by a continual exercise of wisdom and virtue, it is likely that these inclinations, although instinctive and undigested, were always important and worth following. Everyone feels within himself some likeness of such stirrings of a prompt, vehement, and accidental opinion."[15]

Jillian and her colleagues found themselves unable to articulate what the point of the hospital was, but some of them did have a stirring sense of it. They knew in a way they couldn't quite articulate, like having a word on the tip of the tongue. Perhaps only when they returned to this intuitive sense, in ignorance of their rationalized sense, were they truly approaching the real meaning of their work. Could this sense, this mysterious voice, be a cousin to Socrates's *daimonion*? Admittedly, Socrates's voice says only no, whereas the voice I'm suggesting has a larger vocabulary. But I wonder if Socrates isn't just further along than most of us. He often talks about his divine mission to engage in philosophy. Perhaps once we've found a mission that is "divine"—meaning, among other things, beyond our capacity to dictate—when we're on our path, perhaps then our guardian demon is necessary only in keeping us from deviating.

*

The jurors vote 280–220 that Socrates is guilty. Not unlike our own system, both parties get to suggest a penalty. The prosecution proposes death. At no point in the trial does Socrates seem worried about its outcome, and now he is particularly unconcerned—shockingly so. His request for a "penalty" for his "crimes" (he doesn't accept the latter so the former makes no sense) is that he should receive free room and board at the Prytaneum, where the most celebrated victors in the Olympics stay. Since Socrates makes the Athenians really happy, whereas the Olympic victors give them a superficial happiness, the "punishment" would fit the "crime."

Plato appears only once in all the dialogues; and it is here. (His name is mentioned twice, once also in the *Phaedo*, as we shall see.) He stands up in the trial and tries to soften what Socrates has said; he tells his teacher to propose a fine, which his friends would gladly pay. Is the young Plato being foolish, bowing to the charge of guilt when there is no basis for it? Is he trying to push against destiny? Is Plato the author portraying his younger self as still having a lot to learn? Or is Plato the wise one here, understanding when the philosopher must adopt what my teacher used to call "the logic of the mask"? Is he trying to present Socrates in a more acceptable light to the city and posterity? If so, it's too late—at least for the Athenians. The jurors vote overwhelmingly for his execution.

Socrates's response to having the death penalty thrust on him is one of my favorite moments in literature. He calmly replies,

> Death is one of two things. Either it is an annihilation, and the dead have no consciousness of anything; or, as we are told, it really is a change: a migration of the soul from this place to another. Now if there is no consciousness but only a dreamless sleep, death must be a marvelous gain . . . because the whole of time, if you look at it in this way, can be regarded as no more than one single night. If on the other hand death is a removal from here to some other place, and if what we are told is true, that all the dead are there, what greater blessing could there be than this, gentlemen? . . . Put it in this way: how much would one of you give to meet Orpheus and Museus, Hesiod and Homer? . . . Above all I should like to spend my time there, as here, in examining and searching people's minds, to find out who is really wise among them, and who only thinks that he is.[16]

His "punishment" is even better than free meals at the Prytaneum.

PHILOSOPHICAL PATRIOTISM

The drama of the *Crito*, the third act of Plato's four-act drama, is that one of Socrates's rich friends offers to break him out of jail. Socrates—a man who believes that he's innocent—responds to Crito's request in typical fashion. Let's examine it, he says, and see if breaking out of prison is a good thing to do. In this case, getting out of prison is far from an escape from Alcatraz and involves no more than paying a guard to look the other way. Crito makes it sound like it's expected of him to bust Socrates out. His main rationale for doing so is that he'll look bad if he doesn't, for people will say that he cares more about his money than his friends. He's armed with a couple other reasons, too, including the implausible one (which nonetheless pulls on readers' heartstrings) that he should do it for his kids, as if their lives would improve with a seventy-year-old man in exile. Socrates's response to such rationales is that he should be concerned with doing what's right, for that's how to be a good friend or good father. If breaking out of prison is unjust, then to do so would be to set a bad example. If breaking out of prison is the right thing to do, then that's reason enough.

On the question of the justice of escape, Crito has one pertinent argument. Socrates should escape because the verdict is unjust, and a just man doesn't need to respect—in fact, may even have a duty to violate—an unjust pronouncement. Simply that it was arrived at by a majority of Athenian jurors should be irrelevant. Doesn't truth stand beyond popular opinion? Shouldn't Socrates obey his god rather than the men of Athens? What do thirty swing votes have to do with justice?

Socrates then imagines a more profound dialogue than the one he finds himself in, between him and what he calls the Laws. What emerges is that citizens have an implicit contract with the Laws. The Laws provide Socrates (and us, too, for the form of the contract that Socrates describes would be the same, if he's right, for Americans as for Athenians) with all the benefits of living in a political system: the marriage codes that provide for our birth and upbringing, armed forces to protect us, education, health codes, roads, and so on. It's hard to think of a single aspect of our lives untouched by the Laws. In return, we must do no more than follow the law: pay our taxes and not break the rules. If we don't like the deal, there are two important provisions to the contract: (1) we're allowed to leave, or (2) we may try to change the system through legal means. Our very presence in the state, at least after legal age of adulthood, provides what the philosopher John Locke calls "tacit consent" to such a contract. If Socrates didn't like living in a democracy where one can be charged for unholiness, then he shouldn't have stuck around for seventy years.

*

Imagine a dictator in a far off country whose existence we believed posed a threat to us; further imagine that we decided to depose this dictator and install a democracy there, which we believed would be beneficial to both of our countries' long-term interests. Let's even say that we could write up a solid constitution and set of legal codes for that country. We then select a government and put police, judges, et alia, into place. Would the Laws be now in existence?

We still need one absolutely crucial ingredient: the people's willingness to follow those laws. The citizens might not recognize the justice of our divine constitution; at least some of them might form an insurgency, refusing to accept the authority of the laws and the people the laws put in power. They would have legal codes but no order, for laws are meaningless unless people generally abide by them. They would have laws but not the Laws. In some sense, the Laws are our willingness to abide by the structure of law itself; without that general willingness to respect law or custom, all we have left is raw power to create order.

The Laws make an even stronger claim on us than a contract. Socrates makes the case that the Laws are like our parents in that they have given us our whole life. Yes, we can speak of the Laws as an independent entity with which we make a contract, just as I suppose children can speak of their parents as authorities whom they've agreed to honor in exchange for room and board. But in both cases, our identity is much more fundamentally formed by them. It's shallow to believe otherwise. There's an important truth, partial though it may be, in Alasdair MacIntyre's claim that "I can only answer the question 'What am I to do?' if I can answer the prior question 'Of what story or stories do I find myself a part?'"[17] Socrates understands that he is part of the story of Athens. He is also, of course, a part of the story of philosophy and the story of justice, both of which take precedence, for Athens like all cities boasts a basis in justice and humanity. Socrates has taken his stand; now his deep respect for the city that has born and raised him compels him to accept the consequences of taking that stand.

*

Scholars sometimes talk about "the *Apology-Crito* problem" as if Plato didn't know exactly what he was doing. The apparent problem is that, in the *Apology*, Socrates says, "Men of Athens, I respect you and I love you, but I will obey the god rather than you, and as long as I live and breathe, I will never stop doing philosophy, not even if I were to die many times over."[18] Whereas in the *Crito*, he argues that we should follow the laws, even when we disagree with them. In a nutshell: Should we obey our "god" or the laws of our community?

The "problem" is resolved in what we call civil disobedience, which, it seems to me, is powerfully embodied in Socrates. Civil disobedience involves breaking a law out of a piety toward the spirit on which the laws are based. If your examined sense of justice diverges sharply from the laws of your community, our best models of justice recommend that you should violate the individual law you oppose (this is the disobedience part), but you should respect the form of the law (the civil part). When the police come for Rosa Parks, she doesn't flee the scene. In essence, she says, "Yes, you should arrest me, for I've broken a law, and those who break the law are subject to penalty. But while I respect the structure of the law, I reject the justice of this particular law, which my examined sense of justice refuses to acknowledge."

True philosophy is not tyrannical or even disrespectful of the community—just the opposite. The great Confucian official Hai Rui once agonized over what to do about an abusive Ming emperor. His sense of respect demanded obedience; his sense of justice demanded that he air his grievance. The solution he lit on? He remonstrated with the emperor—and brought his coffin along with him.

RISKING ETERNITY

In the dialogue named after him, as he's reeling off all the friends present during Socrates's last hours, Phaedo says to Echecrates, "Plato, I believe, was ill."[19] It's a touching moment in a dialogue full of beautiful moments. Was Plato really not there? How sad, if the man able to see furthest into the most expansive human spirit couldn't have been there for his teacher's culminating moment.

In one of the dialogue's first images, Socrates's chains have just been removed, and he's massaging his legs. He remarks that pleasure is a funny thing, deeply connected to pain, its apparent opposite, like one mythological beast with two very different heads—or, as we might say, two sides of the same coin. It is to be hoped that more familiar to you than having chains removed is taking off your uncomfortable shoes after some formal occasion. In such cases, the pain prepares the way for the "ahh!" of pleasure, just as pleasure can prepare the way for pain after the glow of the fourth martini wears off. I think of the apocryphal bit of verse often attributed to Dorothy Parker:

I love a martini, two at the most;
Three, you're under the table;
Four, you're under the host.

Oddly enough, if you never wear uncomfortable shoes, you're less likely to feel real pleasure in your feet; and if you want to become a connoisseur of pain and regret, you should learn to mix yourself an irresistible Gibson.

Socrates's casual remark suggests the theme of the whole dialogue: the relation of opposites—most pertinently, life and death. As the body underlies the cycle of pleasure and pain, perhaps the soul underlies the cycle of life and death.

Death appears at first to human consciousness as a startling interruption of a seemingly continuous flow of life. Nowadays, after having developed a science that sees everything as built out of lifeless units of matters, we're apt to regard the origin of life as the great mystery. But the origin of death is the central perplexity of our primitive minds. Many early myths grapple with just this question, and they usually posit that it happened by accident—for instance, from having eaten the wrong piece of fruit. The philosopher Hans Jonas perceptively conjectures that "metaphysics arises from graves."[20]

Think back on your first uncanny time looking at a corpse, especially if it was the body of someone you once knew and loved. The body is all there: same face, features, and limbs as always. But where's the body's character? Where's the one you knew and loved? Whatever it is that lit up that face with its unmistakable expressions is no longer there. Let's call that mysterious whatever "the soul"—or, in Greek, the *psyche*.

Maybe the soul is just an "attunement" of the body, to use the language of the *Phaedo*; or, to speak in contemporary terms, the mind is no more than a brain that's hooked up and firing. At the moment of death the soul dissolves, in the words of the Roman poet Lucretius, like "the sweet perfume of an ointment [that] has escaped into the air."[21] Or, as the British poet Philip Larkin more brutally puts it, death is "total emptiness forever, / The sure extinction that we travel to / And shall be lost in always."[22] This view is generally called materialism.

The other view—usually referred to as a form of dualism—holds that the soul is, in some ultimate sense, separable from the body. If materialists hold that the soul is a function of a minimally healthy body, like running is a function of a working car, dualists, in contrast, believe that there is a soul steering the car and that, after the final wreck, it's perhaps able to get out and walk away. Death, on this view, is a translation of the soul from the body—either into another body (reincarnation) or into another zone of existence (for instance, Valhalla or one of the nine circles of hell). In the *Phaedo*, Socrates argues—or seems to argue—for a version of dualism. The soul is deathless and its true home is elsewhere.

In all his most otherworldly dialogues Plato presents Socrates as a sensualist. In the *Phaedo*, as Socrates collects himself to try once more to prove the immortality of the soul, he begins to stroke Phaedo's lovely locks of hair. It's a powerful moment, in part because the act is performed so purely, without a trace of wistfulness. One could easily imagine a death-row inmate stroking something lovely of this world and thinking, "Poor me, this is last time I'll ever experience such a thing!" Socrates, conversely, simply savors the young man's curls as he usually savors the things of the world, without self-pity, without overrating the experience, with a natural, spontaneous relish of the thing itself.

The overall impression of the dialogues is a profound concern for how we live now. The practice for death is the practice for life. It's true that Socrates speaks of how the philosopher should despise the "nominal pleasures of food and drink," not to mention sex. But given the sensuality of Socrates (a seventy-year-old who has just fathered a child), I wonder if he means something other than monkish abstinence. A poem by D. H. Lawrence illustrates my hunch:

> They call all experience of the senses *mystic*, when the experience is
>   considered.
> So an apple becomes *mystic* when I taste in it
> the summer and the snows, the wild welter of earth
> and the insistence of the sun.
> . . . .
> If I say I taste these things in an apple, I am called *mystic*, which
>   means a liar.
> The only way to eat an apple is to hog it down like a pig
> and taste nothing
> that is *real*.[23]

The distinction here is not between fasting and eating, but between considering and not considering experience, between tasting how the sunshine and raindrops of the universe have knotted together into an apple, and pigging the thing down to satisfy a transient desire—in short, between the examined and the unexamined life. When our minds are focused on the universal we get the richest physical experience; when we're focused on the passing world we get only the most abstract kind of pleasure. Socrates drinks deep of friendship, wine, and conversation because he lovingly savors solitude, discipline, and contemplation.

*

After listening carefully to Socrates's arguments for the immortality of the soul, Simmias claims to be intellectually satisfied, and yet "the subject is so vast, and I have such a poor opinion of our weak human nature, that I can't help still feeling some misgivings." Socrates replies, "Quite right . . . and what is more, even if you find our original assumptions convincing, they still need more accurate consideration."[24] But rather than revisiting the original assumptions, Socrates switches gears and begins to tell a detailed story about the nature of the afterlife—after just having admitted that the immortality of the soul hasn't been completely proven!

Most visions of the afterlife contradict our true worldly struggles. The highest values they set before us are nothing more than projections of our basest desires and fears into the unknown. In paradise we crave, irrationally, pleasure separated from pain. After 9/11 it was said—dubiously perhaps—that the terrorists believed they'd have sex with seventy virgins in heaven. Seventy virgins in heaven would very quickly turn into seventy wives in hell! In the folk song "The Big Rock Candy Mountain," a hobo imagines a place where the bulldogs have rubber teeth, the jails are never locked, the policeman hobble on wooden legs, hens lay soft-boiled eggs, and there are lakes of whiskey and springs of lemonade. It dawns on us that the hobo's paradise is a place precisely without hobos, just as the terrorists' paradise is a place without the religious conviction they prize—a place very like the licentious fantasy of America they're trying to destroy. Alexander Pope sums up the problem: "Will Heaven reward us there / With the same trash mad mortals wish for here?"[25]

Despite some interestingly odd details, Socrates's image of an afterlife is intricately connected to how we live now. The character we develop is morally clarified, and the wicked suffer, the morally mixed must undergo a purgation of their souls, and the righteous go on a blessed journey—essentially, hell, purgatory, and heaven. The crucial idea seems to be that what we do matters—matters infinitely—and can be regarded from a perspective outside the ups and downs of the passing moment. Unlike his predecessors' versions of the afterlife, it's not random where you end up: we make our beds. Inside everything we do lurks an eternal destiny: something that exceeds time is dissolved into our experience of time. Life isn't about having our egos live on in people's minds, or even in a zone unlike our current existence. The moral of the story, as he tells it, is that we should leave "nothing undone to attain *during life*"—my emphasis—"some measure of goodness and wisdom."[26]

Does Socrates really believe the myth he's told about souls and the afterlife? Or is he just giving imaginative flesh to his idea of living well in the here and now? Socrates answers, "Of course no reasonable man ought to insist on the facts exactly as I have described them. But that either this or something very like it is true . . . is both a fitting contention and a belief worth risking; for the risk is a noble one."[27]

*

The inevitable time of the hemlock arrives. The poison begins to take effect, slowly paralyzing Socrates from the toes all the way up to the skull's precious cargo. He lies back and pulls the sheet over his face—then pops up to deliver his final words, "Crito, we owe a cock to Asclepius. See to it, and don't forget."[28] Asclepius is the god of healing. A cock is a fitting thanksgiving on being healed. The most common way of reading this pious and humorous command is that life is a disease and death its remedy, which is half right. Poison in Greek is *pharmakon*, which means both poison and cure: a drug is both, depending on the dosage. Just as the entire drama could be read as a comedy or a tragedy, so too could the word in its context be seen as referring to the poison that kills Socrates (if he is his body) or the remedy that cures him (if his arguments are sound, and he truly is his soul).

Origen, one of the great early Christian theologians, complains that Socrates and company "pass from those great topics which God has revealed to them, and adopt mean and trifling thoughts, and offer a cock to Asclepius!"[29] I have to say, with great trepidation, that

Origen seems not to grasp the essence of Christianity here, for Socrates's joke about owing a cock to the healing god strikes me as a kind of naturalized Christianity. After lying down, presumably dead, Socrates pops up—resurrection-like—to deliver his holy joke, his lighthearted piety. There's nothing funny, of course, about the death and resurrection of Jesus, but the structure of his death and resurrection is the very structure of comedy, essentially a pop-goes-the-weasel routine. Dante, you might recall, names his poetic summation of the Christian worldview the *Commedia*. Socrates once dead is dead (whatever that means!), but Plato, ill for his teacher's final hours, gets better and writes the dialogues. We sure do owe a cock to Asclepius!

INTERLUDE ON LAUGHTER AND TEARS

The gist of it was that Socrates was forcing them to admit that the same man might be capable of writing both comedy and tragedy—that the tragic poet might be a comedian as well.   PLATO

Is life tragic or comic? Is our common lot better bewailed or chuckled at? Tradition has it that the philosopher Heraclitus, who held that all things are on fire, was constantly weeping; whereas the philosopher Democritus, who held the ridiculous theory that all things are built out of tiny tidbits called atoms, was always laughing. Which one was the wiser?

Once I taught a class that I spent more time bewailing than chuckling at, a course my institution calls Encounters in Humanities, which I structured around the theme of comedy and tragedy. We read Sophocles's *Ajax*, Aristophanes's *Lysistrata*, Plato's *Symposium*, and Shakespeare's *Tempest*; we listened to Louis Armstrong; we looked hard at some pictures by the artist Katsushika Hokusai; we watched Charlie Chaplin's *Modern Times*; we read humane essays by the likes of Henri Bergson and Arthur Schopenhauer ("The pleasure in this world, it has been said, outweighs the pain; or, at any rate, there is an even balance between the two. If the reader wishes to see whether this statement is true, let him compare the respective feelings of two animals, one of which is engaged in eating the other").[1] These masterpieces fell—to borrow an image from the Sermon on the Mount—like pearls before swine. That is, on all but two bright-eyed students, one who would occasionally write and perform songs on the essay topics I assigned, and another by the name of Shannon McBride, a woman in her midtwenties with bright eyes that sometimes trick you into thinking she's innocent of the world.

Once, after giving the class Montaigne's "Of Democritus and Heraclitus," I asked point-blank, "Is life tragic or comic?" and made each student prepare an answer. Maybe the question is just too broad or lofty, but the responses ranged from the inane ("Sometimes it's happy, sometimes it's sad") to the wicked ("Maybe some people have horrible lives, but I just like to look at the bright side"). And then Shannon spoke up. In her speech, she told of having moved to Bosnia in 1992 because her mother was working with the International Rescue Committee to aid refugees of the recent conflict. Just eleven when she arrived, Shannon spent the next four years of her adolescence following the civil war's increasing brutality across the region into Sarajevo. As most people who have witnessed real horror, she spoke in a classical style, without needless adjectives, without sentimentality, with a quiet precision. While many tears were shed in Bosnia, laughter was slightly more common there, she observed. Life is so tragic it's funny. "When you're right in the middle of suffering, it doesn't always feel comic," she admitted, "but comedy is necessary and usually available to us." This gentle, bright-eyed, good soul then quoted a little of Montaigne's conclusion, "I do not think there is as much unhappiness in us as vanity, nor as much malice as stupidity. We are not so full of evil as of inanity; we are not as wretched as we are worthless. . . . Our own peculiar condition is that we are as fit to be laughed at as able to laugh."[2] I should have assigned Kierkegaard's *Stages on Life's Way*: "The more one suffers, the more, I believe, has one a sense for the comic. It is only by the deepest suffering that one acquires true authority in the use of the comic, an authority which by one word transforms as by magic the reasonable creature one calls man into a caricature."[3]

A year or so after our class, I ran into Shannon at the local restaurant where she was a waitress. Like many of my students, Shannon had been working her way through school. Moreover, she had to support her daughter as well as her brother. When I asked her how she was doing, she told me in her dry style that she'd been recently diagnosed with cancer. When I expressed my concern, she smiled ever so slightly, "I've seen worse in my life. I'll manage."

I'm happy to report that her cancer has been successfully treated. Shannon is now looking into graduate school in psychology. When we last talked, I asked her what she thought of those years when she had to juggle school, cancer, work, and family. She looked at me with her bright eyes and said, "I just got through it at the time. Now I look back and think, 'Oh my God, that happened to *me!*'" And we both laughed.

*

Poets who told stories in Plato's time were either tragedians or comedians. Tragedies are stories with unhappy endings; the appropriate response to them is pity and fear, expressed physiologically by tears. Comedies, conversely, are stories that culminate in a celebration; the mood appropriate to them is associated with laughter. Do the four dialogues that culminate with Socrates's death in the *Phaedo* constitute a comedy or a tragedy? Let me remind you of the plot: a good man, prosecuted for a crime he did not commit, is forced to poison himself. Clearly, a comedy.

Oddly, Socrates's friends interpret it as a tragedy. They begin to weep as the prisoner calmly drains the hemlock. Socrates chastises them for misreading the drama. In the *Crito*, Socrates wonderfully declares that Meletus and Anytus can kill him, but they can't harm him. Among the few principles upheld by the man who knows he knows nothing is the idea that we can't be harmed by anybody but ourselves. To lead a good life is all the soul needs: the rest is incidental. He has always known—and so should his friends—that he was going to die. He's lived well right up to the end. If there was ever a happy ending, here it is.

*

The most consistent theme of Plato's dialogues is the character of Socrates, who blithely transcends all debates about Platonic philosophy. Not a year goes by that I don't have a Christian student write about how Socrates is a closet Christian, a Muslim student write about how Socrates is a Muslim, an atheist argue that Socrates is an atheist, a liberal emphasize the liberalism of his character, and a conservative sniff out the conservatism of his character. And they are all right. And they are all wrong. Right, because each has fastened onto a part of his character; wrong, because they've failed to see the whole. *C'est la vie.* But they're all forgivably wrong on this score, for nobody but Plato seems to understand that character fully.

Socrates is an idealist and a realist; a lover of the otherworldly,

who enjoys this world more than any seizer of the day; a defender of
free speech and of censorship; a social butterfly and a monk; an anarchist, who defends the law; equally at ease with slaves, sophists, poets, politicians, generals, soldiers, children, and prostitutes; a heavy
drinker and an ascetic; a rationalist and a poet; the proudest man
ever and the humblest; the most apparently contradictory, and yet
someone whose contradictions all reconcile into a believable whole.
I can't think of a character trait of his that doesn't contain some of
its opposite. If you don't see something of yourself in Socrates, it's
because you haven't looked, though generally our characters are better embodied by his bumbling interlocutors. Not long ago a literary
scholar published a book in which he argued that Shakespeare, the
master of both tragedy and comedy, portrayed in the many characters of his plays every aspect of human nature. Plato, it could be
boasted, did the same thing, but it took him only one character to
do so. Plato succeeded in writing a story that, like life itself, could be
regarded as a tragedy or a comedy, depending on how you hold it up
to the light. And he found a way of summing up human nature into a
personage of wisdom. Socrates's wisdom is not simply his awareness
of his ignorance: it's his ability to live our full humanity without the
shackling of half-truths.

PART 2 * *What Is Happiness?*

What is at stake is far from insignificant: it is how one should live one's life.
PLATO

I'm guilty of having asked my students: If the doctor told you today that in all likelihood you had only a year to live, how would you spend your time? The best answer I've so far received—best in the sense of most revealing and entertaining—came from Dan Wickenkamp, one of my favorite students.

Dan came to my attention the first moment I saw him. He's a big man, tall and strong, with a shaved head, somewhere between handsome and spooky, foreboding and fatherly. I believe he'd served in the military as well as worked in construction. It was when he started talking to me after class one day that I first saw the sparkles of intelligence and curiosity inside his imposing exterior. I'd mentioned some bizarre case history from Oliver Sacks, the Scheherazade of neurobiology, and he asked me—with real intensity—where I'd read it. I told him to check out *The Man Who Mistook His Wife for a Hat,* and that *Anthropologist on Mars* was also a terrific book. It was a Friday afternoon. The next Monday he cornered me again after class and asked what he should read about neurobiology. I reiterated that he should read *The Man Who Mistook His Wife for a Hat* or *Anthropologist on Mars.* He shook his head with impatience. He'd read those two books over the weekend. He wanted to know what else he should read.

One time I brought to Dan and the class photocopies of Philip Larkin's "Aubade" and passed them around, hoping that the poem would give voice to the darker side of Epicurus's materialism—"I work all day and get half-drunk at night. / Waking at four to soundless dark, I stare"—a poem I thought would speak for itself. After we'd read it aloud, I asked the class what they thought, a class with good chemistry and high spirits. All of a sudden the best and the worst lacked all conviction; the passionate intensity of the class was drained; the rest was silence. I made some final point about the poem and moved quickly on, thinking the whole thing a big flop.

Four years later I got a knock on my office door: it was Dan, wanting to catch up. He'd become a chiropractor, traveled across Australia, fallen in love, gotten married. "You know that poem you gave us—'Aubade,'" he said. I'd been suppressing the memory, but it all came back to me, and I braced myself for whatever he had to say next. "That poem really mystified me when you handed it out—why are postmen like doctors, for instance," he told me, "but certain lines grabbed me, and I could tell you thought the poem had something to say. So, I taped the poem to my mirror, and whenever I've shaved over the past four years, I read it and mulled it over. In the meantime, I read more stuff by Larkin, and that led me to W. H. Auden, and he led me to all sorts of stuff, including this philosopher by the name of Rosenstock-Huessy. Now I think I'm ready to talk about the poem." And did we ever.

When four years earlier Dan answered the question of how he'd spend his final days, his voice had the baritone playful growl characteristic of him at his most inspired. He said, "For the first nine months, it would be all orgies: I'd do all the drugs I wanted, I'd have as much crazy sex as possible, feast on big bloody steaks, gorge on chocolate, skydive, drive fast cars, smoke; then after I'd come out of my hangover, I'd spend my last three months donating all my time and money to charity. I'd convert to Christianity and beg for forgiveness, just in case." I wouldn't put it past someone with Dan's vivaciousness to live just that large in the face of imminent death. He'd get drunk all day and then half-saved at night! Dan's answer, which unleashed in the classroom the laughter of revealed truth, crystallizes Plato's insight into the problem of human happiness.

In the *Republic*, Plato's brothers provoke Socrates with one of the great myths: the story of Gyges and the ring. An earthquake opens a rift in the ground. Gyges, an upstanding shepherd to the king of Lydia, finds inside the rift a large corpse wearing a ring, which he takes. Playing around with it, Gyges discovers that by twisting the collet inward he can turn invisible, and by twisting it back can turn visible once more. Plato leaves some intermediary steps of the story to our imagination. It's hard not to imagine the shepherd ogling naked beauties, stealing baubles, pulling pranks, and what not. In any case, Gyges eventually uses his power to seduce the queen, kill the king, and become king himself. The beauty of it all is that he never has to lose his reputation as a decent man. He can do whatever wicked thing he likes under the cloak of invisibility, but to all appearances he's simply a lucky shepherd who pulled himself up by his bootstraps. Isn't that the best life of all, the happiest circumstance we could imagine: to be able to get whatever we want without ever having to pay any price we don't want to pay?

Like many of the seemingly fantastic myths of Plato, we realize on reflection that the magical story of Gyges is more naturalistic than an Italian neorealist movie, more realistic than reality TV—especially in our age. The computer and the TV *are* magic windows that permit us to see whatever we desire, as we hide invisibly behind their glowing screens. What are most talk shows but our chance to savor private domestic squabbles we have no right to see? We pull pranks and steal baubles when nobody is looking. Pornography has been the secret engine of photography, TV, and now computers. When its voluptuous beauties turn to look us in the eyes, they don't see anything at all. Recently, a powerful member of our government spoke, with unsettling honesty, of having "to work the dark side." We get so invisible we sometimes don't know what we're up to. Is Gyges happy? You tell me.

One insight Socrates draws from the story of the magic ring is that our souls are complicated. We can want conflicting things at the same time, including good and evil. He identifies three parts in particular: appetite, spirit, and reason, which can be symbolized by the gut, the heart, and the head. The gut wants to consume things and fears being deprived or hurt. The heart wants recognition, honor, praise, and success, and fears their opposites. The head longs for truth and goodness, for their sake alone. In short, our gut wants Dan's first nine months (probably about three-quarters of our psychology is devoted to the pursuit of pleasure); meanwhile our head, a smaller part, desires the goodness symbolized by Dan's last three months of charity. In the meantime, our heart vacillates in between; our willpower sometimes enforces the demands of reason, but mostly energizes us to pursue transient pleasures and to seek approval rather than the genuine worthiness of approval. When our soul is out of whack, and it usually is, our reason becomes mostly a way of rationalizing and strategizing, as our appetites tyrannize our lives.

According to Socrates, most of us conceive of a happiness of the part but have never imagined a happiness of the whole. We need some answer to the question of how to spend our time that isn't about satisfying a gut or a heart or a brain—or any other organ of the body for that matter. Real happiness pertains to the complete human being, the whole soul.

The central issue of philosophy in the wake of Socrates is how we can become virtuosos of being human, harmonizing the conflicting parts of our soul, a discipline Plato regards as essentially similar to harmonizing the conflicting voices of politics. The lovely ancient Greek word usually translated as happiness is *eudaimonia* (with our friend "daimon" at its center), meaning something like being in the good graces of the divine, well-being in all walks of life, having a good spirit. Plato's great student Aristotle even wondered whether a lifetime was enough. Perhaps before we call you happy, we should see how your children act after your death, for your life ripples on in theirs.

3 The Exquisite Materialism of Epicurus

Pray for peace and grace and spiritual food,
For wisdom and guidance, for all these are good,
But don't forget the potatoes.
J. T. PETTEE

We furnish plenty of support for Plato's insight that life in a democracy is ruled by the gut. "Consumerism" is our common word for our affliction. The gut aspect of our psyche wants to eat, excrete, and eat again. Somehow it's acquired a Midas touch that turns everything into consumables. We go through styles of clothing, furniture, art, politics—devouring them, growing bored, and then frantically searching for the next new thing. We crave scandals, drama, news—and after wolfing them down, complain of a bellyache, purge, and almost immediately crave more. We consume songs, TV shows, movies, celebrities; the very definition of popular culture seems to be "entertainment not meant to last longer than yogurt." Given the money/power, we consume cars, houses, yachts, skyscrapers, the earth itself. The contemporary philosopher Michael Sandel, in his book *What Money Can't Buy,* tells of rich lobbyists paying poor people to hold their places in line for congressional hearings, elementary school students being paid to read books, and—horrifyingly—a strapped single mother who earned money for her son's education by permanently tattooing the Web address of an online casino on her forehead. I'm sorry to report that a certain crowd has transmuted even poetry and philosophy into consumables: disciplines too often dominated by "rock stars" of the things of the spirit. As the bluesman W. C. Handy observed nearly a century ago, "From milkless milks to silkless silks, we're growing used to soulless souls."[1]

One reaction to our insanity, probably inseparable from it, is the turn to a certain species of religion, a kind of therapeutic "spirituality." Particularly popular in this regard are various Westernized forms of Buddhism and Daoism, which preach a letting go of desire and mindfulness to the moment. Isn't it a touch ironic to witness "Buddhist" retreats for corporate employees, or wealthy suburbanites paying for a half hour of nirvana before returning to their restless pursuits? The Western monotheisms have also mated with psychotherapy to beget their fair share of bastards. Ours is a complex medication of the spirit, not unlike when someone addicted to an upper has to take a downer to get some rest. Of course, many people skip the "opium of the people" and go straight to the drugs themselves.

It's in this context that proponents of more stringent forms of religion criticize modernity and offer their spiritual hierarchies as an alternative. For all their differences, orthodox believers in God agree that materialism is a central problem that undermines the well-being of the soul. What I find infinitely curious and wonderfully hopeful is that Epicurus offers just as deep a criticism of how we live and gives us an alternative that doesn't turn away from the rich, enchanting reality of the material universe.

*

Epicurus (circa 342–270 BC) was born on the Greek island of Samos, seven years after the death of Plato. As a young man he found his way to Athens, but a year later was banished with twelve thousand other poor citizens by Antipater. He migrated to the city of Colophon, and there studied materialist philosophy, returning to Athens in 307 BC. For the rest of his life, he lived and taught in a villa with a lush garden, dodging political life and cultivating an exquisite, humane form of happiness. His charming commune was brightened by his wife, his brother, and a few dear friends, male and female alike. "It is possible," as one of the anonymous authors of the renowned *Encyclopedia Britannica* (11th edition) delicately puts it, "that the relations between the sexes were not entirely what is termed Platonic. But there is on the other hand scarcely a doubt that the tales of licentiousness circulated by opponents are groundless."[2]

Epicurus died of kidney stones, which, mirabile dictu, he seems to have suffered gracefully. On his deathbed he wrote to a friend, "On this truly happy day of my life, as I am at the point of death, I write this to you. The disease in my bladder and stomach are pursuing their course, lacking nothing of their natural severity: but against all this is the joy in my heart at the recollection of my conversations with you."[3] His last will and testament provided for his birthday to be celebrated every year after his death, a fact I find interesting because of how committed he was to the idea that death is the dreamless sleep of Socrates—and hence shouldn't concern us at all. One of Epicurus's modern students, Jeremy Bentham, the nineteenth-century British utilitarian, demanded in his will that while his body should promote the general good by being used for science, his head should be carefully preserved atop his straw-stuffed clothes; the resulting "auto-icon" should then be brought to meetings of the College Council to be marked "present but not voting." As you might imagine, the head has been stolen and abused so many times by students that it has been locked away for good. A wax head now presides at the meetings. It is almost enough to make one a dualist.

The term "Epicurean," to those outside the philosophical circle, suggests a lover of exquisite food and good wine, admirably embodied by someone like Yves Mirande, the twentieth-century French playwright and life-lover, immortalized by his friend A. J. Liebling in the masterpiece memoir *Between Meals*. Here's an anecdote of Mirande's heroism:

In the restaurant on the Rue Saint-Augustin, M. Mirande would dazzle his juniors, French and American, by dispatching a lunch of raw Bayonne ham and fresh figs, a hot sausage in crust, spindles of filleted pike in a rich rosé sauce Nantua, a leg of lamb larded with anchovies, artichokes on a pedestal of foie gras, and four or five kinds of cheese, with a good bottle of Bordeaux and one of champagne, after which he would call for the Armagnac and remind Madame to have ready for dinner the larks and ortolans she had promised him, with a few langoustes and a turbot—and, of course, a fine civet made from the marcassin, or young wild boar, that the lover of the leading lady in his current production had sent up from his estate in the Sologne. "And while I think of it," I once heard him say, "we haven't had any woodcock for days, or truffles baked in the ashes, and the cellar is becoming a disgrace—no more 'thirty-fours and hardly any 'thirty-sevens. Last week, I had to offer my publisher a bottle that was far too good for him, simply because there was nothing between the insulting and the superlative."[4]

But Mirande, in fact, is not a good Epicurean by the standards of the philosophical school, for "the pleasurable life is not continuous drinking, dancing, and sex; nor the enjoyment of fish or other delicacies of an extravagant table," as Epicurus says.[5] The pleasurable life involves the clear-headed calculation of what will actually produce a stable, authentic pleasure. Too often we act like the child who wants to eat ice cream for every meal of the day. The taste of ice cream is assuredly pleasurable, but the experience of eating ice cream doesn't end with the melting sensations experienced by the tongue; and when we factor in all the effects of sustaining oneself on ice cream, we realize that the child's proposal backfires on its own terms: it isn't a pleasurable experience. Though I'm sure Liebling would prefer Blake's "the road of excess leads to the palace of wisdom" to Epicurus's moderation, he nonetheless faithfully chronicles the breakdown of Mirande's body, the lingering effects of his staggering meals, the pains that ripples long after all their original pleasures have vanished.[6]

But we misunderstand Epicurus if we take him to be saying, "It would be wonderful if we could eat like Mirande without suffering any ill effects, but given our physiology that's impossible; so we have to practice moderation." His real point is that the deepest pleasure comes from the satisfaction of our desires with the most basic nourishment. I myself am something of a cook, hardly immune to a luxurious table, but my favorite gustatory experience is always the first strawberry of the season plucked from the small strawberry patch in my backyard. Each one has its own unique little shape, ripe red but for the occasional moon-white splotch, golden seeds, a soft green hat. The faint scent makes my mouth water and my gums ache. I pop it in and—squishing, squishing—taste in the sweet clot what the French call *terroir*, the spirit of its earthly origin. The warm flesh of the berry calls to mind both sunlight and rain. My imagination gets the best of me, and I believe I'm experiencing the architecture of the previous year. One is plenty. I let my kids and the rabbits devour the rest.

Epicurus's preferred diet was barley bread, spring water, and fresh vegetables. A diet that leans on the staffs of life is easy to obtain and promotes our health; and "barley cakes and water provide the highest pleasure when someone in want takes them." Raw Bayonne ham washed down with Veuve Cliquot has its place, for "frugality too has a limit, and the man who disregards it is in like case with him who errs through excess," but luxuries should remain luxuries, the occasional adornment to a healthy diet.[7] Epicurus's occasional feast, it is said, was a slice of Cythnian cheese and a half pint of wine.

The foundational principle of Epicureanism—perhaps the sanest in all philosophy—is: pleasure good; pain bad. In a sense, all his philosophy amounts to is the rigorous, reasonable application of this elementary truth, which even newborns seem to have deduced. Epicurus sees no other way to give meaning to the concept of goodness, "Nor yet for my part can I find anything that I can understand as good if I take away from it the pleasures afforded by taste, those that come from listening to music, those that come from the eyes by the sight of figures in motion, or other pleasures produced by any of the senses in the complete person."[8] We can't, that is, imagine the bodiless existence of heaven without trotting out giant bird wings, sex with virgins, and Bach cantatas; or of hell without employing the instruments of the torture chamber.

But the pleasure-good-pain-bad principle is immensely complicated by the structure of our desires. Epicurus identifies three types of desire: (1) natural and necessary desires, which sustain our health and provide for our mental tranquility (like our hunger for food or our desire for companionship); (2) natural and unnecessary desires, which are extensions of our natural desires (like our wish to have artichokes on a pedestal of foie gras, or a Coke); and (3) unnatural and unnecessary desires (like our cravings for money, fame, or power). The big problem is that our desires tend to slip from the first category into the other two. Our natural desire for mother's milk becomes a mighty yen for ice cream. The discipline of Epicureanism is to contain and then weed out all our overgrown desires, to return to the basic, nourishing desires that do indeed provide for our happiness. As Thoreau once said, "Simplify, simplify," though based on that logic he should have just said, "Simplify."[9]

One easy way to tell a good from a bad desire, according to Epicurus, is to ask if it's limited or unlimited. Limited desires are the good kind and really do bring us happiness. We need no more after having attained the object of the desire. Water really does quench our thirst, and after we've drunk our fill, we want no more. Potato chips, on this account, never bring us real happiness: we always would prefer another, sometimes even after we start feeling sick. But the point needs to be expanded beyond food. A good pair of shoes should satisfy us as long as it holds out. But when we start wanting multiple pairs of shoes, we're headed down a path paved of potato chips, where no amount of Franco Sartos will ever be enough.

Almost all of us are in this boat. We "need" our morning cup of coffee. We "need" our car. We "need" the Internet. Yet we all know with a little reflection that we don't really. What we need, strictly speaking, is what nourishes and delights the body and the mind. Obviously, people unaddicted to caffeine who walk to work and spend their time elsewhere than on the Internet are not thereby disqualified from a happy life.

It's no great revelation that we live in a society with a deeply vested interest in unlimited desires, a society of *more*. If Epicurus is right, most societies are societies of more, for the problem is built into the structure of human desire. But surely we've raised the problem to new heights, for all our technological power and economic prowess have been harnessed to unleash it, to manipulate our desires from the cradle to the grave. It's interesting that, though occasionally ads simply give us information about a sale or a product, most of them have a metaphysical message. "You know when it's real." "Obey your thirst." "Live better." "Just do it." "Coke is it." One web engine's creepy slogan is: "We search what you think." Ads try to reshape how we fundamentally perceive reality because their nature is to make us want something we don't need—and usually don't even want.

But there's an irony to the Epicurean critique of our society. We are, in fact, bad consumerists. We aren't materialist enough. Only idiotic consumers stuff themselves with things that make them sick, fat, and unhappy. Only idiotic materialists fill their lives with disposable crap. A wise consumer enjoys exactly what the brain and the gut can agree is most enjoyable throughout a lifetime. A true materialist values things and seeks out the best. The authentic materialist-consumerist finds a reasonable way of relating to the desires of the body and shuns the desire that extends far beyond what anything in the physical universe can provide.

We don't even value money properly. We ought to regard it as nothing more than a medium of exchange, necessary only to the extent that it helps procure the things we need. We who must possess and use at least one credit card in order to participate in our economy are shocked that most of human history has inveighed against usury, the charging of interest on loans. But the desire to see money as something more than a convenient form of exchange is very powerful and—if our traditions contain any wisdom—ruinous to healthy forms of life. There has been much talk recently about the derivatives market, where investors can bet on the market itself. But there's a sense in which money is the original derivatives market. As soon as money becomes an object of desire rather than simply a tool for the procurement of a desire, then we've entered into an abstract world of value that will never really satisfy our psyches. If the idea of a million-dollar windfall excites you, then you're not a true materialist: you're an abstractionist, more taken by fantasies than by realities. You should greet winning a million dollars like winning a million tubes of toothpaste. The wise response is, "I don't really need a million tubes of toothpaste (or a million dollars); I need only enough to brush my teeth (or satisfy my true desires) and maybe a few spares. The rest is a big nuisance."

The deepest form of our pathological desire for more appears in our relationship to death. According to the Epicureans, immortality is a bad desire, regardless of the form it takes, whether as the wish for an endless heaven or the materialist version of the immortality of the soul: living as long as possible—as Woody Allen says, "I don't want to achieve immortality through my works. I want to achieve it through not dying." Or, as Studs Terkel used to joke, "Who wants to be ninety?! Anybody who's eighty-nine." But the fact that life is limited is exactly what makes it good. When we live on credit, we squander all our riches. Epicurus's natural desires are not those necessary to survival. Yes, natural desires sustain our bodies over time, but the desire simply to survive, according to Epicurus, is pure foolishness. He marvelously says, "Some men throughout their lives gather together the means of life, for they do not see that the draft swallowed by all of us at birth is a draft of death."[10] To embrace life with his rational gusto is to accept that life comes to an end.

As a materialist, Epicurus argues that death is nothing to us—literally, nothing—and so shouldn't be upsetting. Remember what it was like before you were born: was that at all a hard time for you? You should be no more scared of death than regretful of the days before your birth. "While we are, death is not; when death is come, we are not." Why fear something you won't be around for? You've been given a bottle of the most marvelous wine. Enjoy it for what it is. There's no need to demand an endless supply in your cellar, nor to fret over the fact that it will eventually be gone. Especially because you're going to pass out precisely at the moment you drain the lees. You won't even have to suffer the hangover.

*

As materialists, not just in the moral but also the metaphysical sense of the word, Epicureans are committed to the idea that the world is no more than atoms, the void, and the creative principles of movement, which they marvelously name "the swerve." Everything, in short, is the product of chance, which is a view often criticized in our society by certain religious believers who claim that the world—or at least certain irreducibly complex features of it, like the flagellum or the eyeball—are so wondrously formed that they must be designed by a capacious intelligence, namely, God. Such believers have the sense that if the world were just the product of chance, it would be drained of meaning and value, that an atheistic materialism dries up our wellsprings of gratitude for the intricate beauties of existence.

I wonder, though, if atheistic materialism and traditional theology don't converge on the same basic point. According to the Christian theologians, God creates ex nihilo; in other words, His act of creation is an act of grace. He creates rhinoceroses much like a child draws unicorns: the horned creatures of the world are the result of their overflowing creativity. We should feel thankful, the religious believers argue, because every moment is pure gravy, a gift of God. But the Epicurean also greets the world as the result of unthinkably marvelous luck. Imagine, a bunch of atoms randomly swerving around the universe somehow produced out my window—at the moment of my writing—a thrush singing notes that somehow strike against the contraption of my ear in such a way as somehow to remind me of the sound of water dripping on stone. The material of this purposeless universe miraculously pumped out me and you, purposeful beings, not to mention all the rhinoceros-bizarre menagerie of being. "The secret of Epicurean joy and serenity," as Pierre Hadot says, "is to live each instant as if it were the last, but also as if it were the first."[11]

Another common fear that religious believers harbor about materialism is that it undermines morality. Epicurus argues the exact opposite: the rigorous pursuit of pleasure leads straight to the life of a
moralist. Why shouldn't we tell a lie? Simple: lying makes us unhappy.
Telling the truth, like exercise, may sometimes hurt at first, but one
always feels better overall. Immorality is one more form of childish
reasoning: we do wrong to extricate ourselves from some difficult
situation, but wrongdoing simply multiplies our difficult situations.
In fact, justice and pleasure reinforce each other: the more pleasant
our life, the less likely we are to do others wrong; and when we do
others right, the more pleasant our life. Carlo Petrini, the founder
of Slow Food, a modern-day Epicurean movement, slowly discovered
the same idea, "I came to understand that those who suffer for others do more damage to humanity than those who enjoy themselves.
Pleasure is a way of being at one with yourself and others."[12] The idea
is nobly expressed by Wendell Berry, that champion of small farms
and human pleasures, "Moral, practical, spiritual, esthetic, economic,
and ecological values are all concerned ultimately with the same
question of life and health. To the virtuous man, for example, practical and spiritual questions are identical; it is only corruption that can
see a difference."[13]

What we need in life, according to Epicurus, is relatively simple.
We need human companionship. Not so much the brief heroin ec-
stasies and long junkie lows of romantic love, but the steady joys
of friendship or, at least, family and romantic relationships alloyed
with friendship. "Of all the means which are procured by wisdom to
ensure happiness throughout the whole of life," Epicurus declares,
"by far the most important is the acquisition of friends."[14] We need
good work in order to find meaning and provide for our essentials.
An ideal job would be subsistence farming, which does both simultaneously. But any job (I happen to know of one) that is satisfying and
doesn't upset our tranquility will do. We need food and drink, simple
clothes, the pleasures of conversation—ideally about philosophy. A
roof over our heads would be nice, though in the right climates the
stars do fine. Avoid politics, which is a royal headache, but if you have
to live with a lot of people, then work to have good rules that promote everybody's well-being, for "the just life is inseparable from the
pleasant life."[15] To have these things, none of which is particularly
difficult to obtain, is to be filthy rich. "Thanks be to blessed Nature,"

Epicurus prays, "because she has made what is necessary easy to supply, and what is not easy unnecessary."[16]

I have to admit that the Epicurean ideal is a bit harder to attain now than it was back in its day—or even sixty years ago. What Epicurus calls "natural wealth"—bread, friendship, humane culture, water—is supposed to be easy to acquire. But if you stalk the supermarket aisles in search of calories that are inexpensive to buy, crying out to you will be not the fruits and vegetables, but—due to what we might ironically call the "free market"—the potato chips. Moreover, if you're searching for these cheap calories because of your economic straits, then it's also likely that your third-shift job and your spouse's first- and second-shift jobs make it less likely that you sit down to break bread with those you love. Sometimes it can seem that only the upper middle class or above have the money and time to enjoy a meal of the simple products of nature with friends and family.

Despite our commodified common life, I take heart in the wisdom of Epicurus. Even in Athens, he advised unplugging oneself from the bustle of "the political life"—what we're more apt to call "the dominant culture." It's not about what those around us value or peddle. It's about our attitude. We must work on reversing the trend of desire, refocusing on what matters, and living sane lives; and ultimately it doesn't take much money to do so. Insofar as we do enter into politics, it should be to make the laws a little less crazy and a little more suited to the real well-being of our fellow citizens. I often have students who toil below the poverty level, just as I occasionally have students of decent means. In my experience, neither group has a notably larger advantage when it comes to finding the good life.

*

I've been lucky enough to know and work for Simone Delaty. Originally from France, she taught French language and literature at the University of Iowa for many years, retired, moved out to a small house in the country, and opened a peculiar restaurant with the Epicurean name of *Simone's Plain and Simple*. Currently, she's cut back on how frequently it's open (in her seventies she's taken up extreme outdoor photography); but when it was going full steam, the restaurant was open late March through November on Friday, Saturday, and sometimes Monday nights; you had to reserve all of her "restaurant"—it is her house—for a party of between eight and twenty people, usually months in advance. I'd eaten there a couple of times; and Simone and I had hit it off. When she found out I had a serious interest in French cooking and was capable of whipping up *gougères* and a *lapin à la moutarde*, she asked if I would be available to help her out once in a while.

The place is something else, a French restaurant on a gravel road, a bistro in the middle of nowhere (i.e., the steeply rolling hills of farmland several miles from Kalona). She built a brick oven—engraved "Vive le Pain!"—in which a blazing hardwood fire works on her exquisite breads and pizzas. On warm nights, guests dine on her giant screened-in porch and look out at wildflower fields. As her restaurant's name suggests, there's nothing particularly fancy about the food, though guests whose concept of luxury is party potatoes would disagree. She makes the patés, braised meats, *batards*, spiced vegetables, and pastries of her native France, using, when she can, ingredients from her extensive gardens. She agrees with Rousseau that it's only at great expense that we've succeeded in having bad fruits and bad vegetables on our table the whole year round. She doesn't completely disdain la nouvelle cuisine; in fact, she prefers Alice Waters to Auguste Escoffier. But she doesn't like modish attempts to muddle and complicate flavors. What she seeks is the richest taste of the highest-quality ingredients, insisting on what the Italians call *insaporire*—the enflavoring of food, the drawing out of the food's deepest flavors, which involves careful cooking and the use of minimal, albeit perfect, seasoning. Plain and simple. The essence of a dinner, Simone insists, is only partly related to the food. It's really about providing the essentials necessary to elicit the conviviality of the company, the enflavoring of human culture itself. As Epicurus says with admirable plainness and simplicity, "Before you eat and drink anything consider carefully who you eat and drink it with: for eating without a friend is the life of a lion or a wolf."[17]

After working a dinner at Simone's, I'm dead tired. The work is not simply cooking several courses for twenty people, which itself can be a day-long exhausting affair, particularly after teaching. Whoever works at Simone's, including the now seventy-year-old Simone, does everything: setting and waiting on tables, washing dishes, weeding, picking vegetables, feeding the brick oven, and some shamefully un-common activities like killing and plucking pigeons (in this case, for the wonderful pie the Moroccans call *bisteeya*).

So there I was one night, after a long day of work, the dessert served, and nothing but some dishes left to do. My body, tired and satisfied, was registering what I'd accomplished. I'd reserved a bit of dough to make myself a pizza and had just slid it off the wooden pad-dle into the dying light of the oven. The sun was all but set, and the giant Iowa sky was full of intensifying pinks and purples—a more dramatic version of the colors in the brick oven. Simone's house sits atop a high hill, and I looked out on miles and miles of rolling fields where a million fireflies were blinking on and off in their novel con-stellations. All around me there was the silence of the country—a si-lence made up of insect hums and vegetable rustlings, though I could also hear from Simone's porch the talk and tinklings of civilization.

Nature is not opposed to culture, just to bad culture. At that mo-ment nature and culture were mingling beautifully: the aroma of fire and bread (mixed, as Epicurus's, with barley), the harmony of crick-ets and human laughter, the friendship of Simone within walking distance of my native solitude. I felt in possession of an almost em-barrassing amount of natural wealth. But I had no desire to cry out to the moment, "Verweile doch, / Du bist so schön" (Stay awhile, / You are so beautiful—Goethe), even though I was filled to the brim with the passage of time.[18] I was glad to have done what I had done; I was looking forward to sleep; and I was perfectly content with a few minutes of fireflies and the prospect of pizza. Besides, the half pint of wine Simone had poured me was really hitting the spot.

Could I have done better for myself?

4 The Mysterious Freedom of the Stoic

Grant me a soul to which dullness is naught,
knowing no complaint, grumble or sigh,
and do not permit me to give too much thought
to that domineering creature called the "I."
My Lord, endow me with a sense of humor,
give me the grace of understanding jest,
that I might know the joy that life harbors
and were able to grant it to the rest.
THOMAS MORE

I won't ridicule—it's too easy—the dressing up of our crass wishes in the robes of religion, students praying before exams and what not. But sometimes prayers are of the utmost profundity. The torque of reality can become so intense that the inclination to pray is almost irresistible. On hearing that a beloved child is in a coma, even the most hardened atheist may waver in faith and risk a petition upward. If my soul encounters God in the afterlife, and He tells me that, yes indeed, all the atrocious evils of life are essential pieces in some great puzzle of goodness, I believe I'd still pray that they not happen. Is it piety or impiety when Alfonso, in the twelfth century, proclaims, "If I had been of God's counsel at creation, many things would have been ordered better"?[1]

Having our prayers answered is an intuitive idea of happiness, and we're certainly unhappy when things don't go our way. Yet the Stoics, conceivers of the most influential ancient vision of happiness, hold that happiness is just the reverse. Epictetus sums up the essence of Stoicism in one command, "Do not ask things to happen as you wish, but wish them to happen as they do happen, and your life will go smoothly."[2] Happiness isn't having our wishes granted, and freedom isn't doing what we want. The only prayer, as far as our happiness and our freedom are concerned, is: Thy will be done.

*

Sometime toward the end of the fourth century BC Zeno of Citium crawled to Athens after his ship wrecked. He stumbled into a bookshop, began reading about Socrates, and was so inspired that he asked where he could meet a living example of such a marvelous man. The bookseller directed him to Crates the Cynic, a wise, cheerful philosopher who lived in abject poverty. Zeno promptly became his student. One day Crates gave Zeno a bowl of steaming lentils and told him to carry it around, which the student obediently did. Suddenly, Crates whacked the bowl with his staff, spilling the soup all over Zeno, who began to run off in embarrassment. Crates called out, "Why run off, my little Phoenician? Nothing bad has happened to you!" Zeno was immediately enlightened, and Stoicism was born. "I made a prosperous voyage," he wryly observes, "when I suffered a shipwreck."[3]

Because Zeno began teaching at the "painted porch," which in Greek was called the *Stoa Poikile*, the doctrines associated with him were called Stoicism—Porchism. It quickly became the most popular philosophy among the educated in the Hellenistic world, and by the time of the Roman Empire had spread to all walks of society. The philosophy's surviving texts date from the later Roman period and include the *Meditations*, the masterpiece by the emperor Marcus Aurelius; essays and letters by Seneca, the great playwright, financier, and tutor to Nero; and the *Discourses*, the masterpiece by the slave Epictetus, the most eloquent, direct expositor of the Stoic ideal.

Can we control our anger, excitement, sadness, anxiety, grief, envy, pity, and so on? Don't good and bad emotions sometimes overwhelm us and carry us away? Say you walk out to your car and find that it's been stolen. If I told you, "Stop being upset right now; you're in charge of your emotions," you'd likely respond, "I can't help how I feel right now; my car has just been stolen," even if not in so many words. But the Stoics hold that your emotions in that situation, and even much worse situations, are indeed completely in your control, because, in the words of Shakespeare, "There is nothing either good or bad but thinking makes it so," or, as Epictetus says, "It is not the things themselves that disturb people but the judgments about those things."[4]

Our emotions, the Stoics claim, depend on our beliefs. Being upset about your stolen car depends on the idea that your car's being stolen upsets your plans and offends your sense of justice. But if you hate your car and are an honest-to-goodness anarchist, or even if you just have very good insurance, your reaction to a stolen car will be different. Epictetus's prime example is Socrates: "Death . . . is nothing terrible, or else it would have appeared so to Socrates."[5] Because most of us have the idea that death is terrible, it stirs up negative emotions in us whenever we're forced to confront it. But Socrates honestly regards death as a necessity of life, in no way intrinsically bad, a blessing in fact; thus he's merry as ever at his sentencing, in essence responding, "You haven't sentenced me to death; life itself did. All you've done is given me a date."

"Some things are up to us, and some things are not," as Epictetus says at the beginning of the *Handbook*, the distillation of his *Discourses*.[6] Because our beliefs are up to us, we can eventually get our emotions under control. We determine our plans. We can weed out irrational ideas. We have the mental muscle, even if it's grown flabby from lack of use, to govern our mindset. Thus, by eliminating the ideas that generate negative emotions, we're capable of being permanently happy, if we so choose. To use an image from Plato, our emotions are strong horses, and our reason is the charioteer. Though few charioteers exert the discipline necessary to master the horses, it's possible to channel their energies properly and get them to go exactly where we demand.

Everything else, however we try to influence it, is ultimately out of our hands. We can *try* to influence our reputation, our possessions, our job, our family, our world, our body. But we don't ultimately *control* what happens to them. The best-laid plans o' mice and men gang oft a-glee; and when they do, if we've tied our hopes to those plans, we're unhappy. Life is trying its damnedest to make us Stoics, everyday spilling coffee on our favorite shirts, putting kinks in our necks, blowing the winds of politics in an unfavorable direction, sometimes even snapping our spines or taking loved ones from us. In fact, after one of my lectures where I had used a stolen car as a handy example of something that the Stoics believe shouldn't upset you, I walked out to my car and—it had been stolen. (I leave to your imagination the extent of my Stoicism.) Yet we still head off every morning with the brave, stupid hope that we'll be able to organize the infinitely vast vicissitudes of the universe to fit our whims and quirky projects, regardless of everything that happened yesterday. This time around things will be different!

The great Stoic metaphor, going back to the Greek philosopher Chrysippus, is that we're like dogs leashed to a powerful chariot. When the chariot begins to move, we have two choices: trot or be dragged. Either way, we go the same place. The exact same place. After your car has been stolen, you're welcome to kick the curb, swear, and generally be dragged, but it won't magically bring back your ride anymore than a rebellious poodle will change the course of a Mack truck. It's not been given us to dictate the ultimate fate of our lives. No, it has been given us only to be miserable or happy. It's quite the story of humanity: all these dogs behind their carriages, some trotting, tongues wagging in happiness; others being dragged, yelping and growling until they finally get sick of it and start trotting. Then, when the carriage turns, some trotters start dragging miserably, and some draggers get up and suddenly trot happily for a spell.

The secret of happiness is to make up our mind to trot: to bring our thoughts in accord with "nature," to use the word the Stoics employ. Nature, which is also sometimes called "Zeus" or "Destiny" or "God's will," means more than just what goes on in national parks. It's how everything goes. When a mug breaks, that's nature, for ceramic objects are fragile and often get bumped. When you get in a car wreck, that's nature, too, because it's inevitable that when humans fly around at breakneck speeds in large metal carriages they'll occasionally run into each other. Nature, in other words, isn't difficult to fathom or even predict. In fact, I can make any number of Nostradamus-like prophecies about your relationship to nature: a dish of yours is going to break; the Cubs are going to lose; you're going to get sick sometime this year; someone you love is going to die; your car is going to need work; something you hope for will come true; something you fear will too—oh, and there's no hope for you, you're going to die, though the exact date is a little fuzzy.

Why, then, are we unhappy and even shocked when my prophecies come to pass? Isn't it absurd to get angry when you're tackled, if you signed up to play football? Imagine a running back dusting himself off and complaining it's unfair that he of all people should have to be knocked down. Getting tackled—and even injured—is very much part of his game, just as having a glass means having something that very well could be shattered, just as living a life means dealing with sickness, disease, and death. As in football, it's fine to do one's best to avoid getting tackled by cancer, but if it does trip you up, you should accept it as part of the game you're playing.

You might protest that unlike the football player you didn't sign up for the game. True, but as Epictetus observes, "Remember that the door is open. Do not be more cowardly than children, but just as they say, when the game no longer pleases them, 'I will play no more,' you too, when things seem that way to you, should merely say, 'I will play no more,' and so depart; but if you stay, stop moaning."[7] Nobody compels you to play football, drive on freeways, or collect breakable items. If you're unwilling to play such a harsh game as life, where even children die of cancer, then you should be grateful that you have options. Your parents may have signed you up, but you are free to quit.

The contemplation of suicide may seem macabre, but in truth it's just the opposite. Nothing could be more liberating than saying, "Today I'm not going to kill myself; I'm going to face the world in all its power." Can you ever really say yes until you realize that you can say no? To go on living with the possibility of suicide clearly in your mind is to embrace life with real gusto. I think of the wonderful lines from Victor Hugo,

> Personally, I don't expect God to keep himself under control, not
>   always,
> You have to put up with some vibrant excesses
> From such a great poet, and not lose your temper
> If the master who tinges peach-blossom so subtly
> And arches the rainbow right over the ocean he pacifies
> Should give us a hummingbird one day, and next day a mastodon.
> Bad taste is one of his quirks,
> He likes to add dragons to chasms and maggots to sewers,
> To do everything on an astonishing scale,
> To be a combined Rabelais-Michaelangelo.
> That's what the Lord is like; and I just accept it.[8]

That's what you're signing up for. Just accept it. Or don't. You're welcome to be dragged.

*

Nobody's saying that controlling your mindset can be accomplished overnight. In spending the lion's share of our energies trying to control what's not up to us, most of us have let our mental muscles atrophy. The Stoics, like most ancient philosophers, appreciate just how hard it is to carry through with the project of changing your life, even when you're convinced of a goal. As Tom Sawyer observes, it's hard for most of us, even on hearing the best preacher on Sunday, to stay saved past Tuesday. Thus, Stoicism is a goal, but it's also a process of progressing toward the goal. If you believe that Stoicism is a worthy philosophy to live by, then you must train like an athlete in preparation for the big tournament, even if, as Epictetus says, "Now is the time of the contest, and the Olympic games have arrived."[9] Here are some techniques for the Stoic-in-training.

Study

When possible, make friends with real philosophers and spend time conversing about how to achieve what's best in life. Remember, a philosopher isn't necessarily someone with a degree in philosophy; it's someone who cuts through the crap and pursues, in word and deed, what really matters.

Short of philosophical conversation, find some time every day to read philosophers who have your happiness in mind, the ones interested in getting you to see the world as it is and not as you wish it to be. Plato's Socratic dialogues are unbeatable because they don't simply tell us the truth—they are exercises for us to seek truth ourselves; besides, they give us the ultimate model of the Stoic sage in the character of Socrates. Then, of course, there are the Stoics themselves. I'd recommend starting with Epictetus, who is the clearest and in some ways the firmest: "If you want your children and your wife and your friends to live forever, you are stupid."[10] After his bracing dose of Stoicism, then turn your attentions to the mellower Seneca, who says a few reassuring things, like, "There is a healthy moderation in wine, as in liberty. Solon and Arcesilas are thought to have liked their wine, and Cato has been accused of drunkenness; whoever accused him will more easily make the charge honorable than Cato disgraceful."[11]

Meditate in the Morning

One of the most important Stoic disciplines involves the regular contemplation of what you dread. Every morning engage in what Seneca calls a *praemeditatio*: picture the things that you fear happening sometime in the upcoming day—your favorite mug gets broken, your car is stolen, you're fired from your job, a loved one is diagnosed with cancer, and so on. For these things are real parts of the games you're choosing to play if you decide to get out of bed. Marcus Aurelius says: "Say to yourself in the early morning: I shall meet today ungrateful, violent, treacherous, envious, uncharitable men. All of these things have come upon them through ignorance of real good and ill."[12]

You might be thinking, "If being happy involves spending your breakfast imagining your best friend dying of cancer, thanks but no thanks." But visualizing what we fear isn't simply thinking about bad things so when they happen they're not surprising, nor do I believe it's a recipe for a glum mood. Remember, there's nothing good or bad but thinking makes it so. In imagining what we fear, we're training ourselves to see reality clearly. It's only then that our true emotions will be unleashed. If in the morning you imagine in vivid detail that your friend will die, and then you see your friend that afternoon, how will you feel and act? Wouldn't you feel a kind of gratitude? Wouldn't you be less likely to squander your time together? Contrast that with how you feel without the Stoic practice. Far from depressing us, the confrontation with our fears is most likely to make us grateful for all we're given. It's when you take your friend for granted, assuming that you have infinite time to savor together, that you live poorly and are unable to face death, your own or others'.

By the way, if your friend does indeed die, the Stoics aren't asking us to respond, "No big deal: I always knew it was going to happen." As Seneca says, "Nature requires from us some sorrow, while more than this is the result of vanity. But never will I demand of you that you should not grieve at all."[13] Grieving is a complex thing. Much of our grief over someone's death is selfish, a feeling of, "I don't deserve this; I want more time with my friend; life is so unfair." Imagine if I loaned you a book and said, "You can have this a while, but I may need it back at some point." If I see you in three weeks and say that I need the book back now, wouldn't it be absurd to clutch onto it and whine, "I don't deserve this; I want more time with it and expected to have it longer; you're being so unfair"? As the Stoics point out, that's precisely the situation we're in with everyone and everything we love: they've all been loaned to us for an uncertain period of time. It's our job to do right by them when we have time together and to be graceful when the time comes to give them up. Whatever grief remains after our vanity has been extirpated is fine and good. Only after having made significant progress toward the Stoic ideal can we really pay our respects to one who has left us and feel the natural sorrow that's symbolized in our rituals of letting go. To grieve for ourselves when someone else dies is nothing to be proud of.

Start Small

Being able to accept with grace the death of a loved one is hard to do—agreed. The Stoics rarely claimed to be able to do so. Just as genuine Christians strive to be like Jesus, the Stoics strive to be like the Stoic sage. (When in doubt, Epictetus says, ask yourself, "What would Socrates do?"—WWSD.) But just as most Christians are far from being able to take up the cross, so too are few Stoics fully realized in their Stoicism. The subsequent practical advice is that the Stoic initiate should start small. We can't lift the heavy stuff yet, but we can work out with the light weights, which are usually all we have to cope with anyway. What vexes our days is rarely theft and death; it's usually a broken mug, an in-law's cutting remark, a bad time at the pool—things that we all are mentally strong enough to accept, if only we exert ourselves. When the mug breaks, say, "It's just a mug: I knew it wouldn't last forever." Tell yourself before your visit to the in-laws that you refuse to allow them to control your emotions: prepare yourself to transcend all pettiness. When you go to the pool, think, "I might be splashed inadvertently, my towel might be dropped in a puddle, and if it's not a private pool, it's a public restroom."

Pay Attention

Turn off autopilot and pay attention to what you're doing and why. We need always to remember that we're signing up for the life we're leading. Where you can, sign up for what is truly meaningful. But look to uncover the significance of *any* activity you participate in.

Remember that all around you is the majesty of nature and the mystery of humanity. Be conscious that you have the power to control yourself in all areas of life. Treat the tough times as good opportunities to advance yourself. As Marcus Aurelius says in the *Meditations*, "Everywhere and at all times, it is up to you to rejoice piously at what is occurring at the present moment, to conduct yourself with justice towards the people who are present here and now, and to apply rules of discernment to your present representations, so that nothing slips in that is not objective."[14]

Have a Sense of Humor
Don't be hurt or offended when people act poorly, or upset when things don't go your way. Instead, chuckle at the discrepancy between our human ideas and how reality plays out. For that matter, you should also chuckle when things do—miracle of miracles—go your way. Epictetus says, "If [a philosopher] is praised, he laughs within himself at the person who is praising him."[15] The true Stoic sage is likely above the necessity of humor, for there would be no discrepancy in the sage between how things go and the sage's will. But until we reach those lofty heights, laughter is a good way of transcending our dependencies.

My mentor, Dr. Donald Phillip Verene, taught me to look out on life as a nonstop carnival, where colleagues and even complete strangers perform as freaks and clowns, free of charge. As Seneca says,

We should make light of all things and endure them with tolerance: it is more civilized to make fun of life than to bewail it. Bear in mind too that he deserves better of the human race as well who laughs at it than he who grieves over it; since the one allows it a fair prospect of hope, while the other stupidly laments over things he cannot hope will be put right. And, all things considered, it is the mark of a greater mind not to restrain laughter than not to restrain tears, since laughter expresses the gentlest of our feelings, and reckons that nothing is great or serious or even wretched in all the trappings of our existence.[16]

Review in the Evening
At the end of the day, review what you have and have not accomplished. Seneca recommends asking, "What ailment of yours have

you cured today? What failing have you resisted? Where can you show improvement?"[17] It's not unlike what good store owners periodically do, asking where they might do things better, how they might cut costs or increase productivity. If you've failed in some way, you're hurting yourself. The goal is the opposite of religious guilt, which the Stoics would regard as silly excuse making: just change what you're doing or, if you find that you're committed to what you're doing, change your goal. The object of the evening review is honest reflection about what you believe in, and ultimately self-improvement.

After the review, the famous serenity prayer of Reinhold Niebuhr might be appropriate, at least the part that goes, "God, give us the grace to accept with serenity the things that cannot be changed, courage to change the things that should be changed, and the wisdom to distinguish the one from the other."[18] Or you might consider saying the prayer that Epictetus so heartily recommends:

Lead me, Zeus, and you too, Destiny,
Wherever I am assigned by you.
I'll follow and not hesitate.
But even if I do not wish to,
Because I'm bad, I'll follow anyway.[19]

Essentially the dog's prayer to the chariot.

*

The most common complaint that people make about Stoicism is that it seems to demand a completely passive relationship to life. We need to get upset at what happens, they say, in order to make the world a better place. We shouldn't sit on our hands as the world crumbles, shrugging, "Oh well, what can I do about it?" The most vehement version of this criticism was made by a burly student of mine named Robert, a wrestler who hadn't spoken up in class until we got to the Stoics. He raised his hand and declared that it's absolutely crucial for him never to tolerate his defeats because his anger at himself and the wrestlers who beat him is necessary for his self-improvement. Accepting defeat is what losers do.

Robert's point is similar to Aristotle's, who describes anger as a "desire accompanied by pain, for a conspicuous revenge for a conspicuous slight at the hands of men who have no call to slight oneself or one's friends . . . It must always be attended by a certain pleasure—that which arises from the expectation of revenge."[20] As long as anger is directed properly it's healthy and useful, according to Robert and Aristotle.

It must be said right off that the great Stoics were anything but passive in their lives. Seneca, the mellowest of them all, was a tutor of the emperor, a senator, one of Rome's greatest playwrights, and a financier who made a fortune. Are words like "passive" or "lazy" appropriate to describe Marcus Aurelius who vigorously ruled an entire empire, commanded a vast army, and presided over what the magisterial historian Edward Gibbon describes as "the period in the history of the world during which the condition of the human race was most happy and prosperous"?[21]

The Stoics believe that wrestlers should work to do the best they can at wrestling—and we're all wrestlers. As the emperor says, "The art of living is more like wrestling than dancing," or, "A wrestler in the greatest contest of all: not to be overthrown by any passion."[22] Or as Epictetus phrases it, "It is difficulties that show what men are. Consequently, when a difficulty befalls, remember that God, like a physical trainer, has matched you with a rugged young man."[23] But when you choose to be a wrestler you are choosing to engage in a sport of winning and losing. It's wasted energy, the Stoics claim, to be angry at losing itself. If your loss was the result of cutting weight too quickly, making a dumb mistake, not giving it your all, or failing to prepare, then you should resolve to make improvements. If, conversely, you wrestled at the top of your game and lost anyway, what is there to be upset about? If your participation in wrestling is contingent on winning, then the Stoics claim you're being childish. Anger, if one wants to call it that, is appropriate when directed at something you can change—namely, what you're willing to do; but once you've lost, the only option you have is to accept it or be dragged.

Anything truly worth doing is worth failing at. In fact, the test we should use to recognize what the Stoics call our duty is to ask of any endeavor: Would it be worth doing even if our utmost efforts will amount to worldly failure? If it is, then that's what you're meant to do in this life. If your participation in an activity is contingent on being successful, then it's not your destiny. You shouldn't go into wrestling thinking, "I'm going to do this in order to be a national champion." You should ask yourself, "Would this be worth giving my all to, even if I lose my most important match?" (I happen to be a former wrestler and long-time wrestling fan; so Robert and I got into a long discussion after class about our hero Dan Gable's famous loss in the final match of his senior year, the only one he'd ever suffered up to that point. He argued that it was Gable's refusal to accept the loss that led to his illustrious career as an Olympian and a coach.) Rather than wrestle for a gold medal, the Stoics recommend we wrestle to be our best. (Maybe I shouldn't give away the secret, but I have a hunch that the Stoic wrestler is the one most likely to get the gold.)

*

If we follow the logic of Stoicism to its natural conclusion, then we end up at the startling idea that a human could be happy even while being tortured. Our bodies, after all, aren't up to us. The Stoic sage—admittedly rare—should be able to say, "You may torture my body, but you can't harm me. I alone can harm myself." At first glance, the idea that happiness is compatible with torture strikes many people as a deal breaker. If happiness is torture, perhaps we should stick to our "unhappy" lives.

Real torture victims are likely to be more sympathetic to Stoicism. There's a wonderful essay called "Courage Under Fire: Testing Epictetus's Doctrines in a Laboratory of Human Behavior" by James Bond Stockdale, probably best known as Ross Perot's running mate in the 1992 presidential election, the one who wandered aimlessly around during the vice-presidential debate, musing, "Why am I here?" The essay is largely about Stockdale's experience as a fighter pilot who was shot down over North Vietnam during his second tour of duty. He parachuted down into enemy territory and spent six years in a prison camp, two of those years in leg irons, and four in solitary confinement. He was brutally tortured fifteen times. When he was released, he was not a broken man. In fact, he quotes Aleksandr Solzhenitsyn sympathetically, "Bless you, prison, for having been part of my life."[24] He attributes it to the luck of having studied the philosophy of Epictetus in Philosophy 6: The Problems of Good and Evil with Professor Philip Rhinelander at Stanford University.

Stockdale annotates with his own experience Epictetus's famous idea of what's not up to us:

For starters, let's take "your station in life." As I glide down toward that little town on my short parachute ride, I'm just about to learn how negligible is my control over my station in life. It's not all up to me. I'm going right now from being the leader of a hundred-plus pilots and a thousand men and, goodness knows, all sorts of symbolic status and goodwill, to being an object of contempt. I'll be known as a "criminal." But that's not half the revelation that is the realization of your own fragility—that you can be reduced by wind and rain and ice and seawater or men to a helpless, sobbing wreck—unable to control even your own bowels—in a matter of minutes. And, more than even that, you're going to face fragilities you never before let yourself believe you could have—like after mere minutes, in a flurry of action while being bound with tourniquet-tight ropes, with care, by a professional, hands behind, jackknifed forward and down towards your ankles held secure in lugs attached to an iron bar, that, with the onrush of anxiety, knowing your upper body's circulation has been stopped and feeling the ever-growing induced pain and the ever-closing-in of claustrophobia, you can be made to blurt out answers, sometimes correct answers, to questions about anything they want to know.[25]

It was not that stoical Stockdale was able to whistle blithely as they broke his bones, but he did find that he was able to train himself to maintain his dignity even in the darkest holes of human depravity, whispering to himself, "control fear, control guilt, control fear, control guilt." The torture of the body is simply the most effective way of breaking the soul. In the isolation chamber after being tortured "what we [Stockdale and his fellow inmates] actually contemplated was what even the most laid-back American saw as his betrayal of himself and everything he stood for. It was there that I learned what 'Stoic Harm' meant. A shoulder broken, a bone in my back broken, a leg broken twice were peanuts by comparison."[26]

As the ranking officer, Admiral Stockdale was in charge of all the American soldiers in the camp. He scrapped the usual commands (for instance, to say no more than "name, rank, file, and date of birth"), instead issuing the order BACK US, an acronym meaning: "don't Bow in public; stay off the Air; admit no Crimes; never Kiss them goodbye. 'US' could be interpreted as United States, but it really meant 'Unity over Self.'"[27]

After four years in solitary confinement, Admiral Stockdale was caught with an incriminating note (he'd already staged a riot to get fellow prisoners out of leg irons—so much for Stoic passivity). His experience had taught him that extreme torture would eventually get out of him any information they knew he possessed. So, as "even a child knows when to stop playing," he took advantage of a moment alone in an interrogation room to break a window and slit his wrists with a shard of glass. Because his wife that very week had been in Paris demanding humane treatment for prisoners, the North Vietnamese feared the international consequences of allowing him to die. They got a doctor and saved him in the nick of time. When the bandaged Stockdale returned to his cell, a fellow prisoner gave him a covert signal that there was a note in a hidden location, which he quietly scooped up and read later that night. His friend had written with a rat dropping on a sheet of toilet paper the last verse of Ernest Henley's poem "Invictus":

It matters not how strait the gate,
How charged with punishment the scroll,
I am the master of my fate:
I am the captain of my soul.

*

What is happiness? It's not, according to the Stoics, a chipper mood. We're welcome to try to avoid torture, cancer, and premature death. We're welcome to riches, booze, and friendship. But true happiness is something deeper than lucking into a beautiful state of affairs. It's the dignity of mastering the blessed gift of the mind. It's tranquility. It's an ability to bear up under the most difficult circumstances. It's the deeply satisfying sense of doing what we're supposed to be doing. Stockdale's hero Epictetus calls it freedom.

Epictetus's reflections on freedom are especially poignant, for in his early teens—in the first century AD—he was enslaved and carted off to Rome. His master abused him horribly, at one point shattering his kneecap for fun and permanently crippling him. In Rome Epictetus was sold cheap to Epaphroditus, the secretary of Nero himself—Nero being the emperor who busied himself with acting, charioteering, playing music, debauchery, burning Rome, scapegoating Christians, and murdering members of his family. Interestingly, Epictetus's master was the one who brought an end to Nero's reign, assisting the cowardly emperor in slitting his own throat. Epaphroditus, after fumbling his own suicide, was banished and eventually executed. Epictetus got lost in the shuffle, and he used his newfound freedom to attend lectures on Stoicism, apprenticing himself to the Stoic Musonius Rufus. After ten years of study he became worthy of the name philosopher.

So it's with the experience of having been tortured and sold, as well as having enjoyed the liberty of studying philosophy, that Epictetus considers the true nature of freedom. The limping Epictetus argues that the only person who can enslave you is—you. It happens all the time. We enslave ourselves to a mug when it breaks, giving our emotions away for free to a few ounces of ceramic. We enslave ourselves to drivers who cut us off, colleagues who needle us, in-laws, random noises, late students, passing clouds, a cruel Roman. It's another Stoic technique to say, when things upset us, "I've decided now to sell my soul to this shattered mug, this random noise, this jerk." There is a fable in Hegel known as the master-slave dialectic. It culminates with the slave's realization that all the master is capable of doing is bossing someone else around. The slave is capable of doing everything else. As soon as the slave realizes that, he's no longer a slave. Karl Marx loved that story.

A great twentieth-century Turkish poet named Nazim Hikmet spent years in prison for his Marxist political activities. A short poem of his in the form of a letter to his wife articulates, clear as water, Epictetus's concept of freedom.

> They've taken us prisoner,
> they've locked us up:
> me inside the walls,
> you outside.
> But that's nothing.
> The worst
> is when people—knowingly or not—
> carry prison inside themselves . . .
> Most people find themselves in this position,
> honest, hard-working, good people
> who should be loved as much as I love you . . .[28]

INTERLUDE ON WINE AND BICYCLES

You can't get drunk with the labels on the bottles.   PAUL VALÉRY

A rearguard position on happiness is put forward by Sextus Empiri-
cus, who argues that the real impediment to human happiness is
philosophy itself. It's our ideas about happiness that keep us from
ever being happy! It's trying that keeps us from success! In a series
of books all of whose titles begin with "against," Sextus goes about
refuting every possible claim to knowledge in the hopes that we'll
eventually grow tired of philosophizing and return to the unreflec-
tive music of common life, where we can be happy without struggle
and strife.

One doesn't need to go that far to wonder if any theory of happiness is complete. Some Roman thinkers—most famously Cicero—
adopt the position of eclecticism, taking a little of the best from all
the philosophical schools. From skepticism they take the idea that
no theory is final; from Epicureanism, the idea that under favorable
conditions one should pursue a reasonable amount of pleasure; from
Stoicism, the idea that favorable conditions don't last forever, and we
should prepare ourselves to maintain our dignity. Essentially, Epicureanism when you can, Stoicism when you must, and a little skepticism always.

Whether eclecticism is coherent or not, I think it maintains the
spirit of the schools it combines. Epicureanism and Stoicism are intended to be useful mental tools for leading a meaningful, satisfying
life. If they don't work, don't use them. We shouldn't care about being
Stoics, we should care about living well. Philosophy is a practice first
and a theory second. In the ancient Greek tradition, it's not so much
about being right as about being happy. Alfred North Whitehead is

probably right—and surely interesting—in saying, "It is more important that a proposition be interesting than it be true. . . . But of course a true proposition is more apt to be interesting than a false one."[1] For the ancients—for you and me too—what makes a proposition interesting is its ability to quicken our spirits, to enhance our lives.

*

The most indubitable inductive conclusion—that we have to die—is truly and legitimately unsettling if we realize we're not living up to our value. Is the good life something down the road, something we'll start working on mañana? Or is the good life the life we've found and are committed to right now?

One time, as I was fielding answers about how students would spend their final year, I noticed a twinkle in the eye of Kimberly Gress, another of my great "nontraditional" students, with close-cropped slightly graying hair, though still relatively young and in terrific physical shape. A few weeks later, after class, she approached me, because I'd mentioned that I have a soft spot for wine. She, too, was something of a connoisseur, and our conversation revealed that we had similar evaluations of the bottles we had in common.

Talking about wine is almost as good as drinking it and has a similar effect on the tongue. So I inquired why she twinkled when I'd asked what people would do if given a year to live. With a half-smile, she told me that she'd been in pretty much just that situation. A few years previous, she'd been diagnosed with myasthenia gravis, a very rare neuromuscular disorder—"the most aggressive case seen," according to the doctors. They told her there wasn't much they could do.

Kimberly eventually made up her mind, she explained, to take matters into her own hands, seeking out alternative practices to the drug taking the doctors prescribed. Most of all, she refocused on what she found most beautiful in life. She loved wine; so she got into the habit of savoring a few glasses a night. She loved bicycling; so she threw herself into the world of cycling. She had a curiosity to learn more—and she'd never finished college; so she decided to go back to school and study whatever subjects she fancied. For her, Epicureanism and Stoicism were simply the logic of living. You seek out what is truly pleasurable. You do all you can to improve your body but accept the ultimate limitations of fleshy existence. You commit yourself to what you love. You pursue knowledge to deepen yourself. She quoted Descartes to me—"I think; therefore, I am"—as if to say, "because I listen to what people have to say and try to understand the world around me, I lead a meaningful existence."

After her classes with me, Kimberly moved to Boulder to cycle in the Rockies, help out the US Women's Cycling Development Program, take more classes ("I think I may just be a non-traditional student forever"), drink wine, regularly attend the symphony, and work at the Boulder Center for Sports Medicine. She's found a way to have a sound body and a sane mind, a way of making a living by doing something she believes in, a way of adorning her days and nights with music, philosophy, and wine. In one sense, nothing extraordinary. Yet I find a life like hers to be miraculous: a demonstration of an all-too-rare sanity of soul.

There's a preternatural calm about Kimberly. When last I talked to her, she informed me that she'd had to take a break from her job because she was enduring chemotherapy. "Considering I was on hospice care last summer," she twinkled, "I'd say that things are looking up—not that they ever look down. I'm on the fast track to racing my bike again!" The only sign I've ever seen of her aggressive myasthenia gravis is how she talks out of one side of her mouth, and has an interesting smile—somewhere between the Sphinx and the Mona Lisa, like she knows something everybody else should but doesn't.

PART 3 * *Is Knowledge of God Possible?*

We thank thee, Father, for these strange minds that enamor us against thee.
EMILY DICKINSON

Aren't you outraged by simony? What kind of policies for its regulation do you favor? Are you, for instance, a proponent of the Second Plenary Council of Baltimore?

On a different note, do you have any opinions about our health care system? Have you ever been disgruntled about a bill from the hospital? Any feelings about socialized medicine? Are you aware that the government recently passed some legislation concerning health care?

My point is that in an age where spiritual things are the central focus of society, health care is left to quacks, and the great debate concerns how money should play a role in the religious life (simony, by the way, is the sin of paying money for spiritual things; it was a major concern of the Middle Ages); whereas in our age, the situation is reversed: the spiritual life is mostly left to quacks, and we debate if people have a right to health care. Consequently, my typically aged college students who've been raised in a religious tradition are more likely to be searchers than are eighteen-year-olds who've been raised without religion. Atheists, at least in the youthful stages of life, have an easier time reconciling their faith that there is no God with our society of democracy, consumption, technology, and science.

I was so tickled by the frankness of one such searcher that I jotted down a few of her reflections in my journal. "I remember going to parties," Crystal once said to me, "and seeing teens from my youth group doing things that were both immoral and against a religious view. Then I saw them at church preaching against the very things they did at the party. I also hated the scare tactics they used to make people accept Jesus. They told the most heart-wrenching stories, and then if that didn't work they used descriptions of Hell. They asked, 'Where would you go if you died right now?' I just couldn't take it anymore!" The charming thesis of one of her papers was: "Religion is useless traditions and ceremonies that you practice just in case there is a God."

If you got through your religious training without enduring hypocrisy, caricatures of goodness and evil, and scare tactics altogether opposed to your prophet's message, count yourself lucky. Unfortunately, I don't know of any big institution, regardless of its position on the supernatural, that doesn't commit the very same sins. But for reasons it's fun to guess at, nowadays people like Crystal find that they can live perfectly well without "useless traditions and ceremonies," feeling at sea only when they want to get married or somebody dies.

Still, it's hard even for the most ardent atheist not to wonder if there isn't something to religion. A sufficiently distracted, good-looking eighteen-year-old in the buzzings and bloomings of youth can often dance above the wonder and terror at the roots of religion. But it becomes increasingly hard to do so as age forces us to confront the bizarreness of time, the frailty of the body, the bigness of the universe, and the sucking black hole of death. Besides, for nearly the whole of our history we humans have lived with some formal relationship to divinity. There's a poem by Czesław Miłosz ("Either-Or") where he says,

> If a poor degenerate animal
> Could have reached so far in his fantasies
> And peopled the air with radiant beings,
> Rocky chasms with crowds of devils,
> The consequences of it must be, indeed, serious.
> We should go and proclaim without cease
> And remind people at every step of what we are:
> That our capacity for self-delusion has no limits
> And that anybody who believes anything is mistaken.[1]

A big if. Have those who have freed themselves from bothering about the divine corrected several millennia of mass delusion? Or is it possible, as Milosz intimates, that they've taken a fateful step in the wrong direction? What does the tradition of philosophy have to say to Crystal about finding God?

5 The Ecstasy without a Name

It was objected against him that he had never experienced love. Whereupon he arose, left the society, and made it a point not to return to it until he considered that he had supplied the defect. "Now," he remarked, on entering, "now I am in a position to continue the discussion."   ROBERT LOUIS STEVENSON

Before that fateful moment on the playground, the belief in Santa is a certainty of all certainties. Everyone in the world—so it seems to the believing child—speaks of Rudolph and the mystery of the elfin gifts. Moreover, fresh evidence turns up at a million houses every Christmas morning: presents wrapped in unfamiliar paper, drunk milk, nibbled cookies, a letter in curious penmanship, powdered-sugar hoof prints. It's not that children have considered the data and arrived at the belief; Santa is simply a feature of the world, like iPods and the sun. What happens when the believer is told by a classmate that Santa doesn't exist? Once, when I asked my class that question, a hulking student with laughter-freezing bitterness replied, "I gave the dick a black eye and got suspended."

After the dick on the playground delivers the news, the believer doesn't stop believing but does develop a problematic relationship to Santa. How can it be that a seemingly sane classmate thinks anything but the obvious? What's really going on? Beating the kid up does make some sense: best just to silence the problem. But inevitably the believer-in-crisis must formulate a method to discover the truth, which usually involves asking mom or dad, the source of the eternal verities, though I suppose a more entrepreneurial child might set up a hidden video camera inside the tinseled tree. In any case, the truth must come out. When I ask my students if it's worthwhile for parents to perpetuate the myth of Santa, almost to a person all who once believed think they should, and those who never believed think they shouldn't. Mom and dad are still the source of the eternal verities.

The Santa-doesn't-exist experience leads to what we might call an epistemological crisis: a crisis in the order of knowledge. Despite the unusual name, epistemological crises are common as grass. They occur whenever we realize that what we take to be natural is not what someone else takes to be natural. Our first thought is usually that the other person must be barbaric—and perhaps should be physically overmastered. But, if we have a shred of sensitivity, we come to realize that from the other's perspective we're the weird ones. As the civilized Roman poet Ovid was compelled to admit in exile, "Here I am the barbarian."[1]

My favorite example of an epistemological crisis, related by Voltaire, concerns a certain Simon Morin who, believing he was Jesus Christ, was thrown into a madhouse, where he met someone else who thought he was Jesus Christ. "Simon Morin," Voltaire says, "was so struck with the folly of his companion that he acknowledged his own, and appeared, for a time, to have recovered his senses."[2]

As a young man, Abu Hamid al-Ghazali experienced his own epistemological crisis when it dawned on him that "the children of Christians always grew up embracing Christianity, and the children of Jews always grew up adhering to Judaism, and the children of Muslims always grew up following the religion of Islam."[3] The problem is not unlike that of Simon Morin or the troubled faithful of Santa! In particular, two difficulties arise. First, our beliefs aren't really ours; as al-Ghazali puts it, we're bound by a "servile conformism," whereby our beliefs are dependent on which side of the street we're born on. Second, somebody must be wrong, and it could be us. The salvation of our soul may hang on whether we regard Jesus as the son of God, a prophet of God, or a dangerous distraction.

It's common for people to recognize their servile conformism, shrug, and stay put in their beliefs, like ground hogs that see their shadow and head right back into their hole. As Voltaire notes of Morin, "Sometime after [meeting the other 'Jesus'] he relapsed into his former nonsense and began to dogmatize."[4] But al-Ghazali's passion for the truth would not let him rest with a childish relationship to his religion. His great spiritual autobiography, al-Munqidh min al-Dalal, the Deliverance from Error, tells of his "daring in mounting from the lowland of servile conformism to the highland of independent investigation."[5] It narrates his magi's journey to find the ultimate truth.

Al-Ghazali was born around 1011 AD in the district of Tus—in what is now northern Iran. His father died when al-Ghazali was still a boy. Having been willed an endowment for his future education, al-Ghazali made superb use of the inheritance, studying under leading theologians in Nishapur and producing, as a young man, textbooks on Islamic law and theology that are still in use—I am told—to this day. After his formal studies, he became an adviser to the vizier of the Seljuk king Malikshah. By the time he was thirty-four he held the highest educational post in the Abbasid Empire, rector of the madrassa in Baghdad. There he wasted no time in producing two major works, *The Intentions of the Philosophers*, in which he carefully built up the theories of the great Muslim Aristotelians (like al-Farabi and Avicenna), and then *The Incoherence of the Philosophers*, in which he demolished them.

At this point, al-Ghazali was on top of the world. He knew Islamic law backward and forward; he had published lasting works of theology and jurisprudence; he was respected and revered; he had the ear of important politicians. But in the middle of life's way he found himself lost in the dark wood, Dante's *selva oscura*, and had something of a breakdown. It dawned on him that though he knew as much as anyone about the outer form of Islam, he didn't understand what it was truly about. To all appearances a model Muslim, he found in himself the things we all find in ourselves when we bother to look: ambition, lust, vanity, anxiety, boredom. For the following six months he was pulled in two directions. The inertia of a human lifestyle kept him tethered to his job, his family, his misery; but another part of him longed to change his life completely. Finally, he summoned the courage and folly to embark on the journey that he narrates in *Deliverance from Error*.

*

Remembering his unsettling observation that our parents determine our beliefs, he decides to seek out a completely firm foundation for the truth. "What I seek is knowledge of the true meaning of things," al-Ghazali says to himself, "therefore, I must inquire into just what the true meaning of knowledge is."[6] Like the kid who's told that Santa doesn't exist, he realizes that he needs a method for determining what's really going on. The strategy he devises is to put our normal mentality into reverse. We usually accept what we're told until presented with overwhelming truth to the contrary. Our regular thought process resembles our judicial system: innocent until proven guilty. But for al-Ghazali's purposes this process is too lenient; it practically guarantees that we'll never advance far from servile conformism. Al-Ghazali, seeking complete certainty, employs the opposite principle. He shall try to doubt the sources of his beliefs, and if even a little doubt sticks to them, then he shall set them aside until he's able to discover their certain foundation. Guilty until proven innocent.

Is any belief innocent beyond a shadow of doubt? Is anything in this life completely certain? Other than death and taxes, my students generally come up with the same candidates for certainty al-Ghazali considers. First, there's the "my book is on the desk" sort of certainties, which al-Ghazali calls sense data. Second, there are the beauties of math and logic like "2 + 2 = 4" and "all unmarried men are bachelors," which al-Ghazali calls self-evident truths. The first are certified by immediate experience; the second flow from the structure of reason and language. Both varieties of truth *seem* certain, but al-Ghazali carefully applies his method to them to see if they're as firm as they appear. Are we building on a firm foundation when we build on our senses and our reason?

Does any doubt cling to sense data? On reflection al-Ghazali decides that it does, and offers two supporting examples to show how. First, the senses tell us that the shadow of a tree is standing still, when in fact it's slowly moving with the angle of the sunbeam. Second, the senses tell us that the stars are relatively small, but after careful geometrical calculation we realize that in fact the stars are enormous. The conclusion he draws from these examples is that sense data are not completely reliable.

In both cases, one could argue that the doubt clinging to sense data arises only when sense data are used carelessly. Wouldn't a deliberate use of the senses in both cases lead to certain truth? Even though the examples he gives to support this conclusion lack a certain amount of philosophical rigor, they contain a kind of poetic truth. First, our senses show us a constantly moving world. Nothing ever stays put. The tree, which appears stable but for the occasional gust of wind, is really in a constant state of flux: its leaves are changing color, another ring is materializing in its trunk, its branches are stretching sunward. So how can we grasp anything if it changes as we perceive it? Everything is a moving shadow—of a tree we never fully observe! Second, our senses are calibrated to our human scale. Even within the dimensions perceived by the senses there are un-believable layers of swirling complexity, which but for increasingly powerful microscopes we'd never behold. Moreover, it's possible that the cosmos is even more complex than what can ever be observed by the senses alone. From a different perspective (a bee's, a Martian's, an angel's, God's), we likely lack some crucial organ of perception. There is a theory seriously entertained by contemporary physicists that the universe is stitched together with vibrating strings, one-dimensional objects that have length but no height or depth. I don't know about you, but my frail mind has enough trouble imagining three-dimensional objects!

But what about self-evident truths like $2 + 2 = 4$? Does any doubt cling to them? To answer that, let's review. We began by trusting the judgments of our parents, but we found that parents can be mislead-ing. The senses looked to be a more certain source of truth—"I'll be-lieve it when I see it," we like to say; but on scrutiny, it turned out that the senses, too, can be misleading—or at least not totally forthcom-ing. Just as the "sense judge" corrected the "authority judge" when you saw through a cracked closet door your parents writing Santa's note, the "reason judge" corrected the sense judge when it came to matters like how big the stars are or how many dimensions some-thing can exist in. Now the candidate to be inspected is reason itself. Can we trust the quintessential formulations of pure reason, which seem beyond all doubt? Is reason the ultimate judge? At this point al-Ghazali wonders if there couldn't be a higher judge than the reason judge, which if it were to appear might correct even the pronounce-ments of reason. Simply because we can't fathom what that higher judge would look like doesn't necessarily imply it couldn't exist. If there's an afterlife, imagine your winged self asking God, "So I always wondered if my confidence in $2 + 2 = 4$ was beyond reproach. Was I at least right about the basics of math? Was what my own earthly reason told me about arithmetic a firm, basic truth of Your creation?" Isn't it possible that Mr. Unfathomable might answer with a chuckle, "Well, I can see why you'd think that, given the structure of your mind. But, in fact, you need a math that goes far beyond the truths of your arithmetic to structure a universe, just as a human scientist needs a truth that goes far beyond the idea that stars are smaller than the moon to do accurate astronomy"? Hopefully, you and God would have other matters to discuss as well.

It's in the name of the most rigorous collaboration of the senses and reason—namely, science—that many people now reject religion. The purest form of this rejection is expressed by the question, "How can you believe in God if you never see Him?" But, if al-Ghazali is right, our senses can't be trusted to reveal the whole of the universe. Even with the most carefully calibrated reason, the human mind does not necessarily unlock the ultimate truth. It's at least possible there's more to the story than meets the eye or the mind. Imagine a sighted traveler discovering an isolated island of blind people. Though they'd be mystified by the traveler's descriptions of the hues of coconuts and the loveliness of sunlight breaking on the water, they'd be in error to assume that sparkles and the color brown were total lies.

At the same time, how can they trust the traveler's wild tales of a sense beyond the standard four? How can we trust the religionists with their mind-blowing ideas like angels and the trinity? All al-Ghazali has demonstrated is that our human faculties are limited. He's far from pulling the curtain on reality and witnessing the ultimate clockwork. He's labored mightily to get to an early page of the Socratic story: all he knows at this point is that he knows nothing. Religion is built on authority, which could be wrong. Science is built on the senses, which could be wrong. Mathematics and logic are built on reason, which could be wrong. Because al-Ghazali embarks on his quest out of a burning desire for certainty, he now finds himself in total despair. The one thing he wants may be the one thing he cannot by definition have. He describes his recognition of human ignorance as a "mysterious malady," and he becomes "a skeptic in fact, but"—he's careful to add to his audience—"not in utterance and doctrine."[7]

Nevertheless, he heroically continues down the Socratic path and decides to question those who lay claim to the truth: various religious groups and philosophical schools. Perhaps in his scrutiny of human knowledge he's overlooked a crucial step; maybe there's some faction out there that really does know the secret. But what he finds, unsurprising to students of Socrates, is that those who claim to possess wisdom are self-deceived. Religious and philosophical groups must begin with a blind faith in some unquestioned source of truth.

For religious groups it tends to be the authority of some combination of a book, an institution, and a leader. Philosophical schools, even though they claim to be free of the errors of religion, also begin with blind faith in some combination of reason and the senses. In this sense, religion, which emphasizes faith, is more honest than the theories of philosophy, which claim to be self-certain.

Once you accept that pleasure and pain are the ultimate guides to action, or that the rigorous examination of sense data is the only sure way to truth, or that "there is nothing good or bad but thinking makes it so," or that the word of God is in the Koran, or the Bible, or the Book of Mormon, then you can build up a coherent religion or philosophy. But why accept one starting point rather than another? This is how al-Ghazali profoundly characterizes the moral of his story: "One should be most diligent in seeking the truth until he finally comes to seeking the unseekable."[8] The problem is that people who seek the truth take the easy way out and invest in some unquestioned source of truth, whereas they ought to go to the very limits of their search. Just like Socrates, al-Ghazali realizes that the wise aren't so wise after all.

At last al-Ghazali stumbles on a very different kind of group: the Sufis. Whereas all the other religious and philosophical sects explored by al-Ghazali, when asked about their central truth, respond with a credo or their principle doctrines, the Sufis tell him that, while they do have a dogma they could expound, their guiding principle is that searchers must experience the truth for themselves. If al-Ghazali wants to find certainty, it will never be enough simply to be presented with a doctrine, which his mind could always doubt. He must enter into a state of certainty.

He must experience—for lack of a better word—God. Imagine a young man who wants to know about drunkenness, who's given pamphlets from Mothers against Drunk Driving (MADD), physiological explanations from various scientists, promotional materials from Budweiser, and some poems by Charles Bukowski. At last, someone takes him aside and says, "You want to know about drunkenness? Here's a bottle of Jim Beam: have at it." The Sufis say that if al-Ghazali wants to find certainty, he must become drunk on God. Let me reassure religious teetotalers that the analogy to drunkenness is al-Ghazali's own. Another of my favorite analogies he employs to describe the experience of God is sex; he imagines "a small boy or an impotent person" asking: "What is the way to know the pleasure of sexual intercourse, and to perceive its essential reality?" Describing it, al-Ghazali rightly claims, won't quite do; it's better, he says, to "wait patiently."[9]

Sufism is an Islamic variety of what religious scholars call mysticism. It can be distinguished from institutional religion, which refers to the kinds of Islam, Christianity, and Judaism that most of us are familiar with. At the heart of institutional religion is the idea that God has been directly revealed—but to others: a prophet, the disciples, Moses. The institutions of religion—readings of the holy text, prayers, rituals, and so on—are in place to connect everyone else, indirectly, to the divine. Churches, mosques, and temples are like post offices where people go to exchange letters with God. Mystical forms of religion, by contrast, claim that it is possible for you and me to transcend this long-distance relationship and meet God face to face.

For roughly six months, al-Ghazali hems and haws: "In the morning I would have a sincere desire to seek the things of the afterlife; but by evening the hosts of passion would assail it and render it lukewarm."[10] But eventually he recognizes enough desperation in himself to take the Sufis up on their offer. He gives up his family, wealth, fame, and comfort and spends ten years subjecting himself to their discipline of purifying the soul in preparation for God. Such discipline, sometimes called asceticism, is necessary to reorient us from our normal way of being in the world, for it's unlikely we're going to experience God at the grocery store.

To make a long story short, at last al-Ghazali does indeed experience God, and in the mystical experience of God he finds a certainty to which no doubt clings, an existential rather than an intellectual certainty. He finds what he's been looking for: the ultimate foundation of everything. A quest that begins by rising above religion ends by being lost in it.

*

Al-Ghazali, I should say, doesn't use the expression "mystical experience" at all; when hard-pressed, he calls it "the state of ecstasy" or "fruitional experience." Even calling it a "state" might be misleading. As he says in a marvelous passage,

Then [the Sufis'] "state" ascends from the vision of forms and like-nesses to stages beyond the narrow range of words: so if anyone tries to express them, his words contain evident error against which he cannot guard himself. But speaking in general, the matter comes ul-timately to a closeness to God which one group almost conceives of as "indwelling," and another as "union," and another as "reaching": but all that is wrong. . . . Really one intimately possessed by that state ought not to go beyond saying, "There was what was of what I do not mention: / So think well of it, and ask for no account!"[11]

Though the "state" goes beyond language, a few things become clear beyond all doubt to al-Ghazali: first, God is real; second, at our innermost point we are connected to God (in other words, the soul is immortal); and third, God wants something of us, namely, for us to be and do good. These are, of course, the homely truths of re-ligion that the Muslim al-Ghazali has been privy to all along. But now he knows them from the inside, as if the poor child with face pressed against the bakery's window was finally waved in to eat the pastries.

It's interesting that al-Ghazali does not detail any of his mystical practices. To those of us with minimal knowledge of Sufism we're apt to think of whirling dervish dances: spinning around in a circle until we come into contact with the infinite dizziness named God. The idea of experiencing the divine, especially in our postpsychedelic age, conjures some kind of "derangement of the senses," to use the French poet Rimbaud's phrase, which opens "the doors of perception," to use William Blake's. But even when real mystics do use hallucinogenic drugs, they do so under the careful guidance of the myths and rituals of a religious tradition. Ted Hughes, the great British man of letters, says: "The journey [of traditional mystics] was undertaken as part of an elaborately mythologized ritual. It was the mythology which consolidated the inner world, gave human form to its experiences, and connected them to daily life. Without that preparation a drug carries its user to a prison in the inner world as passive and isolated and meaningless as the camera's eye from which he escaped."[12] It is true that al-Ghazali alludes to a certain amount of trippiness in Sufi practice: "Even when awake, the sufis see the angels and the spirits of the prophets and hear voices coming from them."[13] But his "state of ecstasy" seems to be something very different from perceiving a positive image of God: the mystic "ascends from the vision of forms and likenesses to stages beyond the narrow range of words."

My sense is that God, for al-Ghazali, isn't a thing—like a pleasant evening or favorite song—to be latched onto, nor is God simply the penthouse of experience. Only after al-Ghazali has given up on what his society tells him, what his senses tell him, what his reason tells him, what even religion tells him, when there is nothing left at all, is he filled with the fullness of God—or emptied with the emptiness of God. Yes, God is above the levels of reality accessible to our reason and our senses, but God is not, as our childish minds tend to picture, just a bigger, more powerful Someone—a *Nobodaddy*, to use Blake's splendid name for our false image of God. God is above, but God is also the whole, something like a pyramid of champagne glasses at a wedding ceremony, where the champagne pours from a bottle above them all and yet tumbles fizzingly through every tier. I think that al-Ghazali, who lovingly explores the "ninety-nine beautiful names of God," would appreciate this meandering sentence from the English poet John Donne:

> My God, my God, thou art a direct God, may I not say a literal God, a God that wouldst be understood literally and according to the plain sense of all that thou sayest? but thou art also (Lord, I intend it to thy glory, and let no profane misinterpreter abuse it to thy diminution), thou art a figurative, a metaphorical God too; a God in whose words there is such a height of figures, such voyages, such peregrinations to fetch remote and precious metaphors, such extensions, such spreadings, such curtains of allegories, such third heavens of hyperboles, so harmonious elocutions, so retired and so reserved expressions, so commanding persuasions, so persuading commandments, such sinews even in thy milk, and such things in thy words, as all profane authors seem of the seed of the serpent that creeps, thou art the Dove that flies.[14]

Sufi discipline involves overcoming all the passions that alienate us from the divinity of the dynamic whole. One of the most profoundly alienating passions is the need for a belief, the need to cling to some claim on the truth. It's only once al-Ghazali has truly let go of such claims that he's able to access the ultimate root of all truths. It's only once he's returned to the pure desire for truth itself, shunning all temporary satisfactions of it, that he's allowed to have his desire fulfilled. Simone Weil uses the Eskimo myth of the origin of light to illustrate the point: "In the eternal darkness, the crow, unable to find any food, longed for light, and the earth was illumined."[15] Ultimately, al-Ghazali's real mystical practice stares us right in the face. It's the philosophical process he himself describes, which fertilizes the ground with skepticism and despair, seeds it with the study of religious and philosophical schools, waters it with Sufi practice, and bears fruit in the soul's discovery of God. His hallucinogenic drug is philosophical thought.

*

Admittedly, when discussing immersion in the divine, we're in far over our heads. So let's construct an analogy a little more to our human size. As al-Ghazali says, "Perhaps your aspiration does not rise high enough for these words, but rather falls short below their summit. So take for yourself words that are nearer to your understanding and more suitable to your weakness."[16] Let's compare al-Ghazali's journey, his "deliverance from error," to the process of falling in love—an analogy used often by mystics themselves, one that goes such a long way it's hard not to wonder if it's more than an analogy.

First, imagine two sorts of people who have never fallen in love. The first kind is the romantics, who believe it's possible to fall head over heels. In our analogy, they're like religious people who have never experienced God. The second kind is the love skeptics, who think that love is no more than glorified lust and the tall tale of hormones. They're like atheists.

Sometimes there's a special variety of the romantic, a dreamy romantic, who really wants to fall in love, who looks everywhere for love. This is analogous to the philosopher, in our case al-Ghazali (who is a philosopher—a lover of truth—by the traditional definition; al-Ghazali himself tends to speak of philosophy—*falsafa*—as schools of rational thought derived from Greek sources). But, as I'm sure you know, looking to fall in love is a sure way of not falling in love. Of course, it does happen that many romantics and philosophers trick themselves otherwise. But a true love-searcher refuses anything less than true love and, unable to find such a beloved, eventually falls into despair. Just so, al-Ghazali is unable to find the certainty he deeply desires, despite being given all sorts of decent-looking candidates for the truth.

The good news is that once you've abandoned all hope, you have a reasonably good chance of running into your soul mate on the subway. "In the eternal darkness, the crow, unable to find any food, longed for light, and the earth was illumined." In some sense, everybody has the chance of falling in love, believer and atheist alike. If God or Love wants to become manifest, they have the power to knock anyone off their horse. When you do fall in love, you know it, whoever you are. No doubt clings to the experience, to use al-Ghazali's litmus test. If a skeptical friend says, "Come off it, you're just an animal in heat!" you can only smile and sing the old standard "It Could Happen to You." Likewise, to those rare souls truly in the grace of God, no doubt clings to their bond with the divine. Unlike the average believer (or atheist), they don't seize on whatever plank of proof they can find to buoy their belief.

So, however it comes to pass, let's say that you have fallen in love. You want to tell your beloved just how you feel, so you say, "I love you so, so, so much. Deeper than the deep blue sea, higher than the stars above, bigger than a . . . God, am I sounding stupid! I just can't put the experience into words! You're just going to have to think well of it, my dear, and ask for no account!" Al-Ghazali himself judiciously advises, "The speech of lovers in the state of intoxication should be concealed and not spread about."[17] The problem is that the experience of love is different from all the experiences you're used to naming. Your love extends forever, yet somehow it's right there, in your arms. And this is where al-Ghazali finds himself after the culmination of his mystical practice. He's unable to put words to an experience that breaks the boundaries of language.

Maybe because you're human, you can't quite give up trying to put your experience into words; so you crack open a book of poems and find lines like John Milton's "With thee conversing I forget all time" or Alfred, Lord Tennyson's

> Changed with thy mystic change, and felt my blood
> Glow with the glow that slowly crimson'd all
> Thy presence and thy portals, while I lay,
> Mouth, forehead, eyelids, growing dewy-warm
> With kisses balmier than half-opening buds

Of April, and could hear the lips that kiss'd
Whispering I knew not what of wild and sweet,
Like that strange song I heard Apollo sing
While Ilion like a mist rose into towers.

Or William Shakespeare's "the more I give to thee, / The more I have,
for both are infinite" or Emily Dickinson's

Rowing in Eden,
Ah, the sea!
Might I but moor—Tonight—
In thee.[18]

And you think, "How right they are! That's exactly what I was trying
to say." Even otherwise level-headed accountants have been known
on Valentine's Day to shell out twenty-four dollars for a very slim
volume from the poetry section.

Likewise, al-Ghazali opens up the Koran, reads its words afresh,
and says, "How right it is!" The "servile conformist" accepts a book as
holy because an authority says it's holy. The mystic accepts it because
it really is holy. The Koran speaks in an inspired way of the same
truths that become manifest in al-Ghazali's mystical experience, just
as Shakespeare and company give local habitations and names to
passions that seem otherwise wildly beyond language. Not only did
Mohammed have the same experience of God that al-Ghazali does,
Mohammed was blessed by the ability to articulate it in human language. It's such a blessing that it can be talked about only as the result of sheer inspiration, dictation from the angel Gabriel.

Just as poets can speak of love only by employing metaphor,
rhythm, and imagery, so too a holy text can articulate God only by
"indirect" means. I put indirect in scare quotes because I think of poetry as language in its active sense rather than as a merely decorative
way of saying what could be put in plain terms. Poetry is as direct as
it gets, precisely because it contains a little indirection in it. When
we consider language to be either "literal" or "just a metaphor," we're
completely misunderstanding how words work, especially in a holy
text. When the Koran says (in a passage beloved of al-Ghazali), "God
is the light of the heavens and the earth; the likeness of His light is
as a niche wherein is a lamp, the lamp in a glass, the glass as it were

a glittering star kindled from a blessed tree, an olive that is neither of the East nor of the West, whose oil well-nigh would shine, even if no fire touched it," Gabriel's secretary is being careful not to box us into literalism or pure metaphor.[19] We're presented with a paradox that is an invitation to the inmost experience of the universe. We're presented with a holy poem.

If I may extend my analogy between mystical experience and falling in love yet further: the final moment involves turning to ritual practice in order to sustain in our fallible lives the infinite truth that we've been entrusted with. In the case of love, this tends to mean marriage. When all your desire throbs for your beloved, you don't need a commitment to stay true. You don't need it, but you pledge it anyway, as a way of articulating the fountaining infinity of your affections. Marriage is a way of taking the experience of love seriously, for when we love truly, all our being swears to love forever. Marriage is the public commitment to that inward pledge and also an institution that helps us stay true to each other over time, to remember the heavenly moment when the scales fell. In the case of mysticism, at least for al-Ghazali, this final moment involves his return to his religious tradition, for only within a religious tradition can fidelity to the God experience be sustained by our frail personalities.

*

For ten years al-Ghazali lives in solitude, diligently practicing Sufism. He purifies himself. He lives in the presence of God. He is happy in the most stringent sense of that word. But something in the divinity of his new life prods him to return to teaching, to his family, to the unhappy place we call the world. It is his destiny, he realizes, to use all he has discovered about himself to minister to the weak of faith. He comes to see himself like a scientist who has searched his whole life for a cure to a disease. Now that he has found that cure, he must cease being a scientist and begin work as a doctor to the afflicted. Whereas at the threshold of Sufism he dawdled fearful of submitting himself to God, now he dawdles before the prospect of returning to the dubious comforts of everyday life. Finally, God acts and, through the command of a Sultan, demands that he return to his old post. So al-Ghazali returns to teaching. As in all true journeys, his return is not simply a circling back but a spiraling forward. He now teaches out of humility rather than for his own glory. He now teaches out of love for his students and the truth rather than self-love. He calls himself a "doctor of hearts."

In the deep solitude of his own heart this holy cardiologist has found something of everyone: the submissive believer, the skeptic, the rational philosopher, the tepid searcher, the God-intoxicated mystic, and finally the wise man. Now he's able to diagnose accurately what people suffer from and proscribe a cure. In the submissive believer capable of deeper experience he must induce an epistemological crisis. The skeptic must be brought to the despair that leads to God. The rational philosopher must be shown how rationality subverts even itself. The tepid searcher must be reminded of all that is at stake in the search. Even God-intoxicated mystics need educating, for they're apt to forget about the necessities of ritual and religion, slowly blurring their experience of God with their own vanity. Perhaps the central mission and accomplishment of al-Ghazali is his reconciliation of mystical and institutional religion. He reminds each of the need for the other. He invests the letter with the spirit. He preserves the spirit with the letter. Arguably, these are the two highest tasks of human culture.

*

In a passing remark about mysticism, T. S. Eliot boasts, "You may call it communion with the Divine, or you may call it a temporary crystallization of the mind. Until science can teach us to reproduce such phenomena at will, science cannot claim to have explained them."[20] Be careful of such passing remarks! It turns out that a certain Dr. Michael Persinger of Laurentian University has recently outfitted with electromagnetic coils a yellow snowmobile helmet that can induce in its wearer a very peculiar experience. Dr. Persinger flips a switch, and the helmet stimulates a certain lobe of the brain in such a way as to make his subjects feel that there's another presence in the room, a presence some identify as God. Based on his experiments, some atheists now feel confirmed in their suspicion that religion is madness: it is, to be precise, the hallucinations of those suffering from temporal lobe epilepsy.

Certainly, our evaluation of al-Ghazali's thought depends largely on the credibility of mystical experience. Let's admit right off that just as al-Ghazali, a thousand years ago, underestimated the capacity of science, we who grow babies in test tubes are too inclined to doubt that there is anything beyond science. To stimulate mystical experience in a lab no more disproves God than opening a window disproves fresh air. Mystics have always known that the body needs to undergo a certain alteration in order to be opened to the divine. So the fact that a certain stimulation of the brain correlates with the experience of God is hardly a surprise. Moreover, mystics know that simply having a God experience isn't sufficient to establish a meaningful relationship to God. "Ripeness is all," as Shakespeare says; or, in the words of the comedian, "Timing is everything." The context of the experience matters. Some of Dr. Persinger's subjects report that their experiences would have been life changing had they not known it was the product of a wired yellow snowmobile helmet.

Science in the yellow snowmobile helmet will never be able to enter into what being alive is *about*. You can't understand the whole in terms of the part. Surely it's the case that experiences of self and other have a biological basis. But that hardly means you and I don't exist. I don't claim to be able to speak authoritatively about God, but my daimon rebels against talking about the divine purely in terms of neural firing as much as it does against proclaiming love purely in terms of hormones. To do so misses the meaning. Emily Dickinson, in reflecting on her own mystical experience in the presence of a shaft of winter sunlight swirling in through her upstairs window, says,

> Heavenly hurt it gives us.
> We can find no scar—
> But internal difference—
> Where the meanings are.[21]

If you must insist that "where the meanings are" is in the brain, then admit furthermore that the whole mysterious cosmos swirls inside its squishy cords: tragedies and comedies far more horrible and hilarious than anything in Shakespeare, stretches of boredom and anxiety worse than anything on TV, supernovas and storks and gnats and octopuses and Himalayas and great clouds of dark matter passing through us as we speak. Repeat after Blake: "To hold infinity in the palm of my hand." Repeat after Emily: "The brain is just the weight of God."

*

I have a hunch that most of us have at least one mystical experience tucked away somewhere in those loopy cords. Since, as al-Ghazali rightly observes, the experience exceeds the borders of normal language, we're not apt to talk about it. Besides, mentioning it threatens to alienate us from everyday life. Luckily poets aren't so abashed. Almost all poets allude to their states of ecstasy, where they stand for a moment with a foot in the eternal.

One of my favorite accounts, because of its discovery of the most exalted in the most humble, comes from the Austrian poet and librettist Hugo von Hofmansthal:

> The other night I found under a walnut tree a half-full watering can that a young gardener had forgotten there, and this watering can, with the water in it, hidden by the tree's shadow, with a water bug paddling from one shore to the other of that dark water: this combination of trivialities exposes me to such a presence of the infinite, traversing me from the roots of my hair to the base of my heels, that I feel like bursting out in words which I know, if I had found them, would have floored those cherubim in whom I do not believe.[22]

Few of us, especially poets, have the wherewithal to follow through with what such experiences portend, much less cultivate ourselves, like al-Ghazali during his ten years as an impoverished Sufi monk, to be open to the profoundest version of them. But in their presence we do feel that the universe is *about* something, that reality is huge and marvelous and terrible, that who we are is connected to that reality, and that its gloriousness makes some kind of demand on us.

I've had my moments of wanting to floor the cherubim. One time, when I was all of nine years old, I was out at noon recess playing King of the Mountain on a huge snow heap made by the town's plow. I'd teamed up with my pal Pam to depose this very stocky kid who, once he'd clawed his way to the top, was almost impossible to budge. He'd throw us all like ragdolls to the bottom. As I was fumbling up from a hard tumble, a scoop of snow drizzling down my scarf, I was overwhelmed by the brightness of the sun on the snow, the sparkles of which burned swirling splotches into my vision. At that moment, Pam was violently and inadvertently thrown into my arms, and I embraced her, trying to rescue her from danger. Her puffy snowsuit depressed into my squishing coat, and like Jack and Jill we went tumbling backward. Though it must have been just a fraction of a second before we cracked against the ice-crusted snow, time froze; I felt something blossoming rapidly from deep inside me: a prickly sensation, like I was going to bust. Surely part of it was a kind of dizzying affection for Pam, an affection my nine-year-old mind had no clue about. I was a puzzle piece holding the puzzle piece that fit me. Everything, so it powerfully seemed, was being created for the first time right then and there: snowsuits, blind splotches, blond curls, our red-brick school building, the king. Everything was full of a precious fragility, especially Pam. We hit hard. She paused in my embrace as we groggily came to. Then she popped up and went zipzopping in her snowsuit after the king. Eventually I must have too, trailing clouds of glory.

What is philosophy or religion—or human life for that matter—but the attempt to relate to the meaningful hugeness revealed in such experiences without sounding or acting like a total fool, at our best with a touch of style?

One afternoon when I was in graduate school, reading the poets and philosophers who've helped me find words, however stuttering and off-the-mark, for such weird experiences, I got a letter in the mail from my mom. It contained a clipping of Pam's obituary. Her car had hit a patch of ice, and she slid instantly into an oncoming truck. Her brother had been driving right behind her and so was the first to stop at the scene. In hindsight I realized that her last heartbreaking moment was also embodied in that mystical fraction of a second in the snow, when I held her in my arms.

6 In Nightmares Begins Rationality

Half our days wee passe in the shadowe of the earth, and the brother of death exacteth a third part of our lives.　　　SIR THOMAS BROWNE

It's strange to have come this far without talking about dreams. I've had my chances. Socrates has a fascinating dream the night before his execution; the Stoics recommend a careful examination of your dreams every morning to see if you're making progress; and al-Ghazali has wonderful things to say about what flickers in the mind during the Arabian nights. Jorge Luis Borges tells the story of a man who sets out to compose a book that includes everything in the universe. At the end of his life, as he's polishing the final lines, he looks up at the night sky to offer thanks for his miraculous accomplishment— and realizes that he forgot the moon! *"Siempre se pierde lo esencial,"* Borges concludes. We always miss the essential.[1]

Anyone with a clear head shouldn't forget that we spend over a third of our lives with sleep, that brother of death, who escorts our minds into some pretty bizarre realms. Immanuel Kant's magnum opus, *The Critique of Pure Reason*, never analyzes dreaming. But what's a more powerful critique of pure reason than a nightmare? "There are more things in heaven and earth, Horatio / Than are dreamt of in your philosophy," Hamlet says; and one of the things that is rarely dreamt of in even the most elaborate philosophical systems is dreams. There's a famous etching by Goya called *The Sleep of Reason Produces Monsters*. But one of the ironies of the history of Western philosophy is that the movement we call rationalism, which matures into our modern age of science, democracy, and technology, is born of nightmares. The dream of monsters produces reason.

*

René Descartes—born on March 31, 1596, in a town called La Haye (now called Descartes)—was a sickly child who the doctors believed would never reach adulthood. He got in the habit of sleeping in late. When he finally did wake up, he liked to lie around in bed and let his thoughts wander. At the age of ten he went to a new Jesuit college at La Fléche in Anjou and learned all sorts of things he later disdained as mere rhetoric and pointless argument, though he always admired the rigor with which the stupid subjects were pursued. He graduated and went on to study law. At the age of twenty-two, he resolved to search for no knowledge beyond what he could find in himself or in the book of the world. He spent his twenties gallivanting around Europe, visiting courts, mixing with peasants and aristocrats alike, courting beauties, and occasionally signing up in an army.

For a while René Descartes was a gentleman soldier in what posterity would call the Thirty Years' War, a conflict comparable to World War I in its murky causes and horrendous consequences. At the root of the war was whether Protestants or Catholics should control the Holy Roman Empire (which, as Voltaire once quipped, was not holy, Roman, or an empire), but power politics splintered most of Europe into numerous factions of dubious alliances. Regions not decimated by foraging armies suffered from disease, famine, and the poverty generated by the vast cost of the war.

In the summer of 1619, Descartes visited Frankfurt to see the coronation of Ferdinand II. In no hurry to return to the chaos of war, he waited until winter to head back to his post in the army of Maximilian of Bavaria. Because of bad weather, he was detained much of November in a cottage near a small town beside the Danube. Free of any responsibilities but deprived of intelligent conversation, he spent his time beside a potbellied stove, where, as he says, "I was completely free to converse with myself about my own thoughts."[2] After one such day of reflection, he nodded off and had three successive dreams—three nightmares, really—that changed world history more significantly than any king's coronation.

In the first dream he's walking down a street and has the impression of several terrible ghosts approaching him. He fearfully and politely crosses to the other side. His body's right half suddenly feels paralyzed, and he's ashamed to continue walking. A violent wind spins him around and around on his left foot. When he stops, he sees a college down the road and heads for its chapel to pray for some relief. After passing a stranger, he realizes that he knows the person and should go back to say hello. Another stranger addresses him by name and hands him a melon, telling him to give it to the acquaintance he's looking for. Descartes is then assaulted by more whirlwinds, which are so intense as to startle him awake. Groggy, he believes an evil demon is trying to deceive him. He rolls over in bed, as if that would help.

Soon Descartes is tossing and turning, unable to fall back asleep, obsessing, as all insomniacs do, over the evils of his life and the world. After a couple of hours he falls asleep again and, dreaming, hears a powerful thunderclap. He wakes up, though it's unclear if he really wakes up or just dreams he does, for he sees a jet of light scattering sparks throughout the room, as if the thunderclap had engulfed him in fire. Summoning all his philosophical power, he slowly calms himself and slips imperceptibly into a third dream.

An unfamiliar, alluring dictionary stands on the table. Before he can peruse it, the dictionary vanishes. Another book appears, an anthology called *Corpus Poetarum* (Collection of poets). Opening it randomly, he comes across the line "Quod vitae sectabor iter?" (What road in life shall I follow?). A stranger approaches and hands him a verse beginning "Est et non" (It is and it isn't), declaring it to be an excellent poem. "I'm already familiar with it," Descartes proudly declares. "In fact, it can be found in this book here." He starts flipping through the pages of *Corpus Poetarum* to prove it. Unable to find "Est et non," he announces that he knows an even better poem beginning "Quod vitae sectabor iter?" Frantically flipping at this point, he notices some marvelous engraved portraits in the book. Before he can find the poem, the book and the stranger vanish. Descartes realizes that he is in a dream and begins to interpret it while still asleep.

He figures the dictionary stands for the sciences, whereas the anthology of poets represents wisdom. Similarly, the poem beginning "Est et non" is about truth and falsity, whereas "Quod vitae sectabor iter?" is about ethics and his destiny. He then wakes up and seamlessly continues the dream interpretation. The melon he takes to represent "the charms of solitude." What do the engraved portraits stand for? When he meets an Italian painter the next day, Descartes figures that his dreaming consciousness must have glimpsed a symbol of his immediate future. The ghosts and the whirlwind of the first dream, he reckons, are the work of an evil demon trying to push him in the direction he was already heading—that is, the wrong direction. The thunderclap and the spray of sparkles symbolize the spirit of truth, which possesses him and carries him into the science and wisdom symbolized in the third dream.

In the wake of his dreams, Descartes feels, in essence, that right on the edge of his consciousness is absolute knowledge itself, like a whole new language on the tip of the tongue. What road in life shall he follow? His destiny is to unwrap the gifts that his three nightmares had delivered. He must find in the book of life the true understanding of what is and what isn't. The book did not completely disappear; it simply melted into his mind, where he can retrieve its divine wisdom with a little intellectual effort. He procrastinates on the task for twenty years.

In the meantime, Descartes renounces the military life, visits the shrine of the Virgin at Loretto (just in case the first dream really was trying to get him to pray), and makes world-historical contributions to geometry, optics, meteorology, and the study of rainbows. Finally, he feels that he can't procrastinate any longer and reserves a week of solitude to rebuild human knowledge on the ultimate foundation hidden just below his consciousness. He sleeps in and then meditates late into the night for six consecutive days, precisely the amount of time it takes God to make everything. For every night he composes one of the meditations collected in his masterpiece *Meditations on First Philosophy*. The scene resembles that of his original dreams: a fire, a wax candle, solitude. For a week he doesn't get out of his pajamas.

*

On the first night Descartes scrutinizes his beliefs and realizes just how rickety they are. Most of what he takes to be true he believes on the authority of others, even though authorities are often wrong and in disagreement with each other: "I thought, too, how the same man, with the same mind, if brought up from infancy among the French or Germans, develops otherwise than he would if he had always lived among the Chinese or cannibals."[3] Even the rigors of education don't seem to rise above the clash of authority. Reflecting on his own thorough education in the history of philosophy and theology, Descartes declares, "I discovered that nothing can be imagined which is too strange or incredible to have been said by some philosopher," surely knowing that some philosopher—Cicero in *De Divinatione*—had already said that too.[4] For his whole life he's been handed belief after belief, and he's uncritically slopped them into the structure of his mind, like a drunk mason. He realizes that if he is to build a permanent structure of knowledge, he must first demolish this preexisting architecture of opinion. He must raze his beliefs to the ground and begin anew, this time building on an absolutely firm foundation and according to an infallible plan.

The method Descartes formulates to find this firm foundation is practically identical to al-Ghazali's. (The whole of the first meditation follows the Sufi's logic so closely as to make scholars wonder about plagiarism. My own view is that not only do great minds think alike, *all* minds think alike, though mysteriously they often come to different conclusions.) Descartes's plan is to set aside any belief that admits of the least doubt until he can be completely sure it's true. Guilty until proven innocent. Rather than proceed like the drunk mason who slops up every belief willy-nilly, he's going to demolish with the sledgehammer of sober doubt all the contents of his mind until he finds a belief that can't be broken, a belief so unshakably solid it can serve as the foundation for all true beliefs. He need not proceed belief by belief; if he can knock out the support beams it will suffice to bring down all beliefs built on them.

It occurs to him that the support beam of almost all our beliefs is the senses. The first muted doubt (the doubt of the first meditation builds in a kind of intellectual crescendo) is that the senses sometime deceive us: for instance, we see water on the road, which proves in actuality to be a mirage. Such examples prove sufficient for al-Ghazali to dismiss the senses altogether as a source of certain truth. But Descartes rightly wonders that, while they surely can be wrong about distant things, are the senses deceived about what is most intimately experienced—for example, that he is by the fire in his pajamas, holding a piece of paper in his hands? Shaking his hands before his face, he exasperatedly asks, "How could I deny that I possess these hands?"

The motif of doubt begins to grow louder. What about the insane? Descartes, in a nightmarish list, speaks of madmen who believe that they're kings when they're paupers, that they're robed in purple when they're naked, that their heads are lumps of clay, that their bodies are completely composed of glass, or that they're not even humans at all but rather human-shaped gourds. Could it not be that his hands have been amputated, and his deluded mind, clouded by vapors of black bile (to use his quaint understanding of insanity), is tricking him into believing otherwise? Sometimes I'll ask a checked-out student at this point, "Can you be certain that you're not a gourd?" The exploration of the mind, even the geometrically sane mind of Descartes, very quickly leads to the border of madness. Descartes himself refuses to go down that road, though on the far side of modernity, two of his greatest critic-disciples do: Nietzsche and Freud.

Though insanity is out of the question, Descartes reasons that even the soundest minds spend a good chunk of their time in dreams so bizarre as to make the "gourd" seem relatively normal. It's farfetched, but not beyond the realm of possibility, that the gentleman soldier did indeed lose his hands in battle and now is having a recurring dream where he wiggles his fingers in front of his eyes as if to demonstrate their existence. As we know, Descartes is more than capable of having extremely vivid dreams, even of believing that he has woken up within a dream. Because he's trying to demolish whatever beliefs are not completely self-certain, he decides to enter into a thought experiment: for the sake of discovering something certain he will assume that he is presently dreaming.

Proceeding with musical precision, Descartes reasons that he can doubt all the specific information of the senses (that his hands exist, etc.) and any science built on that information. Imagine a physics based on dreaming: it would have to account for the fact that I'm sometimes able to fly if I catch a gust of wind just so! But it dawns on the geometrically minded Descartes that there are some beliefs beyond doubt even in a dream: namely, the truths of mathematics, which do not depend on any existing state of affairs. Regardless of how many hands he actually has, $1 + 1 = 2$. Even if his piece of paper is made totally out of dream stuff, a rectangle has four straight sides that meet in four ninety-degree angles. Are the truths of mathematics, which are logically prior to any given experience, the absolutely self-certain foundation he is looking for? It would take a deception far greater than a human dream to cast doubt on mathematics. It would require trickery of divine proportions. . . .

So why not, he figures, start playing around with the idea of God? Could it be, Descartes wonders in a passage that would bedevil him with religious authorities for the rest of his life, that God is not how we're used to thinking of Him? Could it be, in particular, that God does exist and is indeed all-powerful and all-knowing, but not all-good? Could God be an omnipotent trickster? Come to think of it, the possibility doesn't seem that far-fetched. But even if it's highly unlikely that we're being subjected to a divinely powerful deception, Descartes has stipulated that he must be completely certain. Meditating by the flickering fire, he realizes that he can't be absolutely sure an "evil genius," as he calls his hypothetical demon, isn't in charge of his every perception of the cosmos.

So, for the purposes of discovering the absolute truth that his dreams had promised, Descartes assumes the existence of an all-powerful, all-knowing, deceptive God. Under this new and improved thought experiment, not only are the truths of the senses thrown in doubt, so are the most solid-seeming truths of mathematics. It could be that whenever we do a mental operation even as straightforward as $2 + 3$, the evil genius zaps our minds such that we miscalculate the answer as 5 (it's actually 7!)—something like a record skipping when the record player is bumped. While we congratulate ourselves on the certainty of our mathematical abilities, the evil genius in some dark corner of the universe is chuckling, "That one never gets old!"

At this point, a little initial uncertainty has crescendoed into a vast symphony of doubt. It seems that everything is uncertain, down to the simplest mathematical equations and the fact of the body's existence. Deeply troubled, he goes to sleep (or the illusion of sleep) without a truth in the world.

*

At the beginning of the second night's meditation, he reviews what he's accomplished and finds himself—to use his metaphor—drowning in a whirlpool: unable to swim up to take a breath, unable to touch his foot to the bottom. But he doesn't give up. Distantly echoing Socrates, Descartes boldly declares, "I will proceed in this way until I recognize something certain, or, if nothing else, until I at least recognize for certain that there is no certainty."[5] Perhaps there's some truth, so far overlooked, that really is a brick of certitude.

Such a truth can't be found in the outer world, for the evil-genius thought experiment has thrown all objects of sense and reason into doubt. It also can't be found in God, for neither God's nature nor His existence is at all clear to Descartes. What about himself? Is it possible to apply the method of doubt to his own existence?

> But I had the persuasion that there was absolutely nothing in the world, that there was no sky and no earth, neither minds nor bodies; was I not, therefore, at the same time, persuaded that I did not exist? Far from it; I assuredly existed, since I was persuaded. But there is I know not what being, who is possessed at once of the highest power and the deepest cunning, who is constantly employing all his ingenuity in deceiving me. Doubtless, then, I exist, since I am deceived; and, let him deceive me as he may, he can never bring it about that I am nothing, so long as I shall be conscious that I am something. So that it must, in fine, be maintained, all things being maturely and carefully considered, that this proposition *I am, I exist*, is necessarily true each time it is expressed by me, or conceived in my mind.[6]

Or, to use his formulation in the *Discourse on Method*: "Cogito; ergo sum"—I think; therefore I am. Even if an evil genius with infinite power is spending his entire time deceiving Descartes, it still must be the case that an object of deception exists. Philosophers refer to this famous metaphysical lightning bolt simply as the "cogito."

The best commentary I know on this certainty comes from a poet, Paul Valéry: "There is no syllogism in the Cogito; there is not even a literal meaning. It is a piece of shock tactics, a reflex act of the intellect, a living and thinking being who shouts, 'I've had enough of it! Your doubt means nothing to me.'"[7] In other words, it's a lot like al-Ghazali's experience of God. Even with minds set for skepticism, no doubt clings to either the Sufi's mystical experience or the mathematician's cogito. It isn't just that they see the truth with perfect clarity: their minds melt into the truth itself and form the most primordial of unities.

Also, in both cases, the truth must be performed. From the outside, I can doubt al-Ghazali's experience of God, just as I can doubt that Descartes or anybody else is thinking as I am thinking. (Since I've been a child I've wondered if the way I see blue is how others see blue.) But if I have a mystical experience, or if I declare in the solitude of my thoughts, "I'm thinking right now, so I must somehow exist," I've entered a zone beyond doubt.

The comparison between mystical experience and the cogito runs even deeper. When Moses asks for God's true name, God answers, "I am that I am," which is tantalizingly similar to Descartes's "I am, I exist." In fact, Descartes defines the "I" as "the soul by which I am what I am."[8] Also, when asked if the natural light of our reason is sufficient to access the divine, he replies, "In my view, the way to reach the love of God is to consider that he is a mind, or a thing that thinks; and that our soul's nature resembles his sufficiently for us to believe that it is an emanation of his supreme intelligence."[9] In both the experience of God and the experience of our own "I am," thought and the source of thought are unified. In one sense, they are the same ecstatic experience. But whereas al-Ghazali focuses on the divine "I am," Descartes begins with the human "I am"—a difference perhaps metaphysically small but one that signals the world-historical shift from the medieval to the modern age.

*

Descartes is well aware that he's starting from an all-too-human consciousness. Even though he knows for certain that he exists, he can't be sure of who exactly he is. His memories, his name, his body could all be deceptions. The title of the second meditation is "The Nature of the Human Mind, and How It Is Better Known Than the Body." By "body" Descartes means any physical object. In a passage of beautiful prose, he writes:

> Take, for example, this piece of wax; it is quite fresh, having been but recently taken from the beehive; it has not yet lost the sweetness of the honey it contained; it still retains somewhat of the odor of the flowers from which it was gathered; its color, figure, size, are apparent (to the sight); it is hard, cold, easily handled; and sounds when struck upon with the finger. In fine, all that contributes to make a body as distinctly known as possible, is found in the one before us. But, while I am speaking, let it be placed near the fire—what remained of the taste exhales, the smell evaporates, the color changes,

its figure is destroyed, its size increases, it becomes liquid, it grows hot, it can hardly be handled, and, although struck upon, it emits no sound. Does the same wax still remain after this change?[10]

Let's also consider what we more normally call the body, of which the honey-flavored wax is so deliciously suggestive. Imagine a time-lapse movie of your face from birth to grave: your chubby baby mug suddenly phasing through all the ages of childhood, ripening into its most beautiful moment, then slowly growing puffy or gaunt, wrinkling, brightening and saddening by turns, wrinkling yet deeper, hair whitening and falling out, shank shrinking, eyes growing bleary until vision finally leaves them. I really am being brought to the fire! My belly no longer emits a sound when tapped on! Do I still remain? Of course I do, Descartes maintains, but not perhaps in the way revealed by appearances.

At this point it's worth remembering Descartes's larger project: to transform science altogether. Traditionally, science was the contemplation of the physical world as revealed to the senses. Descartes is heading toward a new conception of the physical world as what is known through mathematical physics and can be manipulated by technology. The appearance of the wax changes, but what—in part thanks to Descartes—we've come to think of as its cellular structure remains the same. We sometimes think of science as the mere scrutiny of our experience, though scientists are always telling us things about whizzing atoms and dark matter that far exceed anything we ever access with our normal senses. Consider the heliocentric view of the universe, which at Descartes's time was a major source of controversy. It seems overwhelmingly obvious that the stars revolve around us. It was just this overwhelming obviousness that we needed to get over, according to Galileo and Descartes. If science is to progress, we need to stop fixating on how wax and stars initially appear and plunge into what Descartes will come to call "clear and distinct ideas" of their deeper structure.

At the beginning of this night's meditation, Descartes steeled himself with the bravado of Archimedes, who after figuring out the nature of levers declared that if given a long enough crowbar and an immovable point, he'd be able to pry the earth itself from its course. By the end of the second meditation, Descartes has found his Archimedean point, one absolutely certain truth: the "I think; therefore

I am." The only thing he can be sure of is that he exists as a thinking being: "a thing that doubts, understands, [conceives], affirms, denies, wills, refuses; that imagines also, and perceives."[11] It is a great accomplishment to sleep on. Now all he has left to do is move the whole world.

*

At the beginning of the third meditation, Descartes is locked deep inside his own consciousness. Standing between his certain self and the rest of the universe is the mighty evil genius, who casts a shadow of doubt on every object of sense and reason. Can Descartes with his one little, solid truth defeat the prospect of an omnipotent deceiver? David has found a stone; now he has to face Goliath.

Descartes's own requirement is that he must be sure of every intellectual move. At this point, he's certain of nothing beyond his own consciousness and the modes of his consciousness. So, all Descartes can say for sure about God (who may or may not be evil, who may or may not exist) is that he has the idea of God, a concept of the Supreme Being. Maybe this idea refers to something real; maybe it's complete fiction. Where possibly could such a strange notion as God originate?

You might think that the idea of God comes from our parents or our society. But that isn't a complete answer to Descartes's question; it merely pushes the question a generation back. Where did our parents—and our grandparents, and our great-grandparents, all the way back to the first human offspring of the chimpanzees—get the idea from? Descartes has courted a doubt so radical that it calls into question the existence of all humans but for himself. He's all alone in the wild Eden of consciousness. How does the primordial human mind stumble on the idea of the divine?

Our French Adam identifies three possible sources for all ideas: (1) the world (by way of the senses)—for instance, we derive the idea of a horse from having seen horses; (2) the imagination (by way of combining our sense perceptions)—for instance, we derive the idea of a unicorn from having seen horses and horns and blending them in our minds; or (3) God—for instance, it's possible that any or all ideas are simply implantations of the evil genius, stimulating our minds in his macabre laboratory.

The idea of a supreme being is, by definition, not the kind of thing our senses could perceive as an object in the world. It's possible to see horses, rocks, molecules, and supernovas. It's possible, at least theoretically, to see even unicorns and angels. But it's impossible to see God, for a supreme being would lie beyond the conditions of space and time. One could, I suppose, see a token of God. If an acacia catches on fire, burns without being consumed, and speaks meaningfully to me, I might reasonably believe that God is trying to get my attention. But it would be a mistake to conclude that God is a combustive process of shrubbery. God would simply have used the miraculous bush as a way of communicating from the Unfathomable Beyond to my little human mind, fond as it is of its three dimensions.

Most, if not all, atheists hold that the idea of God comes from Descartes's second possible source: the imagination. We cower at the mystery of thunder and in our ignorance suppose it's caused by a superhuman force that we name Big Dada—or something like that. But Descartes holds the remarkable view that it's impossible for us to have imagined God, for the capacities of our imagination are bounded by the limitations of our senses. We can, of course, imagine things we never experience, like winged angels and giants hurling thunderbolts; but we cannot imagine the unimaginable, a being unlike all other beings we have perceived. We can perceive and imagine finite things, even very big and powerful finite things, but not a supremely perfect being. In unbecoming academic language, Descartes says, "Now it is manifest by the natural light that there must be at least as much reality in the efficient and total cause as in the effect of that cause."[12] In more straightforward terms, only God could imagine God. Since we have the idea of God, it must be the case that God exists. Only God could have put the idea of God in our minds, signing His creation like an artist.

This proof of God, intended to be completely certain, turns paradoxically on the idea that God is incomprehensible. As Descartes says in a letter to a friend, "The greatness of God . . . is something which we cannot grasp even though we know it."[13] Try to picture God. What do you envision? Perhaps you see a severe, bearded Jehovah with flowing white beard and chiseled muscles, something out of Michelangelo or Blake. Maybe you imagine a kindlier creature, a dreamy Jesus or a milk-white dove. It's not impossible that you picture the many-breasted Artemis, or many-faced Krishna on the battlefield, or a fat Venus without a face. Maybe even your mind is overrun by a host of mythological weirdos. The saints, for all I know, have only to look into someone's eyes. But Descartes holds that such images are, at best, fables of the divine, fleshy images of what cannot be framed by a cerebral cortex. Presumably, when we call lightning a god, it's because our minds are groping for an appropriately powerful image for the impossible concept of the divine that's born into them. If we're to maintain total intellectual honesty, we should probably stick to the second commandment not to form an image of God at all. And yet, despite our inability to draw any remotely accurate picture, we have the idea of God. According to Descartes, the very implausibility of having an idea of something none of our intellectual faculties can frame is itself the proof of God.

After the third night's meditation, Descartes doesn't have to go to sleep lonely. Someone else exists for sure in the universe. The little "I think; therefore I am" nods off next to the great "I am that I am."

*

But what is God like? Is God the benevolent creator Descartes is accustomed to trusting, or the evil genius he fears? Descartes, perhaps too easily, concludes that the idea of an evil God is incoherent. A supreme being by definition cannot have any limitations or imperfections. Since evil is an imperfection, God cannot be evil. Sure, God would have the power to deceive, but He would lack the inkling to do so, for "in every case of trickery or deception some imperfection is to be found."[14] Descartes has defeated the evil genius by proving him to be as logically impossible as a round square.

If the cogito is Descartes's immovable Archimedean pivot, the idea of a benevolent God is his sufficiently long crowbar. With very little force, he's now able to lever the world of sense and reason out of the doubt into which it was sunk. Does $2 + 3 = 5$? Yes, with complete certainty. Are the hands he holds before his face really as they appear? Yes, they surely must be. God just wouldn't allow such ideas to form in the mind if they weren't really so.

But what about all the times our senses and reason do form ideas that aren't so? Hallucinations, dreams, mirages, and even the history of science furnish us with examples of how we can indeed have wrong beliefs floating around our minds. Countless red Xs on the math homework of the world seem to prove that reason often goes awry. If God is a perfect being who by definition would never deceive us, why are we so often deceived?

The fourth meditation, in some ways the most radical of all the meditations, concerns a subset of the problem of evil, the great problem first framed by Epicurus: "Is God willing to prevent evil, but not able? Then he is impotent. Is he able, but not willing? Then he is evil. Is he both able and willing? Then where does evil come from?" We'll confront this problem in all its horrible glory in a coming chapter. Here our problem concerns simply mental sins. If the perfect God created our minds, how can they be so imperfect?

In reflecting on this question, Descartes draws—perhaps unfairly —on a longstanding tradition of Christian reflection. Why does a good, all-powerful creator allow us to make mental errors, let alone commit sins as grave as rape and murder? The answer that bubbles up from innocent students and ponderous theologians alike is: free will. God does not create us to go wrong, but He does give us the ability to go wrong. This ability, freedom itself, is a great gift; for it's a necessary prerequisite for having a meaningful life. Imagine if God had made us as robots who always get the right answer and always do the right thing. There would be no triumph or glory in mathematics or morality. There would, in fact, be no point in them at all. So, free will is a gift perfectly compatible with an all-good giver. But it obviously comes with the possibility that we might go wrong. Though God did not program us to commit sin, He did leave room, ample room, for us to do so. Evil, to use theological terminology, is simply a privation, nothingness, a gap left by an all-good God in His all-good creation. Evil is the hole that gives meaning to the whole.

The principle Descartes invokes is that we should accept as true only what can be known clearly and distinctly. As he explains it, "I call 'clear' that perception which is present and manifest to an attentive mind: just as we say that we clearly see those things which are present to our intent eye and act upon it sufficiently strongly and manifestly. On the other hand, I call 'distinct,' that perception which, while clear, is so separated and delineated from all others that it contains absolutely nothing except what is clear."[15] To put it plainly, when we make mistakes, it's because we've accepted a belief as true prior to having an idea of it that's clear as a toothache and distinct as arithmetic. It's not God deceiving me when I believe a mirage is water, or a shadow is standing still, or 13 × 14 = 172, or the sun revolves around the earth; it's me abusing my freedom, leaping to a conclusion without sufficient evidence.

Thus the startling conclusion of the fourth meditation is that we never have to make a mistake. If we work only with clear and distinct ideas, then we can move ever closer to the truth. In particular, Descartes argues that we can understand the things of the universe as objects of mathematics, for maximal clarity and distinctness is achieved when we use mathematical modeling as a basis for the careful scrutiny of the senses. Granted, we'll often have to leave certain questions unanswered, for our minds are limited and the universe is vast. But we should be able to widen our knowledge, and whatever does appear clearly and distinctly in its beam we can have complete confidence in. More specifically, clear and distinct knowledge is based on the cogito and the proof of God, clarified by mathematics, and accessed by a careful scrutiny of the senses. The world as uncritically known to the senses has been demolished, the foundation of the new science of mathematical physics has been laid, and now humanity is ready to build the mansion of clear and distinct ideas.

Already after the fourth night's meditation, Descartes's mission is basically accomplished, and he's able to lie down on a pillow that's probably as downy as it feels, confident that three sheep plus two sheep is definitely five sheep.

*

In the fifth meditation, Descartes proves God—again.

*

In the sixth meditation, he wrestles with the nature of the mind and the nature of material existence. Descartes is often invoked as a case of a simplistic mind-body dualism, where the mind is a ghost in the machine of the body. While he certainly does hold that mind and body are ultimately different substances, his analyses in the sixth meditation, let alone in his book *The Passions*, prove far more subtle than the ubiquitous caricature. In fact, I know of no more accurate description of the problem posed by the bizarreness of consciousness than his observation: "I am not only residing in my body, as a pilot in his ship, but furthermore, . . . I am intimately connected with it, and . . . the mixture is so blended, as it were, that something like a single whole is produced."[16]

But the crucial idea of the sixth meditation, still haunting us to this day, is that the world—including my own body—is a machine that can be known to scientific minds that hover strangely within the system but ultimately are different from it. Descartes has continually been criticized for this dualism, but at least he has the guts to admit his situation. Many contemporary enthusiasts for science insist that the mind is no more than the brain, a machine governed by natural laws, including evolutionary laws, but they often have real troubles in accounting for the knowing and willing qualities of the mind. How is it possible to know and to manipulate and to transform the nature that I supposedly am synonymous with? Wouldn't it be a wondrous irony if science could account for everything but scientific knowledge and technological desire?

After six nights of meditation, Descartes can rest assured that he exists as a thinking being, that God exists and is perfect, that clear and distinct ideas are true, and that the mind and the body are intimately mixed but ultimately distinguishable. As a child, I used to wonder what God did on His seventh day of rest. As an adult, I wonder that about Descartes.

*

Every one of Descartes's conclusions, since their publication, has been subject to unceasing criticism. Has Descartes smuggled in the concept of the "I" in the midst of his hyperbolic doubt? Perhaps, as Hume and various Buddhists hold, the self is an illusion, and all we should conclude is that there is thinking. How, countless others have wondered, can Descartes rationally prove God in the midst of doubting reason itself? It seems that Descartes needs reason to prove God, and God to prove reason. How, for that matter, can clear and distinct ideas be trusted when it's always in principle possible to have clearer and more distinct ideas? How do mind and body interact if they're separate substances? Much of the philosophy of the seventeenth and eighteen centuries is the attempt to answer that last question. Finally, how can we believe that we never have to make a mistake when so much of even the finest science requires mistake making as an intrinsic part of the process?

The nature of a good proof is that it lays a subject to rest: we no longer have to think about it. In this sense, Descartes's rational intuitions and deductive proofs have been a failure among professional philosophers. But they've been a kind of success everywhere else. Even Descartes himself seems not to be much interested in the *Meditations* after their publication. In a letter to an admirer, Descartes writes, "You should not devote so much attention to the *Meditations* and to metaphysical questions. . . . They draw the mind too far away from physical and observable things, and unfit it to study them. Yet it is precisely physical studies that it is most desirable for men to pursue."[17] The foundation, he implies, is poured and set; now is the time to build the house of modernity. Advance mathematical physics and build life-enhancing technology in light of that knowledge. Philosophize only to help move science and technology smoothly along.

It would be an overstatement to give Descartes complete responsibility for modernity; certainly, Copernicus, Galileo, Bacon, and Hobbes—to name just a few—should also be praised and blamed for their role in its creation. Bacon seems closer than Descartes to formulating the spirit of scientific method; the scientific achievements of Copernicus and Galileo utilize that spirit more successfully than any of the Frenchman's experiments; and it is Hobbes, not the generally conservative Descartes, who wrenches political authority away from religion. Yet somehow Descartes still seems to me the true prophet of modernity. At the heart of the Middle Ages, we find al-Ghazali basing knowledge on the mystery of God. At the beginning of modernity, we find Descartes basing knowledge on the mystery of the self. In his lucid writings are the following seminal ideas:

- real knowledge should be expressed in numbers;
- we should utilize a self-correcting method of knowledge about the physical world;
- this method should involve a uniform, repeatable procedure;
- the truth is accessible to anyone who is willing to think clearly;
- values are subjective and private;
- we should use reason to determine the existence and nature of God;

- the body is a machine and hence can be understood and fixed like a machine;
- the universe is a machine too;
- we should utilize scientific understanding to build technologies so we can become masters of our fate;
- and the "preservation of health" is the "chief of all goods."

What is modernity (of which what we boastfully call postmodernity is very much a part) but the follow-through on these ideas, which are themselves the spelling out of a few dreams?

I variously curse and thank Descartes when I see all the ridiculous, wonderful gadgets we amuse ourselves with; when I enter a hospital, where the mechanical body is miraculously fixed and the human spirit must fight for a little concern; when I am told that my educational outcomes must be quantified; when I whir the splendid gadgets in my kitchen; or when I reflect on the deep disconnect between science and the humanities, two "cultures" that have become incompatible as mind and body. Even the greatest words of modernity, "We hold these truths to be self-evident: that all men are created equal," I hear as a powerful echo of "I think; therefore, I am." To be a professional philosopher in the modern period is to have a criticism of Descartes, just as to participate in modernity is to have some kind of gripe against modernity. I don't mean to suggest that Descartes would embrace all aspects of modernity. I do think that much of our current way of life can be recognized in seed form in his reasonings.

The extent to which we've inherited Descartes's approach to God is particularly important. The usual human relationship to God is one that goes beyond human reason. In the beginning stages of human life, we accept the basis of culture on authority. Then, when we go deeper into the ultimate, we find that reason blanks at its sunlike intensity, and we must utilize the mirrors of myth, symbol, and ritual to picture it. Certainly, this usual relationship to the divine still holds in its way—and always will. But Descartes establishes, quite against his intentions, the possibility of a purely rational relationship to nature and the divine. So, when religionists and atheists alike debate as if our connection to God depended solely on fossil records and the usefulness of the appendix, or when every aspect of our common life is subjected to social science, or when nature is glimpsed solely through the lens of technology, I also think of Descartes.

In my opinion, among all the conundrums of Cartesian thought the most wonderful, responsible for these past four centuries of philosophical criticism, is that while Descartes presents his ideas as the certain result of careful reasoning, they originally issue from a daimon. The nightmares of Descartes and the mystical certitude of the cogito, I've tried to hint, suggest that rationality has roots that go deeper than reason. But perhaps the clearest way of making my point is based on the odd phrase that crops up repeatedly in the *Meditations*. Whenever Descartes finds himself at an intellectual impasse, he is apt to say, "Reason now persuades me"—to do whatever it is he needs to advance his thought. "Reason," as it is used in these passages, could be replaced by any number of words: God, an intuition, a dream, my Muse, a Martian. For "reason" speaks as a voice from the ether, a guide from beyond, that shepherds Descartes through the darkest valleys of doubt. "Reason" continues to persuade him even after he puts reason in doubt with the evil-genius thought experiment! I understand that such a guide, particularly in the dark valleys of our life, is necessary. But it's disingenuous to call this guide "reason" if its name could just as well be "unreason." One of my favorite titles of a student paper—which did not, unfortunately, live up to its title—was: "Maybe Descartes Should Have Given More Thought to the Possibility That He Was Crazy."

*

In the splendid, not-very-trustworthy volumes of the third century called *Lives of Eminent Philosophers* by Diogenes Laertius, it's common to find philosophers dying a death somehow befitting their philosophies. My favorite example is Diogenes the Cynic who, aspiring to live a self-sufficient life, met his end while trying to see how long he could hold his breath. We're still counting, Diogenes!

On good historical evidence, we do know how Descartes died. Though his writings contain nothing obviously subversive regarding politics, he was often in hot water with various authorities. In one particularly notable episode, he was charged by the University of Utrecht with undermining orthodox theology and traditional philosophy, thereby leading the young astray—essentially those old charges against Socrates, unholiness and corrupting the youth. So, when the intellectually curious Queen Christina asked him to come to tolerant Sweden to be her tutor, Descartes took her up on it, re-solved to be "a spectator rather than an actor in the comedies of life."[18] Unfortunately, a queen's life is demanding, and she scheduled her lessons at the crack of dawn. On the unpleasant morning walk to the castle, Descartes—who was used to sleeping in till noon—came down with pneumonia. He died on a cold February day in 1650. Strangely fitting in its way. Rather than see Descartes on his own terms, as a man whose reason never sleeps, I've tried to present him as a dream-haunted philosopher and an unwitting prophet of modernity. Thus, denied his best dreaming hours, he wasn't long for the world. The lesson I draw is: don't get up too early because you will die.

7 The Terrifying Distance of the Stars

Distracted from distraction by distraction   T. S. ELIOT

Let's go back to a cloudless night in the Middle Ages and look up at the sky. Though the constellations tingle on our retinas the same raw image as ever (give or take a star), they actually *look* very different, for that delicate dance of light has to be processed by the help of concepts—or, in the absence of concepts, the improvisations of myth. Remember, the earth is not yet a satellite of the sun, the beams of the stars don't yet have to travel light years, and the twinklings we see aren't yet the tail ends of beams whose original sources self-pulverized a million years ago. C. S. Lewis, imagining us in medieval times, explains,

> Remember that you now have an absolute Up and Down. The Earth is really the centre, really the lowest place; movement to it from whatever direction is downward movement. As a modern, you located the stars at a great distance. For distance you must now substitute that very special, and far less abstract, sort of distance which we call height; height, which speaks immediately to our muscles and nerves. The Medieval Model is vertiginous. And the fact that the height of the stars in the medieval astronomy is very small compared with their distance in the modern, will turn out not to have the kind of importance you anticipated. For thought and imagination, ten million miles and a thousand million are much the same. Both can be conceived (that is, we can do sums with both) and neither can be imagined; and the more imagination we have the better we shall know this. The really important difference is that the medieval universe, while unimaginably large, was also unambiguously finite. And one expected result of this is to make the smallness of

Earth more vividly felt. In our universe she is small, no doubt; but so are the galaxies, so is everything—and so what?[1]

So what? Well, if we're sensitive to the tinglings of reality, we're apt to say with Pascal about our modern cosmos, "The eternal silence of these infinite spaces fills me with dread."[2] Whereas the medieval stargazer feels small in comparison to the skyscraping constellations, the modern stargazer is inclined to feel a creeping worthlessness in comparison with universes on universes, the vanishing littleness of it all. I sometimes wonder if it was the change in astronomy that unleashed our modern anxiety, or if it was our anxiety that pressured us into a new model of the universe.

*

Blaise Pascal—born June 19, 1623, at Clermont in Auvergne—lost his mother when he was three, and was raised along with his two sisters by his loving father, a tax commissioner. Like Descartes, Pascal was a genius in any and every sense of the word. By the age of twelve, he'd deduced by himself the first thirty-two propositions of Euclid. When he was sixteen, he published a treatise on the "mystic hexagram," in which he laid out what is still known as Pascal's Theorem. Descartes, when presented with the treatise, refused to believe it had been produced by a teenager. By the age of nineteen, Pascal had invented the Pascaline, a calculating machine intended to lighten his father's workload. This computer was tweaked a few times over the following centuries and in 1971 became the first microprocessor, that great symbol of our times. (One of the first computer programming languages was called Pascal in homage to the inventor.) At the age of twenty-four, he overturned two-thousand years of thinking about hydraulics in his *New Experiments with the Vacuum*. He more or less invented the hydraulic press and—another symbol of our age—the syringe. At the age of thirty, he published his *Treatise on the Arithmetical Triangle*, a pioneering work in binomial coefficients. In the following year, prompted by the gambling problems of his friend the Chevalier de Méré, he invented probability theory.

In the winter of 1647, his father slipped on the ice and broke his hip. Over the next three months, two prominent doctors attended to him, both of whom were vocal members of a small but growing group within Catholicism called Jansenism, associated with Calvinism by its Jesuit opponents and eventually condemned by the pope. Thus, by means of a fractured hip bone, the Pascal family came under the spell of Jansenism, and Blaise underwent what his biographers refer to as his "first conversion," feeling the religiosity of his Catholic upbringing with a new intensity. But he soon backslid into a worldly life, falling in love with a beauty and writing his *Discourse on the Passions of Love.*

In the fall of 1654, Pascal's horses plunged over a great bridge and, had their reins not broken, would have pulled his carriage down with them. While the carriage teetered on the edge of the precipice, he felt the terrifying wonder of philosophy. As soon as he stood on solid ground, he fainted. A month later, on the twenty-third of November, between 10:30 and 12:30 at night, Pascal suffered a mystical experience, which he never published and never forgot. He simply jotted down, "Fire. God of Abraham, God of Isaac, God of Jacob, not of the philosophers and the scholars. I will not forget thy word. Amen." Then he sewed the note into the lining of his jacket which he wore for the rest of his life.

After this second, authentic conversion, Pascal wrote the two great prose works associated with his name: the *Provincial Letters*, the masterwork Voltaire called "the best-written work yet to appear in French," and his greatest work of all, the *Pensées* ("Thoughts" in English, though the title is rarely translated, even in English-language versions of the book, because the French word has a ring to it). Intending to produce a systematic defense of Christianity, Pascal never got around to finishing it, dying at the dispiriting age of thirty-nine. The *Pensées* is a set of notes and jottings on large sheets of paper, which Pascal cut into pieces and arranged and rearranged according to various plans. I've never heard or read of anyone who wishes the text had been finalized into a polished treatise. As it stands (and it has stood in different ways), the book is a cubist portrait of human nature, a sheaf of little lightning bolts, a book that sometimes reads us. Not to say that it's without blind spots, religious defensiveness, pet sayings, odd obsessions, darkness, and quaint ideas. But the more I read the *Pensées*, the more I feel that even its weaknesses are a philosophically significant part of the human whole suggested by the fragments. It's a book productively read by dipping into it at random, particularly if, like me, you resist the tyranny of page numbers.

*

Pascal sums up our condition in three words: "Inconstancy, boredom, anxiety"—a striking outline of the problem of being human.[3] In short, our very being fills us with anxiety; we flee the anxiety by means of some kind of diversion (another of Pascal's pet terms). As long as our diversionary tactic lasts, we have a measure of happiness, but eventually the charm wears off, the diversion becomes boring, and we seek out the newest thing to do—thus our inconstancy.

Not long ago I met the writer Carl Honoré, and he told me of his inspiration for his book *In Praise of Slowness*. While standing in line at the airport, he was flipping through a magazine and saw an ad for *One-Minute Bedtime Stories: Snow White in 60 Seconds*. A father who often read to his sleepy kids, he considered sending away for it in order to save some precious time at night. On second thought, he realized he was being insane—in a particularly modern way. Why was he trying to minimize the amount of time he read to his children? Wasn't that some of the most precious time he had? He went on to write *In Praise of Slowness*, an Epicurean tract on how we shouldn't forget to stop and smell the roses.

Offering a different perspective on Carl Honoré's temptation, Pascal devastatingly observes,

> The fact is that the present usually hurts. We thrust it out of sight because it distresses us, and if we find it enjoyable, we are sorry to see it slip away . . . Let each of us examine his thoughts; he will find them wholly concerned with the past or the future. We almost never think of the present, and if we do think of it, it is only to see what light it throws on our plans for the future. The present is never our end. The past and the present are our means, the future alone our end. Thus we never actually live, but hope to live, and since we are always planning how to be happy, it is inevitable that we should never be so.[4]

"Anxiety"—a word that implies an uneasiness beyond any clear cause—is built into our very being. In part, I suppose, it's the anxiety of having to die, but that's really no more than saying it's the anxiety of being alive. Sometimes we're thrown into the present and must face this fundamental anxiety head-on—for instance, we're forced to wait on a street corner for a friend who is running late. But most of the time the anxiety eats at the periphery of our experience. Even when what we're doing is something we find valuable, like reading our daughter to sleep, part of us is trying to escape the present, to run on to the next thing, even though the next thing may be even less worthwhile. We channel surf our very lives.

The Buddhists make a similar point. The second noble truth, right after "life is suffering," is that we suffer because of our endless desire. The Chan—or Zen—Buddhists believe that the cure to this horrible, universal problem involves nothing more than being able to sit and breathe. If we could just calmly exist, not grasping after anything, even for a moment, we would be enlightened. Though Pascal doesn't go quite so far as inventing Buddhism, he does say, "Sometimes, when I set to thinking about the various activities of men, the dangers and troubles which they face at Court, or in war, giving rise to so many quarrels and passions, daring and often wicked enterprises and so on, I have often said that the sole cause of man's unhappiness is that he does not know how to stay quietly in his own room."[5]

In one Zen anecdote, a man is walking along a cliff, and a tiger suddenly jumps out, startling him right over the edge. On his fall the man catches himself and hangs by a small branch protruding from the cliff. Looking down, he sees another tiger prowling on the beach. Looking up, he sees the first tiger greedily eyeing him. All he can see as he looks around for help is a wild strawberry growing beside the branch he hangs from. What should he do? Should he risk climbing down? Should he try to climb back up? Should he hang there in hopes the tigers move on? Should he try to scare them off? According to Zen wisdom, he eats the strawberry. The end.

Pascal would agree with the presentation of the problem: our lives are anxiously suspended between the two devouring ends of time. But whereas Buddhists and certain philosophers like Epicurus hold that there's a remedy for our anxiety—meditation or the therapy of desire—Pascal is skeptical of a psychological or this-worldly cure. Perhaps we may lessen the effects of our natural suffering, but nobody is able to overmaster the problem fully. In short, while the wisdom of eating the wild fruit of now sounds beautiful, it's damn hard to eat your strawberry in peace when you're on the verge of being devoured by tigers.

Which brings us to an absolutely fundamental question. Is it possible for human beings to be truly happy in this life?

A. Yes, if we take the bull by the horns, we can be happy; moreover, there exist known disciplines (Buddhism, Epicureanism, Stoicism, et al.) that have proven to lead to happiness.
B. Yes, but we're waiting on better political realities for this happiness to be realized (Marxism).
C. No, the only hope for our happiness lies in something beyond this life; lucky for us, the path to this happiness has been revealed by God (Christianity, Islam, et al.).
D. No, the only hope for our happiness lies in something beyond this life; unfortunately, it's wishful thinking to believe in something beyond this life (pessimism).

What's the answer we mostly give to this great question? Which solution—A, B, C, or D—is the most popular of all? According to Pascal, it's:

E. Let's not think about it.

He says with hilarious clarity, "Being unable to cure death, wretchedness and ignorance, men have decided, in order to be happy, not to think about such things."[6]

Instead of facing our misery, we divert ourselves. Ball games and hunting are Pascal's favorite examples: "Men spend their time chasing a ball or a hare; it is the very sport of kings." But the list of diversions is practically endless: not just dramas, gossip, sports, cards, and other obvious trifles but having affairs, having pets, engaging in politics, going off to war, even working and attending to the necessities of life. When I was in graduate school, I knew a student whose apartment was never so clean as when he was supposed to be working on his dissertation. Think of a summer retreat to a cabin. The idea is to get away from the rat race and enjoy the simplicities of nature. After a few minutes watching the geese drift on the glittering water, we start wondering, "Now what?" It's no coincidence that every cabin on Walden Pond is stuffed to the gills with board games. Anything but the simplicities of nature! As Pascal notes, one of the worst punishments we've dreamt up, befitting the most heinous rapists and murderers, is to close a person in a room without diversions.

The beauty of a diversion is that while the charm of it lasts we're happy—kind of. We have the expression "being in the zone," or as one psychologist puts in, "being in a state of flow." This state is as close as we get to happiness—not in the sense of gratification but in the sense of a fullness of being. When LeBron James is in the zone, he may be cursing a teammate's blown coverage, may even be in physical distress, but he's actualizing a large part of his nature and riding on an immense wave of time. In short, he's happy. Games, a pure example of distraction, enchant us by simplifying our being into a zone where nagging anxiety is kept at bay. Even a game as complex as chess or football is wonderfully simple compared to, say, family life. Games have clearly prescribed rules and a clear goal. The only anxiety we feel while playing is if we're going to win, whereas in life we aren't clear about the rules and, despite our burning desire to win, don't know for sure what winning looks like.

The problem with diversions is that the happiness we find in them eventually wears off; their simplified version of life is unable to satisfy us in the long run. You just can't play basketball forever. All games are, in the end, boring. For Pascal, boredom is not a lack of inner resources but, rather, our groggy awakening to truth. If you're at all like me, you've had times when the regular routines—work, booze, TV, sports, books, politics, whatever—seem suddenly tedious and empty. If I remark on my boredom to my companions, they invariably retort, "Snap out of it! What we're doing is important (or fun). What's eating you all of a sudden? Where are your inner resources?" The odd thing is that when I'm in such a mood, I prefer my boredom to what strikes me as their foolishness. If Pascal is right, it's because such moods bring us closer to reality, and ultimately we prefer a genuine misery to a phony happiness (though it sometimes takes a little while to realize that).

What do we do when our preferred diversion becomes boring? Do we snap out of our delusion and embrace a more authentic life? Not according to the inventor of the computer. We're more likely to seek out a new diversion. Thus the human condition is one of "inconstancy," to use Pascal's word. It's not just certain cuts of clothing that suddenly come into style only to become passé; almost every facet of life is liable to the vagaries of fashion: cycles of politics, ways of writing and speaking, kinds of sport, movements in art, modes of transportation, preferred burials ("man is a Noble Animal," Sir Thomas Browne observes, "splendid in ashes, and pompous in the grave"), beautiful body types, and so forth.[7] Though every style up to now has eventually proven as outmoded as the previous, we nevertheless move heatedly on to the next cool thing as if it, at long last, were the secret of our happiness!

*

Let's say that you go to your high school reunion and bump into a former classmate, someone you always thought was a good guy, even though you were never close. You ask him how he's doing, and he answers, "Things are going well—unbelievably well, in fact. Just over a month ago, I'm out in L.A. visiting my cousin. I'm sitting at this cafe, just poking around the Internet, when all of a sudden this guy approaches me and says, 'You're perfect!' Turns out he's casting the new Spielberg movie! Based on my looks alone, he invites me to come read for Spielberg and some other big shots. I figure, what have I got to lose? One thing leads to another, and suddenly I have a $5 million advance and am starring in a big-time movie!"

As you stand there at your high school reunion, how do you now feel?

A. Genuinely happy for this person who's only ever been nice to you.
B. Mostly happy, but strangely a little irritated.
C. Somewhat happy, but more than a little irritated.
D. Just plain irked at his success.

How many people do you think could honestly answer *A*?

Now reverse the scenario. Say you're the one who's offered $5 million and a starring part in a blockbuster. Do you feel the same irritation that a nobody like yourself should be given such a break, particularly right before your high school reunion? Or do you feel, deep down, that finally your true importance has been recognized, and, what's more, just in time for you to gloat about it to your former classmates?

Pascal believes that we have an unrealistic view of ourselves, which he calls vanity, and hence a malicious relationship to others that surfaces in feelings of envy. We unreasonably esteem what we do, despite and often through protestations of humility. Through this lens of vanity we regard the activities of others as competition, regardless of the real situation. If, for instance, you're an aspiring actor who's never gotten a break, you might have cause to be irritated by your classmate's good fortune. But even if you've never shown a lick of interest in acting, even if you're happily married and have a job you like, you're still apt to be at least a little bothered by his success. Oh, well. Smile. Tell him how happy you are for him. As Pascal says, "Respect means: put yourself out."[8]

*

"Wretchedness" is Pascal's shorthand for that part of the human condition he analyzes with the terms "anxiety," "diversion," "boredom," "inconstancy," and "vanity." The good news is that there's another side to human nature, which he describes as our greatness. Let's take another look at those stars. Though we feel dwarfed almost to nothingness by their infinite distances, we nevertheless should take heart that we understand our withering smallness and their eternal silence. "Through space the universe grasps me and swallows me up like a speck," but, Pascal adds triumphantly, "through thought I grasp it."[9] In terms of mind, we're the infinite ones, and the stars, the magnificent stars, are just a few more of our playthings. Even our own overwhelming wretchedness gives us cause to recognize the glory of our nature: "It is wretched to know that one is wretched, but there is greatness in knowing one is wretched."[10]

Furthermore, we're able to imagine unwretched ways of being. The commandments of religion not to kill, lie, cheat, steal, or covet are splendid visions of human greatness. The exhortations of the Greek philosophical schools to live in accord with the divine are inspired by the intuitive height of our nature. In fact, no human society— not even a hermit—lives without an inspiring voice of greatness, expressed in etiquette and morality, which if only followed would make life immeasurably better. Just think if the greatest problems we faced were generated by side effects of following the Golden Rule!

The problem is that we've never set the bar of morality low enough to leap it. Rules, it seems, really are made to be broken. How many nights could you go to bed honestly sighing, "One more day of perfect morality, O Lord!" I don't even mean perfect by some standard you only half-heartedly believe in; I mean perfect by any set of standards at all you've set for yourself. "But Pascal is being too hard on us. I for one don't cheat on my spouse. Sure, I've told a few lies, but it's not like I've ever murdered anyone. There are plenty of rotten eggs out there, but mostly people like me are decent. Let's not go overboard with this wretchedness business!" This voice is another version of what Pascal calls vanity. It's a little like saying, "I have the very best mediocre house in the whole city! Certainly better than most of the shacks on the edge of town!"

Our wretchedness is the shadow cast by our greatness. They're inseparable, both generated by the nature of human consciousness itself. In Christianity, this dilemma is grasped mythologically in terms of the expulsion from the Garden of Eden, which occurs straightaway after we see who we are. But regardless of how we conceptualize its coming onto the scene, by ingesting the pulp of forbidden fruit or the slow zigzaggy work of evolution, the human mind seems to have a weird doubleness, to be haunted by conceptions it can never measure up to, to cast a shadow by its own light.

*

The most famous piece of reasoning associated with the *Pensées* is what's known as Pascal's Wager, the argument that it's a better bet to believe in God than to be an atheist. I think this argument seems a little superficial when severed from the rest of the *Pensées*. It gains in significance when reconnected to his analysis of the human condition, which poses the big problem: What are we supposed to do, given that our existence seems doomed to either honest misery or the superficial satisfactions of diversion? We have an abyss as big as God in our being. In an effort to plug its sucking vortex and alleviate our anxiety, we throw everything we can at it. Nothing really works. Should we turn our lives over to God in hopes that He is real and truly will satisfy us? Or is the solace of religion simply wishful thinking— infinitely wishful thinking?

First of all, Pascal thinks that we can have no intellectual knowledge of God's existence, let alone of what He might be like if He does exist. When we can prove something, reason compels us to believe accordingly. But Pascal denies that anything can be proved or disproved when it comes to the divine: "If there is a God, he is infinitely beyond our comprehension, since, being indivisible and without limits, he bears no relation to us."[11] It's a gross abuse of "the mathematical mind" for thinkers like Descartes to construct proofs of God, precisely as bad as reasoning oneself into atheism. About what could our knowledge be less certain than the possibility of perfect being? Intellectual honesty commands us to confess our complete ignorance of God. When a coin is flipped, and you're asked to call it, the right answer is: "How should I know? It could go either way." Therefore, we should all be agnostic.

The next point Pascal makes is that we can't be agnostic. We must call it. We're not simply intellectual spectators at the coin toss of God's existence. Our very lives hang on if it comes down heads or tails. We're "embarked," to use Pascal's term. Agnosticism, for Pascal, is simply a refusal to admit what you've staked your life on. As he sees it, either you live a life committed to God or you don't. There's no option of waiting until the coin spinning in eternity lands.

Jean-Paul Sartre tells of a French student who was in a bind during the German occupation of France. The student's brother had been killed by the Nazis. His father had proven semitreasonous. His mother was sick and grief-stricken. The student was convinced that his presence was her sole reason for continuing to live. Part of him longed to join the French Free Forces and avenge his brother. Another part of him felt obligated to stay at home and care for his mother. What, he asked his philosophy professor, should he do? We might be inclined to say, as Sartre does, that there is no clearly right path. Intellectually speaking, the best answer could be that there is no correct answer. But the student is embarked. He can't in good faith say, "This is an impossible choice, so I'm going to be agnostic about it." He must either stay home or go off and fight. He can say, "I don't know," but he can't live "I don't know." He's condemned to freedom, as Sartre likes to say. As long as he prolongs his indecisive meditation, he is choosing to stay home. Likewise, according to Pascal, an agnostic is essentially an atheist without the guts to admit it.

Pascal is right that we're embarked. Not just with God, but with every serious issue in philosophy. We must live like we know what love, beauty, justice, and truth are, even though we're clueless about the true meaning of those words. What is the examined life? Basically, facing up to how much of a gamble being human is. Should you get married? Should you have kids? What work should you do? How should you decorate your home? How should you treat others? How selfish should you be? Should you follow your heart, your head, or your parents? One of the wretched, great achievements of modernity is that you need not be a king or queen to have the power to answer such questions. Another of our great, wretched accomplishments is that the questions themselves have been multiplied—almost endlessly. We're now open to troubling ourselves over every choice we make—for instance: should we bike, ride the bus, buy a hybrid, or continue driving our gas-guzzler to work? Every advance in our power brings us new impossible questions.

For Pascal, all such questions come down to a single question. Should you be religious? In other words, should your life be guided by God, or should you puzzle your own life out? Remember, no direction is inherently more rational or ridiculous than the other. Being an atheist is just as intellectually disrespectable as being a churchgoer. Pascal's *Pensées* is one of the first texts I know of—another mark of its modernity—that takes atheism to be a perfectly valid option. Religion appears, as it did not for most of human history, as one sphere among others of human life; we stand outside of it and can choose to enter or not.

When the mind permits us to go either way on a question, we turn to the heart ("The heart has its reasons of which reason knows nothing").[12] But the heart is vain and greedy; so we begin immediately to think about what we stand to gain or lose from our choice. Imagine I flip a coin and tell you, "If you call heads, and it lands on heads, I'll give you a million dollars; if you call tails, and it lands on tails, I'll give you the quarter." Even though tails is just as likely, wouldn't you be an idiot to call anything but heads? The situation with God, in Pascal's analogy, is essentially the same. If God exists, and we devote our lives to God, then we stand to gain the happiness that nothing else in the world provides. In a word, we stand to gain heaven. Moreover, we lose nothing by devoting our lives to God, even if we're wrong. If, instead, we're atheists, and indeed God doesn't exist, what have we gained? Nothing, according to Pascal. But if wrong, what do we stand to lose?

*

One of the first criticisms of the wager that comes up, usually raised by atheists, is that Pascal has unfairly characterized just what we stand to lose if we bet wrongly on God. By devoting ourselves to the supernatural, we stand to lose the pleasures of nature. Religion calls on us to renounce certain parts of who we are. At least, we must waste the time it takes to practice the religion. At most, we might be giving up the only goods we'll ever have.

Pascal has two responses to this criticism. The first is a mathematical point, which is really just an abstract way of expressing the second point about our psychology. The mathematical point is that even if there are potential gains to being an atheist, they are finite goods, whereas the good of God is infinite. Infinity always wins. An unlimited money supply is more than what even Bill Gates possesses. The second rebuttal is rooted in Pascal's view of the human condition. True enough, religion asks us to renounce aspects of who we are—but so what? What do you fear renouncing: your anxiety, your diversions, your boredom, your inconstancy, or your vanity? As one student put the criticism, "You do lose something if you believe in God and are wrong; you'll have wasted all those Sunday mornings!" To which the Pascalian response is, "What else were you going to do on those Sunday mornings? Play video games? Watch *Grizzly Adams*?" With regards to natural goods like love, religion doesn't ask us to give it up: it promises to perfect it.

Another common criticism of the wager, usually made by those who are religious, is that God will not smile on those who are making a selfish bet on His existence. There's no religious worth in the belief generated by the wager, just like there's no moral worth in a business that makes a charitable donation for no other reason than a tax break. But if Pascal's right about the state of our knowledge, I wonder if it wouldn't be cruel of God to scrutinize the genuineness of our belief. Go back to our coin toss. You call heads. Isn't it a bit much if, before I show you the coin's face, I say, "Are you just saying heads, or do you really believe it"? It would be foolish to expect someone to deny even the possibility of tails, when it is, after all, a coin toss. What possibly could "really believing in heads" mean other than betting on it? What does "really believing in God" mean other than betting your life on God?

Nevertheless, Pascal is sensitive to the criticism. His response is: "Custom is our nature," or, as Alcoholics Anonymous puts the same point, "Fake it until you make it."[13] A lush who successfully fakes sobriety long enough is no longer a lush. Similarly, if you go through the motions of being religious, then you will eventually become really religious, for we become whatever we grow accustomed to. Naturally, you must "fake" religion with an open mind, really believing perfect happiness is potentially on the table. At minimum, I take it, this would mean for Pascal: going to Mass, learning the basics of theology, praying a few times every day, trying to do right by your neighbor, repenting, trying harder, and generally trying to live a holy life. Whatever impediments your soul has set against God will slowly break down, just as not doing such things will quickly put those impediments up. We don't become atheists or believers based on any intellectual point. "Custom is king over all," as the ancient poet says.

Another wonderful criticism of Pascal was put forward by one of my students in a paper called "Pascal's Roulette Wheel." He claimed that the metaphor of a coin flip is a bad one because in fact there are numerous possibilities we're compelled to bet on. As in roulette where gamblers must place a bet on either red or black, we must either believe or disbelieve in God; but also, just as roulette gamblers can place a bet on one of thirty-eight numbers, so too must we place a bet on one of thirty-eight or so religions (in fact, quite a bit more, if we start factoring in denominations). Should we go to mass or mosque? Is God more likely to speak Hindi or Hebrew? Should we be Wahabi or Wiccan? My student did struggle a bit with the idea that it might still make sense, according to Pascal's logic, to bet on one of the God numbers, rather than on a form of atheism. But he concluded, not without reason, that because there are so many possibilities, and our odds of winning the cosmic lottery are depressingly low, no bet is really any better than another.

The roulette wheel of religion is probably a better metaphor than the coin toss in eternity, as Pascal himself understands. (Little did my student know that Pascal introduced a primitive form of the roulette wheel as part of his search for a perpetual motion machine!) The founder of probability theory does analyze what he takes to be the "living options," to use William James's term for religions one can regard as real possibilities. In Pascal's case, there are three big religious squares on the layout: Judaism, Islam, and Christianity.

It's common for people to object to a religion because of how far-fetched its dogma seems. Pascal, in contrast, looks to bet on a religion sufficiently far-fetched. His question is less, "Is a religion credible?" than, "Is a religion incredible enough?" Maybe the most common theory of truth is that an idea counts as true when it conforms to reality. In this case, the idea of religion is to be judged against the reality of human nature—that anxious, changeable, wretched, splendid, brave, incredible thing. "What sort of freak then is man!" exclaims Pascal. "How novel, how monstrous, how chaotic, how paradoxical, how prodigious! Judge of all things, feeble earthworm, repository of truth, sink of doubt and error, glory and refuse of the universe!"[14] A sensible religion is absurd because human nature is anything but sensible. We need a paradoxical religion, one that speaks to our wretchedness and our greatness simultaneously. The only dogma that would fit us would have to recognize us for the glorious pieces of trash we are. In short, Pascal thinks that Christianity, the most scandalous of all religions, is our only hope. Islam and Judaism make too much sense. I can only imagine what he would have made of Unitarianism.

Pascal subscribes to a classic Christian take on Islam and Judaism as religions of the law. They both map our greatness along a sacred path, that of Halakha or Sharia. (The upside of Judaism, according to Pascal, is that it implicitly recognizes how our wretchedness and greatness interact and thus prophesies our salvation; the upside of Islam, for Pascal, is that it's a universal religion, like Christianity.) But given our wretched nature, we're unable to lead spotless lives. In fact, most of what religious legalism does, quite opposite of its intentions, is make hypocrites out of us. As Pascal says, "We have established and developed out of concupiscence admirable rules of polity, ethics and justice, but at root, the evil root of man, this evil stuff of which we are made is only concealed; it is not pulled up."[15] As a kid in church, I used to wonder why we said a prayer of confession every Sunday. If we're really so sorry for sinning, why don't we just stop? Imagine a man who beat his wife Monday through Saturday (in fact, I knew one such parishioner who did just that) and like clockwork said sorry every Sunday for doing so? What kind of atonement is that? Why did we as a congregation never pray, "Having sincerely apologized last week, this week we have nothing to confess"? It's an honest puzzlement, but it takes some dark adult wisdom to understand its naïveté. If a religion of the law proves the right bet, we're in deep trouble, for few to none of us, according to Pascal, could face God and honestly boast, "I've followed your law; now let me into heaven." There's a good book on Pascal's theology, the title of which more or less sums it up: *God Owes Us Nothing*. If obedience to God's law is a necessary requirement of salvation, then heaven would self-destruct by not having enough souls in it to play a game of baseball.

What we need is a religion of law and forgiveness, of greatness and wretchedness, not as separate moments but as one great unity. It is Christianity alone, according to Pascal, that synthesizes the opposites of our nature into a believable salvation. By understanding us, only Christianity makes us lovable. Its paradoxical message is readily apparent in the stories of Jesus. When a well-to-do man approaches him and asks, "What must I do to inherit eternal life?" Jesus answers, "Follow God's commandments." The man replies, "No problem: I've always done that." So Jesus says, "Then give all your money to the poor." At this point, the man does the equivalent of looking at his watch and saying, "I've really got to get going. Chat more later." The fact is, we're rarely looking to inherit eternal life, despite our boastings; what most of us seek in religion is to have our vanity flattered. What the well-to-do man wanted was to be told by Jesus, "You're a real model. If only those Samaritans were as good as you!" It's attitudes like this well-to-do believer in the face of our ignorance and wretchedness that puts so many people off religion, young people especially. When people want to play the game of the law, Jesus doesn't flatter their vanity at all; he makes them play it to the very core of their being. If you boast of following the commandments, Jesus says that you should go all the way and give your wealth to charity. If you boast that you don't cheat on your wife, he tells you, "But I say, anyone who even looks at a woman with lust in his eye has already committed adultery with her in his heart." Gulp. The point seems to be that if you're looking to be the perfect one according to the law, then go ahead and perfect yourself. But until you do, be wary of casting the first stone.

Who does come off well in the Gospels, if not the half-pious religious folk? The people Jesus seems most inclined to bless are tax collectors, thieves, and whores—souls who have confronted their wretchedness and ask tremblingly for forgiveness. "Man's greatness comes from knowing he is wretched," in Pascal's fine phrase.[16] We stand a much better chance of winning the forgiveness game than the law game. Yet forgiveness can take place only within a context of the law. It's not the case, as it might seem at first blush, that Jesus is okaying thievery and prostitution, let alone taxation. We must play the games of law *and* forgiveness. Jesus is more judgmental than his fire-and-brimstone preachers *and* more forgiving than his most progressive do-gooders. Only by believing deeply in the law, according to Pascal, are we able to recognize our meekness and inherit the earth.

Christianity is, as I said, a religion that stretches credulity. To be a Christian is to believe any number of paradoxes: that true morality appears in the context of immorality, that God is human, that power is expressed in suffering, and that this human God, uttering the famous cry of abandonment on the cross, is something of an atheist. When students protest that Islam or Judaism is being maligned by Pascal, that the same weird logic of law and forgiveness is at work in their religion, I concede the point. Maybe Pascal is portraying the other monotheisms unfairly. It's possible that Islam and Judaism are every bit as absurd as Christianity.

*

Though it's hard to imagine someone converting to Christianity after reading Pascal's Wager, any number of my students have found in the *Pensées* a description of their lives and their tense relationship to the possibility we call God. Almost all of them, when they think about it, recognize how appropriate the metaphor of gambling is for leading a human life. Modernity itself vacillates on the question of religion, sometimes betting red, sometimes betting black. Regardless of their religious status, they identify with Pascal's analysis of the need for diversion. How could someone in our culture not? In one paper, an older student wrote:

> I've felt in my life just how much of a gamble things are. And I know first-hand what Pascal means by wretchedness. I don't like to admit it, but I've done some things in my time. Mostly to people I loved, too. I grew up kind of religious, but when I left my parents' house, I left the church with it. I can't say that I ever thought it out like Pascal did, but I can't think of a better way of putting my return to the church in my thirties than as a "wager." I wanted forgiveness. I wanted to be part of something bigger. I didn't necessarily believe it, but I wanted to believe it. And I went through the motions, "fake it until you make it," just like Pascal said.
>
> But there's the problem. I faked it for several years, but I never made it. I don't know why. It just didn't take. I never felt at home.

Not that people weren't nice to me at church. If anything, they were too nice. . . .

I try to live a good life. I'm trying to do better. I guess I'm now gambling that if there's a God, trying will be good enough. It's like what Socrates said, how we should do what's right because it's right, not because religion says it's right. I'm hoping God sees things like that.

Amen.

*

I've suggested that Pascal's analysis of human anxiety and his subsequent relationship to religion are bound up with his status as a modern. Let me dispel a possible confusion. I'm not suggesting, as a Marxist might, that the material conditions of Pascal's time are completely responsible for his uneasy philosophy. What I do think is that the conditions of modernity emphasize and even exaggerate our natural anxiety and need for diversion. When philosophers grasp eternal truths, they're wearing the gloves of time. In a sense, we're lucky to be suffering from the anxiety of Pascal. In more primitive ages, we didn't have any time to suffer: life was much too difficult. Bless you, Modernity, for giving us the freedom to be anxious!

INTERLUDE ON CAMPFIRES AND THE SUN

Not till the fire is dying in the grate,
Look we for any kinship with the stars.
GEORGE MEREDITH

So, what do the philosophers have to say to my student Crystal about God and, in her words, "all those useless rituals and ceremonies"? Al-Ghazali attests to the possibility of experiencing God and investing those rituals and ceremonies with their inner meaning; Descartes explores the possibility of proving (and thereby the possibility of disproving) God and turns to the careful use of human reason to solve our problems; and Pascal thinks that God is the cosmic croupier on whose existence or nonexistence we must stake our lives in the hopes that our bet pays off big. Though mysticism, rationalism, and skepticism will always be with us, history reorchestrates them, assigning at least one a minor part in the chorus of an age. Certainly, for you and me in our wired snowmobile helmets, mysticism isn't as publicly available as it was for al-Ghazali. Even Pascal's mystical fire was sewn into the lining of his coat.

Much like how students pester me about what I believe, I used to force them to evaluate which approach to God is best. I've found that such evaluation doesn't amount to much. The poetic types like the mystical approach, the scientific types prefer the rational method, and most people think it's a big gamble. Our society conditions us to be tolerant of all ways or no way at all. (Tolerance is a blessing, but not if it's an excuse to check out. It's good to tolerate the multiplicity of languages, but you have to speak at least one of them!) A lesson I myself have learned is based on the underlying similarity of the main approaches to God and pertains to the odyssey of philosophy itself.

*

According to a seventeenth-century sermon, in lines that inspired T. S. Eliot's "Journey of the Magi," Lancelot Andrewes says of the so-called wise men's travels, "It was no summer progress. A cold coming they had of it at this time of the year, just the worst time of the year to take a journey, and specially a long journey in. The ways deep, the weather sharp, the days short, the sun farthest off, in *solstitio brumali*, 'the very dead of winter.'"[1] We go on the journey of philosophy, the search for wisdom, despite what is comfortable, despite what is sensible, often into the depths of our loneliness—impelled by the force of a truth we don't even know, but that somehow we know we must know.

I say the word "truth" a little nervously, for what we find is perhaps not the whole story but, rather, an expansion, often painful, of our narrow beliefs into a larger swatch of reality. When children find out that parents are the ones who nibble the carrots left out for Rudolph, they haven't learned the whole story of what the myth of Santa means (I can't say I know yet), but they have enlarged their capacity to understand the world. Exactly how much the magi saw in the manger's mewling baby is impossible to say, but it's a safe bet that the truths still unfolding from his rosy flesh these two millennia later were not completely spanned by their wisdom. The curious children and questing magi gain, certainly, but perhaps lose something important, too. The imaginative sparkle of the restless child on Christmas Eve is to some degree extinguished by the truth; and, if the myth of Santa is worth anything, it's to kindle the glimmer of magic that the wise men found in the manger. Perhaps someday, after an adult's quest, that imaginative fire can be rekindled and fanned into something more useful than naïveté or skepticism. To discover the truth is to have our souls disoriented and then reoriented into a higher way of being. In Eliot's poem, the wise man asks in desperation, "were we led all that way for / Birth or Death?" It is a birth and a death. Truth is a birth and a death, if I may put it in such terms.

*

In book 7 of the *Republic*, Socrates asks us to imagine a large underground dwelling, in which people have been imprisoned for their whole lives. Though no sunlight reaches the prisoners, a fire from behind them illuminates the wall they face. Another group of people walk in front of the fire with shadow puppets. Essentially, the scene is like a twisted movie theater. The prisoners constantly watch images cast by a primitive projection unit. Since they've never known anything else, the prisoners' concepts of reality and value are completely based on the pale light and flickering shadows—though they don't think of the appearances as shadows, being oblivious to how they're generated. Big business in the cave would likely involve guessing which image came next. If you had the money, you'd pay $50,000 a year to send your kid to college to major in guessing shadows. (One more far-fetched tale from Plato! Like people would ever stand for doing nothing more than staring at images on a screen all day, or send their children to school for something so silly as the manipulation of information!)

Socrates then invites us to imagine what it would mean to escape the cave. You'd have to have some strange mixture of bravery, curiosity, and lunacy, for you wouldn't even know that you were imprisoned. And if you were to crawl arduously out of the cave and poke your head into the sunlight, you'd be painfully blinded and thus inclined to believe that whatever world lies outside the cave is unfit for human eyes. But let's say that somehow you liberated yourself, wiggled out, and had the chutzpah to stick around. Eventually your eyes would adjust to the illumined world, and the first thing you'd see—your eyes turned as far as possible from the painful sun—would be the shadow of a tree. You'd think to yourself, "Ah, here too they have trees." But as your vision adjusted further, you'd look up and notice that attached to the "tree" was a tree-shaped object much more vivid than your familiar shadow-tree: a three-dimensional, barky, leafy, swaying giant of untold reality. After a long, bizarre, confusing transitional period, you'd finally realize that you'd been seeing shadows all along.

Though you'd be tempted to dwell permanently in the sunlit world, I think you'd eventually feel an obligation to return to the cave and free the inmates you grew up among. Doing so would be no easy feat. You'd proclaim, "What you see in front of you isn't real at all! Your beloved images are just—how can I say this?—shadows, projections, lesser versions of a much more vivid reality. In fact, they're just shadows based on shadow puppets based on real things!" To which your interlocutor would be apt to respond, "That's crazy. Of course they're real. You've got such—*interesting* ideas. Now back to business, what's going to appear next?" You'd say, "You don't get it. You're a prisoner. It doesn't matter what appears next!" Your interlocutor would then snap back: "Doesn't matter? I'm paying $50,000 a year so my kid can figure out what appears next. Better damn well matter. Seriously, what's next? Or has your 'upward journey' spoiled your eyesight, O wise one?" According to Socrates, if you persisted in trying to liberate prisoners oblivious to their imprisonment, the cave dwellers, if they could, would kill you.

It's hard not to think that one meaning of this allegory pertains to the life and death of Socrates himself, who is executed for "corrupting" Athenians by making them confront the fact that their foundational concepts are at best partial truths, flickering images of a more complex reality. What is Socratic method if not the attempt to lead people through the darkness in order to see the truth for themselves? Socrates can almost always get his interlocutors to the point of being blinded by the sunlight of knowledge; this moment in the dialogues is referred to as aporia, where they feel totally confused. But very few ever want to go further. Most of them, like Euthyphro, suddenly remember some pressing engagement elsewhere and burrow back to their spot in the cave.

But the allegory is about more than just the story of Socrates. It maps the philosophical quest itself, corresponding point by point to the journeys of al-Ghazali, Descartes, and Pascal. In each case, the philosopher begins by recognizing that the truths around him are projections of a particular culture. The children of Christians grow up embracing Christianity; the children of Jews grow up adhering to Judaism; and the children of Muslims end up following the religion of Islam. And if images of democracy and consumption are projected on every screen and t-shirt in front of us, we end up being acquisitive and believing in religious freedom. Each philosopher then insists on pressing on to find the original models for the shadow puppets of culture and religion. Each climbs arduously out of the cave and, at the very moment of being freed from tradition, is blinded: al-Ghazali undergoes his crisis of skepticism; Descartes feels that he's drowning in a whirlpool of doubt, certain only that nothing is certain; and Pascal confronts our complete ignorance about the possibility of God. (At the end of a semester of philosophy, most students feel befuddled rather than enlightened. If Socrates is right, that's all to the good. It's a phony education that doesn't completely confuse you at some point, though at this point many students suddenly remember a pressing engagement elsewhere, usually at a business school.) Our philosophers heroically press on and eventually come to adjust to the sunlight in their own way. Al-Ghazali sees God, who is symbolized in the allegory by the sun itself. Descartes recognizes with overwhelming certainty the truth of clear and distinct ideas. Pascal is a more curious case, for he doesn't claim in the *Pensées* to have exited the cave and its diversions. His philosophy bets on the possibility that there is a sunlit world, even if we never see it in this lifetime.

We relate to the truth on different levels: the level of the "servile conformists" in the cave (you and me); the level of the shadow puppeteers who perpetuate and adjust a culture's foundational ideas (artists, politicians, religious authorities, parents, sometimes you and me); and finally the level of freed prisoners, who see by the light of the sun and try to negotiate between their higher vision and life in the cave (revolutionary scientists, philosophers, prophets, occasionally you and me). On first encountering Plato's story, we look down on the prisoners for their misplaced confidence in the shadows. Likewise, many of my cleverest students disdain the meager religion and superficial culture they were brought up in. But the story should elicit our sympathy for them. They're us. Yes, people worship their little campfire when they ought to go looking for kinship with the sun. But that's understandable. It's night out. Moreover, as al-Ghazali realizes, we can't live, at least in our present condition, full time in the sunlit world; we need our little fires in order to remember the great fire.

PART 4 ∗ *What Is the Nature of Good and Evil?*

In sorrow shalt thou eat of it all the days of thy life.   GENESIS 3:17

Because the railroad goes through Ainsworth, Iowa, it was a boom-town at the beginning of the twentieth century, replete with restaurants, taverns, dry-goods store, and opera house. By the last quarter of the twentieth century, when I was growing up there, it had dwindled to about five hundred people. Main Street looked like a ghost town from a spaghetti western, retaining only the taverns. Two of the churches it had once easily supported, one Methodist and one Presbyterian, had had to consolidate into the hybrid I went to every Sunday as a child. For a few years we'd have a Methodist minister, then we'd switch for the next few to a Presbyterian pastor. In the cold months, we'd worship at the church down the block which was better heated; in the hot months, at the church up the block where the air flow was better. The bottom of every folding chair was marked with either a *P* or an *M*, depending on its original home, and several of the older parishioners demonstrated their particular convictions by planting themselves only atop their denomination's letter. In confirmation class, the teacher would often get mixed up about which tradition was which. We got to select, more or less randomly, which denomination we were going to be confirmed into. Like everybody else so educated, I forget which one I chose.

That odd little church's seventy members furnished me with the entire spectrum of human nature, every rainbow gradation from grandeur to depravity. I'm especially glad I was exposed to the Bible, though the church itself did little beyond exposing me to it. In fact, the biblical passages I read in church and Sunday school seemed downright out of place in their setting. I'd read, "I form the light, and create darkness; I make peace, and create evil: I the Lord do all these things," and then hear a sermon, bookended by two jokes, on how we should be nice to each other.[1] I'd sit through a lesson on family values after reading that Jesus said, "If any man come to me, and hate not his father, and mother, and wife, and children, and brethren, and sisters, yea, and his own life also, he cannot be my disciple."[2] The Bible, which seemed full of danger and ancient horrible power, was either overlooked, like a copy of *King Lear* in a kindergarten classroom, or treated with odd calm, as when fools keep a pet tiger.

But when I think of religious institutions and all their foolishness, or of philosophy classes, for that matter, and all theirs, I have nothing but gratitude. They keep us in contact with the tigers of the spirit. The church had enough wisdom to give me a Bible and compel me to read its mysterious, spooky, encompassing passages. And when I did, the stiff pews and laid-back rituals receded, and I entered into communion with the Holy Spirit, though almost always more baffled than illumined. My mind was furnished with stories and injunctions I'm still puzzling out. What kind of God is this, I wondered and wonder still, who boasts of his gargantuan creation, "Canst thou fill his skin with barbed irons? or his head with fish spears?"[3] How can anyone reconcile our images of heaven and hell with: "All go unto one place; all are of the dust, and all turn to dust again"?[4] One of my favorite passages goes, "But Mary kept all these things and pondered them in her heart."[5] As a kid, I too kept all these things and pondered them in my heart. I folded the yellowed obituary of my grandfather, whose final words asked if I had yet been born (I hadn't quite), and placed it in my copy of the Bible. It seemed appropriate.

I didn't have to read long to find one of the most bewildering passages, the famous tale of the apple from "the tree of the knowledge of good and evil." God instructs Adam and Eve not to eat the fruit of this tree, "for in the day that thou eatest thereof thou shalt surely die." The serpent, in contrast, says to Eve, "Ye shall not surely die: For God doth know that in the day ye eat thereof, then your eyes shall be opened, and ye shall be as gods, knowing good and evil."[6] Of course, they do eat of it, and their eyes are opened. God says, "Behold, the man is become as one of us, to know good and evil."[7] After heaping on the couple all the familiar misery of being alive, God drives them from Eden so they don't eat of the tree of life next and become immortal. The "us" that God addresses mystified me: is he talking to the serpent or to other gods? But the real problem was the disconcerting fact, which the Bible goes out of its way to make plain, that God lies (they don't surely die on the day they eat of the tree), the devil tells the truth (they do become "as gods, knowing good and evil"), and we suffer from having violated the powerful half-lie and believed the powerful half-truth.

Sometimes students ask me (they ask me just about everything) if I think the events narrated in the Bible really happened. I think they happen all the time. Every hour Cain slays Abel, Moses stumblingly leads his people out of slavery, Job and God debate, Ruth gleans in the garbage, and four horseman of some kind or another are on our trail. We certainly ate of the tree of the knowledge of good and evil, and in sorrow we keep eating of it all the days of our life. That we missed our opportunity to eat of immortality, the apple from the tree of life, seems true also.

In college I acted in a production of the medieval mystery plays, the dramatic cycle that was once used to instruct illiterate peasants in Christian mythology. I was cast as Cain. Once during practice, right after the expulsion from Eden, as Eve was conversing with the director, Adam finished eating the prop of the apple and then cast it aside as if he really was at liberty in the Garden. It rolled right next to me, as I was trying to memorize my petulant address to God, the one that begins, "Am I my brother's keeper?" My Cain self looked at that gnawed apple with just a bite or two remaining. A fine image of our predicament.

8 The Moral Worth of a Teardrop

These weeping eyes, those seeing tears.   ANDREW MARVELL

On the PBS series *Antiques Roadshow*, collectors bring in odds and ends, which antique dealers scrutinize and spin a history around. The high drama of every encounter is what the junk is really worth. Occasionally, the Japanese bowl a GI got for a pack of cigarettes turns out to be a priceless imperial vase. Other times, the imperial vase that a collector paid through the nose for proves to be a fake worth a pack of cigarettes.

Let's imagine a spinoff called *Antiques Roadshow of the Soul.* Curious people bring in various choices, which you and I, the ethical appraisers, study and evaluate, assigning this one a day in heaven, that one a week in hell, or whatever else our imaginations come up with. On today's episode our task is to pronounce on the word "no." While rummaging in the attic of her psyche, an Austrian lady came across this old refusal, spoken by her grandfather, a man by the name of Franz Jägerstätter, toward the end of World War II. She explains to us that her great-grandfather was born out of wedlock in 1907 in Sankt Radegund, not far from Salzburg. Though raised a Catholic, Franz Jägerstätter was no model Christian; like his biological father, he begat an illegitimate child. But he eventually married, had three daughters with his wife, and grew serious about Catholicism. When the Germans overtook his village, he was the only citizen brave enough to vote against its annexation. He openly criticized Nazism over the following tumultuous years. In February of 1943, he was finally drafted into Hitler's army. Aware that refusal almost certainly meant death, he refused to fight. His relatives, his friends, even his bishop pleaded with him to change his mind. "Do it for your family," they urged. "It's not like you alone are going to change anything." But he stood by his no to Nazism; and on August 9, at the age of thirty-six, he was executed by guillotine.

Now the granddaughter of Franz Jägerstätter places this old, dusty "nein" in our hands and asks us what, if anything, it's worth. What do we have to say to her? Does her grandfather's refusal make him a fool or a hero, a dutiful soul or a negligent father? What is the value of Franz Jägerstätter's "no"?

*

As a matter of fact, *Antiques Road Show of the Soul* has been around as long as we have. One of our earliest appraisers, by the name of Hammurabi (born around 1792 BC), left behind such principles of evaluation as: "If a man puts out the eye of an equal, his own eye shall be put out," and, "If during an unsuccessful operation a patient dies, the arm of the surgeon must be cut off." Another of our more influential experts was known for the wildness of his evaluations, claiming that a poor lady's gift of a few pennies far exceeds the largesse of a Bill Gates and that the crazy son who squanders all of his father's money and then begs for forgiveness is far more deserving of reward than his dutiful brother.

In the tradition of Western philosophy, no appraiser has been more incisive than Immanuel Kant, who was born in 1724 to a saddle maker in Könisberg, a provincial Prussian town that he never left and that furnished him with enough experience to construct one of the deathless philosophical systems. Kant made steady, if unspectacular, progress in school and eventually became a lecturer at his alma mater, the University of Könisberg. Paid by the number of students he attracted, Kant lectured on almost everything, particularly scientific matters. His talents slowly blossomed. He speculated about the origin of the universe from a cloud of gas and correctly deduced that the Milky Way is a spiral galaxy of stars. He never married, taking too long to consider the opportunities he had. Though Kant published a few interesting treatises along the way, it wasn't until he was in his late fifties that his great philosophical work began to appear, particularly the three critiques: *The Critique of Pure Reason*, *The Critique of Practical Reason*, and *The Critique of Judgment*. These works led Heinrich Heine, the wisest of German poets, to conclude that Kant in the quiet of his provincial study was more dangerous to the established order of Europe than Robespierre and all his guillotines, claiming that the philosopher had "stormed the heavens, put the whole garrison to the sword, and left the Sovereign of the world swimming unproven in His own blood."[1]

The story goes that the housewives of Könisberg set their clocks by the professor's unfailingly regular afternoon walk. This myth, which professors of philosophy perpetuate, speaks to the clockwork-like intricacy and precision of the three *Critiques*. Though Kant devastatingly criticized his work, Johann Gottfried Herder wrote, "I have had the good fortune to know a philosopher. He was my teacher. . . . The history of men and peoples, natural history and science, mathematics and observation, were sources from which he enlivened his lectures and conversation. He was indifferent to nothing worth knowing. He incited and gently forced others to think for themselves; despotism was foreign to his mind. This man, whom I name with the greatest gratitude and respect, was Immanuel Kant."[2]

*

Several years ago, I was asked to teach an introduction to ethics over the Iowa Communications Network, where a professor must fiddle with endless buttons in an effort to simulcast a course to a variety of remote sites, where students generally chat, doze, and leave early, since they can't hardly be seen on the professor's little screen and can't be heard at all unless they press a microphone's button. Like an idiot, trying to please a new dean, I agreed. For a few-hundred-dollar bump in my salary, I gave up every waking moment to grading my heavily increased load of student work and to juggling ineptly the roles of director, writer, cameraman, and star of a televised class. Because of a few moments with one student, it was worth it.

Julia never said a word and usually sat out of camera shot in one of the remote locations. The work she handed in was fine but not particularly memorable. One day she came to Iowa City to attend class in my originating classroom. That day we were discussing Kant's moral philosophy, particularly his idea that the consequences of an action play no role in evaluating it, that an action has moral worth based solely on its motive. The spirit of Kant's idea can be found in our "good Samaritan laws," which hold that you shouldn't be held culpable for trying to help the sick if your assistance proves injurious or even fatal. After class, she came up and introduced herself to me. As she began to open up, a technician kicked us out of the classroom: another TV class had to begin on schedule.

Out in the hallway, Julia looked me in the eye and asked with startling passion, "Is it true what Kant says? Is it true"—she glanced at some notes in her notebook—"that the consequences of an action are irrelevant to its moral worth?" I parried with the teacher's ancient irritating dodge, "Well, what do you think?" In response, she told me the story of her son.

A few years back, she'd come home to find that her son had tripped and fallen down a flight of stairs, at least so her husband claimed. Her husband—her ex by the time she was telling me the story—was abusive, and she wondered if in a fit of rage he hadn't pushed their son down the stairs. The injury was severe. When her son finally got out of the hospital, he was in a wheelchair and found it painful to move. Julia did all she could for him. One day a doctor told her of an operation, albeit a risky one, that might improve his condition. She agonized over what to do. Unable to stand seeing him in pain anymore, she finally agreed to it. The operation went surprisingly well. But due to unforeseen complications from the operation, her son died.

Her husband blamed her for their son's death. In part, she blamed herself, too. More than anything she'd wanted to help her suffering boy, and yet it was her decision that led to his death. As the indifferent parade of students and teachers plowed past in the hall, she looked at me, tears rolling down her cheeks, and asked once more, "Is it true what Kant says, that it's the motive and not the consequences that matters?"

Part of what motivated Julia's decision was surely her own suffering at having to see her son broken. Mother love is a knotty thing; its strong, warm affection is complicated with all manner of selfishness. But she wasn't looking for an excuse. We were seriously appraising her soul, human to human. Her tears reminded me of the dewdrop-like tears in one of my favorite paintings, Dieric Bouts's *Sorrowing Madonna*, which portrays Mary as a plain mother, a mom, with eyes bloodshot from having wept for a long time at the hard death of her boy. All I could think to say was, "I never knew if Kant's moral philosophy was right—until now. The consequences of an action, however horrible, play no role in its moral worth. After hearing your story, I believe that's true."

*

On the afternoon of September 11, 2001, officials ordered all commercial planes in U.S. airspace to land. If any plane did not land, it would be shot down. The reasoning behind this decision seems sensible enough. If a plane doesn't land, it has probably been hijacked. If it's not shot down, then it will likely crash into some other important building, killing the innocent people inside. Granted, shooting down a commercial airline would be a horrible thing, involving the deaths of many innocent people; but those people would likely die anyway in the crash. The grim calculus holds that between the two rotten choices, shooting down the plane would cause less overall misery. Our government examined each possible set of consequences and chose the better—or, at least, less bad—one, so the argument goes.

The idea that the worth of an action lies in the consequences it brings about—in short, that the ends justify the means—is called consequentialism. According to most forms of consequentialist moral theory, an action is good when it promotes good consequences, bad when it promotes bad consequences. The president, or whoever was the ultimate source of the command, was almost surely using this common moral logic on the afternoon of September 11 , weighing the deaths of one decision against the deaths of another.

Kant vehemently rejects the logic of consequentialism. One of his main arguments is that it's absurd to locate our worth in something we have basically no control over. Not being gods, we can't control or predict what the consequences of our actions are going to be. If the president really could choose to save a thousand people, he should. But, in point of fact, he can't. All he can choose to do is to kill a hundred people with the hopes of saving a thousand. The consequences of the choice are anybody's guess. Yes, it's possible it would end up reducing the death toll. It's also possible—even perhaps likely, given what happened on Flight 93—that the passengers of our hypothetical plane would have been on the verge of overtaking the terrorists and landing safely.

In Kant's view, all we ought to consider is the action, independent of the consequences. If killing innocent civilians is wrong, according to the firm logic of Kant, then we should not choose to do it—ever. Evil is impermissible, regardless of what good we think will come of it. (Max Weber, the foremost social theorist of the twentieth century, makes a distinction—perhaps relevant here—between what he calls the ethics of intention, which is basically Kantian ethics, and the ethics of responsibility, which involves those in power taking the risky responsibility for how things come out. Is "the ethics of responsibility" more pertinent to our evaluation of political decisions?)

At the beginning of the *Groundwork for the Metaphysics of Morals*, Kant says in a great sweeping sentence, "There is no possibility of thinking of anything at all in the world, or even out of it, which can be regarded as good without qualification, except, a *good will*."[3] By a "good will" Kant means doing the right thing for the right reason. Other good things—like good looks, wealth, courage, even happiness—are good only if the inner content of the person is good. You can have good-looking Nazis, wealthy shysters, "courageous" terrorists, and reasonably happy rapists. All that matters in an absolute sense—whether here, in the afterlife, or on a distant swirling planet in the Milky Way—is the inner quality of the agent, the good will.

After explaining Kant's concept of moral worth to one of my first classes of students, a suave student named Ricky furnished me with a nice example of a good action lacking in moral worth. He explained how a few days earlier he'd been running a little late and was driving hurriedly to get to class. On the roadside he noticed a woman waving for help beside a flat tire. (This was in the not-so-distant days before cell phones colonized every inch of private space.) As he got closer, seeing that the damsel in distress was a fellow student whose beauty he'd been admiring all semester, he proceeded to slam on the brakes and help with her car. "I guess you could say," Ricky said with a devilish twinkle, "that even though I did the right thing, my action had no moral worth."

One interesting upshot of Kant's doctrine of moral worth is that a common religious conception of ethics—using heaven and hell as motivators—actually destroys our moral worth. If what inspires you to do good is the prospect of heaven, then your action is really no different from Ricky's. If the prospect of hellfire is all that stands between you and petty theft or worse, even if the fiery prospect is so powerful in your imagination that you never sin once, then your character is morally worthless, as immature as the child who refrains from bullying only when a parent is around. Kant regards Abraham's decision to sacrifice his son to please God as the essence of immorality.

At the same time, if you're willing to do right even under the threat of divine retribution, then your action clearly does have moral worth. One example from literature is Huck Finn, who has to decide whether to turn in his friend Jim as an escaped slave. Huck's sense of morality—what there is of it—was shaped by religious white folks telling him that slaves are property, and it's against the will of God for them to be free. Though he loves Jim, he writes a letter to Miss Watson, Jim's proper owner, telling her the whereabouts of his friend. At first he feels "light as a feather" about being right with the world. But he eventually tears his letter up. Turning in his friend would violate the deep convictions of his conscience. With his wonderful way with words, Huck declares, "All right, then, I'll go to hell."[4] Precisely then he is worthy of heaven.

Just how often we do the right thing for the right reason is hard to determine. Kant gives the example of a shopkeeper who charges all his customers the same prices. Why does he treat everyone fairly? As the Better Business Bureau once said in a big ad in the *New York Times*, "Honesty is the best policy. It's also the most profitable." If our shopkeeper is being fair because it's right, his action has moral worth; if he's being fair because it's good business, his action is without moral worth. Which is it? Hard to say, even for the shopkeeper himself. Most of the good we do raises this very dilemma. We give to charity because we genuinely want to help out—and get a tax break. We don't steal, because stealing is wrong—and we don't want to go to jail. We're good, because it's right—and we wouldn't mind a spot in heaven. There's nothing intrinsically damning about having these dual motivations. It's fine to fear jail and hope for heaven. But having these dual motivations leaves the true value of our character largely in the dark. The only hints we get are those moments when we're truly tested, when we're wearing Gyges's ring of invisibility, when we think we could get away with it, when our act of charity would remain anonymous and unrewarded, when our opposition to Nazism means our death: then we see what we're really made of.

*

Kant doesn't intend to tell us anything we don't already know about morality. What is right is basically what we've always known and told each other. Do unto others as you would have them do unto you. Or, as Confucius more reticently puts it, "Don't do unto others what you wouldn't want done unto you." Kant tries to give a theoretically clean version of the spirit of these injunctions in what he calls the categorical imperative. When rational beings like ourselves have to decide how the world ought to be, we have nothing to do except apply the bare notion of law, rationality pure and simple. Act on a principle that you could, without contradicting yourself, will everyone to act on. Do unto others as you would have them do unto you, your mom, your best friend, your neighbor, and your enemy. Kant gives several formulations of the categorical imperative, all of which are intended to carry the same weight. "Act only according to that maxim whereby you can at the same time will that it should become a universal law without contradiction."[5] "Act in such a way that you treat humanity, whether in your own person or in the person of any other, always at the same time as an end and never merely as a means to an end."[6] "Every rational being must so act as if he were through his maxim always a legislating member in the universal kingdom of ends."[7] The force of these imperatives, however expressed, is getting at the same elementary principle that your mom was getting at when she asked, "How would you like it if someone did that to you?" Though Kant might find it a bit conceptually messy, my own favorite formulation of the categorical imperative comes from William James: "There is but one unconditional commandment, which is that we should seek incessantly, with fear and trembling, so to vote and to act as to bring about the very largest total universe of good which we can see."[8]

Our formulations of the principle of morality are simply attempts to direct ourselves toward the inner experience of ethics, the magic of an action's being not simply helpful or unhelpful, useful or useless, but right or wrong. Insofar as Kant does have a problem with how the Golden Rule is usually stated, it's that we shouldn't think of morality as being about what we happen to prefer. Morality isn't simply about liking certain things and applying that preference to others; it's about respecting a common dignity. The formulations of the categorical imperative are poems of morality, haikus of decency. They are not computer programs meant to pump out right answers. If anything, they're as difficult to apply to our lives as the Constitution is to the cases before the Supreme Court. The ultimate force of the moral law tells us to err on the side of the good. One bit of sage Kantian advice is that if you worry about your virtue and others' happiness, you improve both; whereas if you worry about others' virtue and your own happiness, you decrease both.

Why should we be good? According to a lovely line by the German mystic Angelus Silesius, "Die Rose ist ohne warum; sie blühet weil sie blühet"—"the rose is without why; it blooms because it blooms." What blossoming is to the rose, doing right is to humans: we do it because we should. If there is an ulterior motive for doing good, as Kant points out, the action's moral character is blemished. We are good when we do good out of pure respect for goodness. The Stoics talk about our duty flowing from our acceptance of nature. Similarly, for Kant there's a common human duty to treat each other fairly and with dignity, a duty that flows right from our rational nature. Marvelous paradoxes follow. Only when we treat each other morally does our existence become necessary. Only when we're doing something for no particular reason at all does our life make sense. Only when we're following the moral law are we truly free.

Like Pascal, when Kant looks up at the night sky, he's overwhelmed by the sheer magnitude of all the galaxies layered on galaxies. When he looks inward, like Pascal, he's filled with equal awe. Our moral nature is, in his words, a "true infinity." We're microscopic specks—not even that—in the vast interstellar spaces. But our moral imagination reverses the telescope, and suddenly the stars appear as tiny motes in relation to the grandeur of our shimmering morality:

Two things fill the mind with ever new and increasing wonder and awe, the oftener and the more steadily I reflect upon them: the starry heavens above me and the moral law within me. I do not merely conjecture them and seek them as if they were obscured in darkness or in the transcendent region beyond my horizon: I see them before me, and I connect them directly with the consciousness of my own existence . . . [The moral law within me] begins at my invisible self, my personality, and exhibits me in a world which has true infinity but which only the understanding can trace—a world in which I recognize myself as existing in a universal and necessary (and not, as in [the case of the stars], only contingent) connection, and thereby also in connection with all those visible worlds.[9]

*

Kant is the philosopher of limits. In most of his philosophical work, he labors to circumscribe just what we can and cannot know and do. It turns out that we can't know or do very much. We can't control the outcomes of our actions. We can't know if God does or does not exist. We can't know if our souls are immortal. We can't know what the world is really like. We can't even be sure that we're really free. Since freedom is necessary for morality to be meaningful, we're compelled in practice to believe that we're free, though needing something to be true isn't much of a reason that it is. When it comes to knowledge and power, Kant's bottom line is that we're not gods.

But with the categorical imperative, Kant comes very close to telling us that we are gods: act as if the rule you were living by could become a law of nature. Who has the power to legislate laws of nature except a god? In essence, morality is about playing God, playing a good rational God. The freedom on which morality is founded is a divine power, albeit a pretty weak one next to the might of nature. But it does have some efficacy in what we now call culture; to some degree, we do shape ourselves as humans. We live in a house made of ideas about who we are, a house that we inherit from our ancestors, a house that we must constantly keep up. Insofar as we want humans to act and live in a certain way, we have the miraculous power to bring that about.

One of the most inspiring aspects of Kant's moral vision is his commitment to the idea of moral progress. He argues that it's possible for humankind to become better, for our house to be upgraded. The moral law is never the blueprint for all human affairs, but we can structure more or less of our lives by it. Since Kant's time, humanity has borne out his commitment to moral progress in a few cases. Consider race relations in America. From September 21, 1862, the day before the signing of the Emancipation Proclamation, to January 20, 2009, the space of 147 years, approximately seven generations, our country has gone from enslavement to liberation, from Jim Crow to civil rights, from glass ceilings to a president with black skin. If there are still a million evils with us, including some horrible racism, we nonetheless have made some significant moral progress in those 147 years. Progress in morality is always fragile, can be undone, and

sometimes involves accompanying sins, but we shouldn't be so cyni-
cal as to believe that our country hasn't done a significant good in
illegalizing slavery and lynching.

So we do have some godlike power. True, we can't change the
course of nature. True, we can't individually command culture to be
as we'd like. True, we are beings beset by powerful inclinations toward sex, power, and pleasure. True, we are enmeshed in social roles
that make profound demands on us. Perhaps we even ought to bow
before divine power. And yet we have this miraculous ability to say
yes or no to God, to nature, to our inclinations, to our social roles,
to the Nazis. Our saying yes or no is expressed at the social level in
our culture, the sum of what humans have made and hence could
unmake or remake. Every time you act selfishly, according to Kant,
you're perpetuating a selfish civilization. Every time you act according to the moral law, you're unleashing our native nobility. When you
tell a lie to extricate yourself from difficulty, you've taken the side of
those who tell lies to extricate themselves from difficulty. When you
tell the truth regardless of the personal consequences of doing so,
you've put on the uniform of those who fight for morality. Kant has
the marvelous notion of "the kingdom of ends," the world where everybody treats everybody with full moral dignity, where the Golden
Rule is the only rule followed. I sometimes imagine the whole earth
with little lights lighting up wherever the moral rule is being carried
out. The darkness certainly exceeds those little lamps of goodness,
but it heartens me that there are those sparkles, probably more of
them than we pessimistically believe. The kingdom of ends is flickering here and there into existence all around us.

*

Sometimes Kant is criticized for being too optimistic, for believing
in a pure morality when humankind is just not constructed for such
a demanding law. As one contemporary of Kant puts it, "Out of the
crooked timber of humanity nothing straight can be made."[10] The
only problem with this line of criticism is that Kant's contemporary is Kant himself: the quotation is straight from him! Kant understands perfectly well the impediments to our morality. In fact,
his view of human nature is so dark that he even wonders if there
has *ever* been a pure moral action in human history: "Reason unre-

lentingly commands actions of which the world has perhaps hitherto never provided an example."[11] But he says that it doesn't matter. What's right is right. Even if our actions are never quite pure, a moral light illuminates what we do. It's no great feat to recognize moral action. Children understand full well when a character in a fairy tale vitiates or upholds our moral nature. We often try to rationalize morality away. We frequently fall into bad habits. We're all too prone to selfishness. But somehow that little moral light manages to keep on flaring up and flickering inside us.

Another—stronger—criticism of Kant is that we aren't moral gods, that we don't create a moral universe, that the lion's share of morality requires an established tradition and place of mores and virtues; thus, Kant's moral philosophy, relying so heavily on human freedom, has to fail. There's some truth in this. In premodern societies there's quite a lot of truth in it. When Aristotle reflects on ethics, he thinks largely about the virtues required to be a good citizen of a Greek city-state. In modern societies, there are still such traditions that bind us, but they are much less substantive and every day a little more diffuse. As our traditions have receded, our individual power has increased. Here we have to invoke a principle I first learned reading Spider-Man comics: with great power comes great responsibility. This applies even in the case of tradition. If our traditions are necessary to upholding our morality, then the moral law indirectly demands that we must work to bring about a world of stronger traditions.

Consider just one feature of our modern world: the news media. One of the perennial complaints of our age is how our media outlets are a bunch of biased, distorting, greedy scandalmongers; how the Internet has wrecked impartiality; how the decline of newspapers has destroyed real reportage; and so on. All these complaints are largely true. But here's a clear case where Kant's moral philosophy is useful. We create the demand that the media fulfills. As one commentator recently declared, "We get the media we deserve." Apply the categorical imperative to the situation. What kind of world would you like to create with regard to the news? What kind of world could you will not just for yourself but for those ideologically opposed to you? What kind of world could you will for your children, your great aunt, your neighbor, your favorite teacher, and your enemy? What kind of world could you will that doesn't contradict the very purpose of the news, that respects the dignity of all parties? How about a world where reporters strive to report the facts, and commentators don't consciously distort those facts to their own ends? How about a world where citizens read multiple viewpoints on the issues? How about a world that errs on the side of respecting privacy rather than reporting scandal? We have two choices before us. We can make a fuss about how the media falls short of our demands, worrying about others' virtue and our own happiness. Or we can change ourselves. When we dislike an outlet's coverage of the news, we turn it off. We start paying for newspapers that strive for accurate reporting. We read multiple opinions on controversial subjects. Maybe we even read more literature and philosophy, what Ezra Pound in *The ABC of Reading* calls "news that stays news," for, as his classmate William Carlos Williams says, "men die miserably every day / for lack of what is found there."[12]

"But I can do all that, and still things won't really change." It's in this complaint that our desire to be gods in the bad sense reveals itself. How things ultimately go, as the Stoics are so good at reminding us, isn't up to us. Consequences don't matter, from the perspective of our character as humans. If it's right to do something, we should do it for that reason alone. And if you need a little hope, remember that "things won't really change" is a motto humankind constantly defeats, even if not always for the good. The question we must answer is which side we're fighting on.

*

We often wince at the prospect of leading a constantly upstanding life. "It's too hard," we're apt to whine. It's true. We can't lead a perfect life. But here, too, Kant's philosophy is helpful. A poet once said that the Buddha's message could be summed up in two words: wake up. In essence, Kant's whole difficult oeuvre can be summed up in two words: grow up. Take a couple of personal issues and a couple of public issues, and resolve to put the categorical imperative into practice. Where you fail, use your imagination to conceive a life where failure is less likely. It's the false dilemma of adolescence to say, "Either it's perfection, or it's nothing doing." Adulthood involves understanding our limits but not being oppressed by them. By the way, changing your life isn't usually that hard; it's deciding to change your life that causes most of the problems.

Just as the Buddha calls waking up enlightenment, Kant calls growing up enlightenment. We as rational beings have a childhood, adolescence, and—let's hope—adulthood. We begin in childhood by accepting everything on authority. In unleashing our freedom, adolescence leads us to a crossroads, where we can either cling to or reject authority. Neither choice is adequate in the end. Clinging to authority is refusing to grow up. Rejecting authority often simply replaces an external tyranny with an internal tyranny, one where our wishes and desires are newly robed as kings and queens. But if we follow through on our rational nature, we come to see the limits of our powers, both our own and that of the authorities, and sometimes even glimpse the basis of a humane existence, such that we're able to make reasoned judgments about where authority accords with or departs from its foundational principles. As adults, we must work to be moral not selfish, rational not clingingly dogmatic, probing but not destructively skeptical, concerned with our virtue and others' happiness not with our happiness and others' virtue, wise rather than foolish in our judgments, self-aware, self-correcting, conscious of our limits, and worthy of our freedom. If it's human nature that we can never be perfectly good, it's also human nature that the very nobility we strive for lies in the striving. As Marguerite Yourcenar's Hadrian says,

> Life is atrocious, we know. But precisely because I expect little of the human condition, man's periods of felicity, his partial progress, his efforts to begin over again and to continue, all seem to me like so many prodigies which nearly compensate for the monstrous mass of ills and defeats, of indifference and error. Catastrophe and ruin will come; disorder will triumph, but order will too, from time to time.... The words *humanity*, *liberty*, and *justice* will here and there regain the meaning which we have tried to give them.[13]

*

Back to the granddaughter of Franz Jägerstätter: What are we to tell her about his refusal to take up arms with the Nazis?

If we judge the act in terms of its consequences, we must say that his "no" was vicious. He left his children fatherless and his wife husbandless and did nothing that slowed Nazism down. He is deserving of whatever ring of hell is devoted to foolish idealists.

If we judge his act in terms of his action's coherence with its culture, we must also fry him in the inferno. His fellow community members all voted for their annexation by Germany. Even the immediate authority of his religion, the bishop, was happy to bend pragmatically to Nazism. Herr Jägerstätter is worthy of whatever circle of hell is devoted to rebellious individualists.

But don't those evaluations seem to miss something essential? Doesn't his refusal of Nazism, even to the point of death, register positively on your internal moral seismograph? If his story were framed as a fairy tale (obviously, the ending would have to be altered to veil its horror: let's give him a magic scarf to protect his neck from the guillotine's blade), wouldn't he clearly be the good guy and not the villain?

According to the Kantian appraiser, Herr Jägerstätter's act is one of those lights, small but intense, that show forth the kingdom of ends. That it brought about no perceptible change in the world is irrelevant. That his community and bishop opposed his decision only further highlights its moral worth. The fairy-tale fabulist in me would like to think that his refusal was enough to redeem whatever sins Franz Jägerstätter was guilty of and ensure him a spot in heaven. The realist in me, as long as he's permitted some poetry, would tell Franz Jägerstätter's granddaughter, "On this 'no,' despite its poor condition, for insurance purposes, I would put a value of—hold on to your hat—one of Julia's teardrops."

9 The Beast That Is and Is Not

In contrast to many other mythological systems, in the Bible the dragon seems to be a consistently sinister image. This is not only because of its antisocial habits of breathing fire and eating virgins, but because, of all sinister animals, it has the unique advantage of not existing. NORTHROP FRYE

Kathy used to come periodically to my office hours, plop down in the chair beside my desk, look me straight in the eye, and ask, "Why does God permit evil? I can't get this question out of my head. You need to tell me the answer. I'm not sleeping." I often have students blithely ask me impossible questions like I just might be able to pull the answer out of my hat. But there's more than simply bright-eyed curiosity behind her question—though there's definitely that. Kathy inquires about "the problem of evil" with genuine, mature desperation. She really isn't sleeping.

Because of her husband's job, Kathy came to Iowa City about a decade ago from a country in the Middle East (she's asked me to blur her identity because she's moved back to a country where the holiness of thinking freely about God is considered unholy). She spent most of her time in her house, doing the work of a mother and housewife, rarely venturing beyond a small community of immigrants. When she came to Kirkwood to take a few classes, her English was good but not perfect. But she absolutely blossomed in an academic context, poring over her books, asking numerous questions in her classes, making friends, and perfecting her writing and thinking abilities. After a semester, her written and spoken English surpassed—and in most cases far surpassed—that of her native-speaking peers. We hit it off because, among other reasons, I grew up eating Lebanese food made by my mother, and Kathy and I would compare hummus recipes.

I first had her as a student in Basic Reasoning, an elementary logic class that I enjoy teaching despite the fact that there's not much romance in its technical subjects. But for Kathy the study of formal logical structures was a marvel and an awakening from the dogmatic slumbers of her prior education. She'd often declare, wide-eyed, as if I'd just dreamt up some novel concept, "You're teaching us how to think for ourselves!"—reminding me of what must have been the original exhilaration of the philosophers who formulated the principles of a well-tuned mind.

When I asked Kathy why she was so passionate about the problem of evil, she explained that her Catholic faith had always been an important part of her life. When she was younger, she had even had a vision of the Virgin. (After Basic Reasoning, Kathy took Introduction to Philosophy with me, in which we studied al-Ghazali. When I asked her what she thought of his mysticism, she wrinkled her nose. If anything, it had put her off mysticism as a basis for religion, reminding her of the antiliberal smugness of the Muslim Brotherhood.) Her vision implanted in her the desire to become a nun, but her parents hadn't allowed it. Her marriage having already been arranged, she settled down, had a daughter, and committed herself to her family and charitable work.

A sincere, practicing Catholic, she nonetheless was prone, as mystics are, to unorthodox wonderings. She once told me how a bird visits her house every morning and pecks on her front door as if knocking. When she opens the door, the cardinal hops back and looks beseechingly at her until she offers it some bread crumbs. She asked me, with her characteristic passion, if it was possible that the bird was the reincarnated soul of a miscarried child, for its persistent peck was reminiscent of how a baby pecks after the mother's nipple.

*

"The problem of evil," which I had brought up in Basic Reasoning as a way of formalizing arguments on each side of a sophisticated philosophical issue, concerns how an all-powerful, all-good God could allow "evil," which is roughly defined as unmerited suffering. It is often broken into two categories: "moral evil," which includes the unfair suffering that humans inflict on each other (rape is a powerful example), and "natural evil," which describes the unfair suffering that appears to be built into the very structure of existence (bone cancer or earthquakes, for instance). To state the skeptic's position in the form of two linked arguments:

If God is all-good, then He should not want any unfair suffering.

If God is all-powerful, then He has the power to eliminate any unfair suffering.

So, if an all-good, all-powerful God exists, then there should be no unfair suffering.

But there is plenty of unfair suffering in the world.

So, an all-good, all-powerful God does not exist.

In less formal terms, imagine if you had a drug that could heal a child suffering from cancer, and you refused to give it to the child, even though you could have freely given it without any trouble. Is there any way we could describe you as good? Surely God, if He exists as reported, could heal such a child, and yet the pediatric oncology wards of the world offer ample proof that He often isn't helping.

The formal problem of evil dates back to Epicurus, though it's certainly present in the book of Job and has occupied theologians, particularly Christian theologians, ever since the dogma of a perfect, all-powerful God was formulated. There are three straightforward logical solutions to the problem. First, one can deny that there's evil in the world. Many religious believers, in their foolish zeal to save God, do just this, insisting that all so-called evil amounts to no more than birth pangs of goodness. The Bible, in its wisdom, repeatedly denies this option. Jesus himself declares, "[God] maketh his sun to rise on the evil and on the good, and sendeth rain on the just and on the unjust."[1] For those who take the crucifixion to be the central event of history it should be especially difficult to believe that nobody suffers unfairly. Second, one can deny that God is all good, as Zoroastrians, Manicheans, and polytheists do. Finally, one can deny that God is all powerful, as Plato does in the *Republic* ("'Then,' I said, 'the god, since he's good, wouldn't be the cause of everything, as the many say, but the cause of a few things for human beings and not responsible for most'").[2] Generally speaking, the orthodox Christian can take none of these logically tidy options and must simultaneously assert the existence of evil and the existence of an all-powerful, all-good God.

Before I articulated the problem in class, Kathy had subscribed to the classic theological position that an all-powerful, all-good God can be reconciled with evil in that He has given us freedom. Despite its potential for abuse and hence evil, freedom is a gift that allows us to enter into a meaningful relationship with God. Furthermore, God has given us a moral law to direct that freedom properly. But the very nature of freedom opens up the possibility that we ignore God's direction. Because we turn away from God and morality, evil is unleashed on the world. In essence, everything God created is good, but He left room for evil. Evil is not a thing but, rather, an absence, a vortex that we could resist but often don't, a beast that is because it isn't.

After giving the matter some thought, Kathy, as Job before her, recognized that this solution goes only so far. Our abuse of freedom is sufficient—at least logically—to account for lies, rape, murder, and war. Even a certain amount of unjust suffering at the mercy of natural events, like cancer and hurricanes, can be reasonably explained by an abuse of freedom. A smoker gets cancer not simply as an act of God, and probably a fair number of the victims of Hurricane Katrina suffered and died because of a combination of bad government and poor decision making. But it's painfully hard to make such an accounting add up in the end. Even though we tend to overestimate how much nature is to blame and underestimate how much we are to blame, the balance of suffering exceeds the result of human choice. Moreover, one can easily be disgusted by how much suffering is allowed even as a result of human freedom.

Kathy's quick mind could think of any number of examples, but she zeroed in on one in particular. She'd had a good friend who'd prayed ardently to have a child. After a long period of trying, her friend's wish was granted. But the hopeful mother developed preeclampsia and died giving birth to a healthy child. Kathy continues to help her friend's husband out and tries to take care of the child as one of her own. But her heart breaks to think of her friend's perfectly natural wish being her very undoing, to think of her friend's husband left without a wife, and her friend's child without a mother. "How," she asks me with a fire in her eyes, "can a good God give a death sentence to a mother for giving birth?"

I gave her excerpts from John Hick's classic statement *Evil and the God of Love*, where the theologian argues that this world is still in the process of being created, that it is a place of "soul-making," where we are tested against harsh, unyielding obstacles. She was unmoved by the argument. After much hesitant reflection, she concluded that God has to be all good but not all powerful. God, she said, must cry like she does, with little power to repair the evils of reality. When push came to shove, she endorsed Blake's cry of innocence,

> Think not thou canst sigh a sigh,
> And thy Maker is not by:
> Think not thou canst weep a tear,
> And thy Maker is not near.

> O He gives to us His joy,
> That our grief He may destroy:
> Till our grief is fled and gone
> He doth sit by us and moan.[3]

*

Throughout the preceding chapters I've been trying to propose what could be winkingly called a pragmatic mysticism. The mysticism is when we stand without limiting preconceptions before certain overwhelming realities. At its most intense, this is the mysticism of al-Ghazali, who tapped into what we tremblingly name God and have given flesh to in holy books. But what I'm calling mysticism also applies to my student Jillian who confronted the elusive purpose of the hospital, as well as to my student Julia who, like Immanuel Kant before her, confronted the mystery of moral worth. What's revealed in such experiences is in some ways beyond words and can never be perfectly conceptualized. There's always a touch of Socrates's "I know I know nothing" about an authentic engagement with reality. Nevertheless, these mystical moments strongly incline us to live in relationship to whatever portion of truth they have unveiled. We must find or improvise beliefs and practices accordingly. This is the pragmatism.

My pragmatic mysticism is particularly applicable to the concept of evil. Think of the blues: you may not be able to define the blues adequately, but if you need a definition to recognize them, your case is hopeless. Likewise, we may never be able to give a satisfactory definition of evil. But surely anyone who's reached adulthood—for that matter, anyone who's reached the age of five—has had their moments in the presence of evil, both as its agent and its witness. The pragmatism here involves finding workable ways of resisting and combating evil, and keeping ourselves honest about what we're really up to.

And yet I've been involved in conversations with any number of students and colleagues who oppose the idea that evil is a reality. Because what one person calls evil can be what another person calls good, they argue, the concept of evil has no meaning beyond a way of expressing extreme dislike of something. It's the Euthyphro problem all over again: do we call something evil because it's evil, or is it evil because we call it so? Even in the presence of the *reductio ad hitlerem* ("Are you saying that even the death camps at places like Dacchau and Auschwitz weren't truly evil?"), they hold firm to a version of Euthyphro's answer ("But the Nazis thought such places were good and thus were so in their eyes").

Perhaps it's my own philosophical limitation that I find this view practically impossible to entertain with any degree of seriousness. I, of course, don't deny that there were Nazis who rationalized their atrocities as expressions of greatness, justice, or even mercy. One Nazi, for instance, prided himself on shooting only children; since his partner killed their parents, he felt that he was taking pity on them. I simply would rather affirm that 2 + 2 = 5 than believe that such thoughts are anything but really wrong. If we can't take as axiomatic that the deliberate dehumanization and murder of over six million people—men, women, and children—for no crime whatsoever is evil, we really are lost in a dark wood of words. A French theologian once said that he could understand not believing in God, but not believing in the devil was completely beyond his comprehension.[4] To which we should add Baudelaire's comment, "Never, my brethren, forget, when you hear enlightenment vaunted, that the neatest trick of the devil is to persuade you that he does not exist!"[5]

The noble impulse in relativism is a healthy suspicion of those who think the line between good and evil is drawn between their side and their opponent's. Often the game of accusing others of evil is bad business. When each side calls the other evil, it's virtually impossible to make any progress toward a peaceable solution. So, it's certainly wise to be on the lookout for demonizing whoever opposes us, and it's politically prudent in many cases to refrain from calling opposing political regimes evil.

Where the relativists lose touch with reality is in giving up on the idea of evil altogether. In the Christian tradition, the standard dogma is that we are all possessed of some quantity of evil. As Aleksandr Solzhenitzyn puts it in *The Gulag Archipelago*,

> It was granted to me to carry away from my prison years on my bent back, which nearly broke beneath its load, this essential experience: how a human being becomes evil and how good. In the intoxication of youthful successes I had felt myself to be infallible, and I was therefore cruel. In the surfeit of power I was a murderer and an oppressor. In my most evil moments I was convinced that I was doing good, and I was well supplied with systematic arguments. It was only when I lay there on rotting prison straw that I sensed within myself the first stirrings of good. Gradually it was disclosed to me that the line separating good and evil passes not through states, nor between classes, nor between political parties either, but right through every human heart, and through all human hearts. This line shifts. Inside us, it oscillates with the years. Even within hearts overwhelmed by evil, one small bridgehead of good is retained; and even in the best of all hearts, there remains a small corner of evil.[6]

"In my most evil moments I was convinced that I was doing good, and I was well supplied with systematic arguments." That fact hardly disproves the existence of evil. If anything, it's a reminder of just how insidious the devil is.

*

According to Susan Neiman's *Evil and Modern Thought*, one of the main catalysts of modernity was the 1755 Lisbon earthquake, which leveled the thriving Portuguese city and killed perhaps a hundred thousand people. To witness such carnage is to confront something horribly wrong, something we have traditionally called evil. The philosophers of the day, in struggling to make sense of this horror, began to articulate more clearly their newly burgeoning concepts of nature and morality. While some fell back on a tradition that regarded such events as "acts of God" and tried to conceptualize the event as part of "the best of all possible worlds," the newly dominant philosophers began to understand the event in different terms, of which we are the inheritors.

The earthquake, on this new view, wasn't evil; it was simply an act of nature; and nature is nonmoral, for nature has no conscious intentions. We should limit the concept of evil to the moral sphere, to the sphere of freedom. Only an act of malicious intent is truly evil. Earthquakes aren't deliberate "acts of God" so much as the results of a rule-governed system. Whatever evil there is in earthquakes pertains to the human choices that exacerbate the suffering or death toll. God, on this view, is no longer a crowding concern. Nature just happens. Only humans can be morally culpable, for only humans are free to do what they do.

But the tradition that left behind the theological problem of evil at Lisbon, after refining itself over the next three centuries and reaching its zenith in the moral philosophy of Kant, developed a new anthropological problem at Auschwitz. The problem was first articulated by Hannah Arendt, who after observing the trial of Adolf Eichmann coined the expression "the banality of evil" to describe it. She came to the conclusion that Eichmann, one of the architects and executors of the holocaust, was no defiant devil but, rather, a family man who was doing his job. His evil, which stands for much modern evil, was less a product of conscious intention than a product of thoughtless participation in a wicked system. But the tradition that developed out of Lisbon reserves the concept of evil for only those who willfully violate the good. How are we to make sense of an everyday guy who just happened to have the blood of millions on his hands? Though the defense of "I was just doing my job" can often be a rationalization, there is also some truth in it. Do we, therefore, let Eichmann and the many other Nazis like him off the moral hook on the grounds of involuntary manslaughter? Just as so-called acts of God become merely the results of a rule-governed natural system at the beginning of modernity, human acts run the risk of becoming just the results of rule-governed bureaucratic systems at the end of it.

After Auschwitz, we are left "homeless," to use Neiman's word. Our purely naturalized account of ethics strikes those who look the Nazi horrors in the face as inadequate. And yet the premodern theological tradition, though it exerted a powerful attraction on many serious people after the war, is difficult, if not impossible, to return to. As Hannah Arendt says of our impasse,

> We refuse, and consider as barbaric, the propositions "that a great crime offends nature, so that the very earth cries out for vengeance; that evil violates a natural harmony which only retribution can restore; that a wrong collectivity owes a duty to the moral order to punish the criminal" (Yosal Rogat). And yet I think it is undeniable that it was precisely on the ground of these long-forgotten propositions that Eichmann was brought to justice to begin with, and that they were, in fact, the supreme justification for the death penalty.[7]

The problem of the banality of evil has been demonstrated chillingly by researchers like Stanley Milgram and Philip Zimbardo. The latter chronicles, in his book *The Lucifer Effect*, how a group of normal young male students were randomly divided into guards and prisoners in a makeshift jail at Stanford University. Though they were simply supposed to be playacting, the guards began to abuse the prisoners verbally, physically, and psychologically. "At the start of the experiment, there were no differences between the two groups; less than a week later, there were no similarities." Zimbardo himself was implicated in the evil, for he continued the experiment even on witnessing the abuse. It required the intervention of his girlfriend for him to discontinue the depraved research into depravity. He concludes, "Any deed that any human being has ever committed, however horrible, is *possible* for any of us—under the right or wrong situational circumstances. That knowledge does not excuse evil; rather, it democratizes it, sharing its blame among ordinary actors rather than declaring it the province only of deviants and despots—of Them but not Us."[8] In essence, the banality of evil is that, without any wicked intentions at all, "decent" people like you and me, when put into a certain social structure, are capable of carrying out atrocities.

Though there's been an understandable debate about the extent to which Arendt is accurate in her characterization of Eichmann, I think her overall identification of "the banality of evil," as Zimbardo's research shows, is illuminating. Even more important is her discussion of the lesson we should draw about the banality of evil. She argues that we need to learn not just that the final solution could happen anywhere but, more important, that it did not happen everywhere. "Humanly speaking, no more is required, and no more can reasonably be asked, for this planet to remain a place fit for human habitation." Or, as Susan Neiman says, "If your reaction to these insights is a quiet murmur—There but for the grace of God go I—you have missed the point entirely. Humility is no excuse for resignation; realizing that any of us might collude in evil is just the other side of realizing that any of us might oppose it."[9]

While humans have always known that we're capable of evil, the expansion of power through technology has made the problem extremely acute. Growing up during the end of the Cold War, I used to live in fear that the whole world was going to be blotted out by a series of nuclear attacks, which could be brought about, the movies convincingly depicted, by one careless hacker or deceptive government agent. Nowadays, my children grow up with the fear that we may have already trashed the environment beyond repair and that numerous animal species, including *Homo sapiens*, may well find the earth uninhabitable very soon. Such fears are mixed with a healthy dose of ancient apocalyptic superstition. But environmental degradation and nuclear weapons aren't figments of our imagination, nor were the gulags of Stalin and the concentration camps of Hitler, nor were Hiroshima and Nagasaki, nor was 9/11. All these events had good old human evil behind them, but good old human evil amplified by the now godlike power of our technology and our vast systems. In some ways, we're back to the old problem of how we make sense of atrocious acts of the gods; it's just that increasingly we're the ones wielding their power.

*

The thinker whose work, in my opinion, most powerfully copes with our impasse is Hans Jonas, who, interestingly, ends up articulating a speculative theology much like my student Kathy's. He was born on May 10, 1903, in Mönchengladbach, Germany. His parents were Jewish in the complicated way characteristic of many of the European Jewry of the time: religiously tepid, culturally committed to the traditions of Judaism, and yet patriotic Germans who were more or less happy to assimilate. From early on, Jonas was skeptical of the possibilities of complete assimilation and began a lifelong support for Zionism. His father, a businessman, recognized his son's superior intellectual gifts and insisted that he should study whatever he wish, unconcerned about finances. So Hans Jonas studied philosophy and theology under the leading German philosophers of the day, names that will never be forgotten in the history of philosophy: Edmund Husserl, Rudolf Bultmann, and especially Martin Heidegger, whom many consider the greatest philosopher of the twentieth century, whose work inspired Jonas's thinking to the very core. Early in his studies he also befriended fellow student Hannah Arendt, and they remained close throughout their long, tumultuous lives, except for a brief row over her book on Eichmann.

When the Nazis proved to be more than a passing fad, Jonas moved to England and then to Palestine, swearing never to return to Germany except as a soldier in a victorious army. In Palestine, he met his wife, Lore, who fell for him because when he first came over to dinner, he delivered a paean to the olives on the table, which began "with the anointing of Homer's Greek heroes, went on to the use of olive oil by the high priests of the Old Testament, and eventually arrived at Goethe's West-Eastern Divan."[10] In 1940, Jonas made the first steps toward fulfilling his promise, heading back to Europe and joining the British Army. His thrilling, boring, restless years of soldiering, in which he was deprived of books, threw him back on "the philosopher's basic duty and his native business—thinking."[11] He regularly faced not only the prospect of his own death but the possible apocalypse of civilization. When he returned to Germany, it was not as a passive victim of Hitler but as a member of a conquering army, and he took an ignoble, though understandable, pride in seeing his homeland desolated. When he finally wended his way back to Mönchengladbach, he discovered that his mother had been deported to Auschwitz and killed.

Jonas couldn't stomach living in Germany and eventually wound up teaching for most of his career at the New School for Social Research in New York City. But his return to his homeland as a soldier filled him with questions about the nature of philosophy. On the one hand, his great teacher, whose work would continue to influence his own for the rest of his life, betrayed the philosophical life. In 1933, Heidegger joined the Nazi party and served it in various capacities. Though he said a couple of mildly critical things about the Nazis after the war, Heidegger never repented of his sojourn into politics or apologized to his Jewish students, among whom numbered Jonas and Arendt. On the other hand, Jonas was heartened by a number of his former colleagues, who had resisted Nazism based on their philosophical principles.

> Among my professors was Julius Ebbinghaus, a strict and uncompromising Kantian, not to be compared with Heidegger in significance. He had passed the test admirably; I learned of this and visited him in Marburg in 1945 to pay him my homage. He looked into my eyes with that old fire of absolute conviction and said: "But do you know what, Jonas? Without Kant I wouldn't have been able to do it." I suddenly realized that here theory and life were one. With which man, then, was philosophy in better hands? With the creative genius whose profundity did not keep him from a breach of faith in the hour of decision or with his unoriginal but upright colleague, who remained pure?[12]

Once again, it's the old Euthyphro problem of power versus goodness. On Euthyphro's side is the powerful philosopher who violated goodness (and yet inspired Jonas to be a philosopher). On Socrates's side is the unoriginal philosopher who refused on moral grounds to participate at all in the evil that brought about the death of Jonas's mother and countless others. With which man was philosophy in better hands? Jonas says, "To this day I do not presume to have the answer to this question."[13]

However, when it came to his theological reflections, Jonas found that he could not let the paradox stand. How could God have allowed the atrocities at Auschwitz? It's here that Jonas solves the problem of evil, like Kathy, like Plato, by refusing to believe in God's omnipotence.

*

In his magnum opus *The Phenomenon of Life*, Hans Jonas argues that there are three important breaks in the order of existence. First, there's the transition from inorganic matter to primitive life-forms. This is the leap of life itself. With this leap, need enters into the universe. Unlike a stone, a plant has needs (for sunlight, water, nourishment) that must be continuously met in order for its existence to be maintained. When these needs are no longer met, the plant dies. Though a stone can be crushed or transformed or even vaporized, it can't, strictly speaking, die. So, with the leap of life, death also comes on the scene. And, in a sense, a bit of value does, too, because it's a little sad when a plant dies from lack of water and hence a little good when a plant flourishes. A stone just is and is and is: nothing is particularly good or bad for it.

Next, there's the transition from vegetative life-forms to animal life-forms, where life begins to feel itself. An animal, like a plant, needs nourishment, but it also experiences that need as hunger. With this leap to animality, pain and pleasure come into being. Life becomes rangier, able to move restlessly about in search of the fulfillment of its desires. The little bit of value that arose with plant life increases immensely, for pleasure is undoubtedly good and pain bad. If it's a little sad when your houseplant perishes from lack of water, it's a calamity if your dog dies of thirst.

Finally, there's the transition from animal life to human life. We are rational animals, able to conceptualize the world and our very existence. Like a plant, we have needs; like an animal, we feel them as desires; but we frame those desires by means of concepts. We grasp our nature only through our culture, so to speak. We feel hungry, but we disallow ourselves from eating certain things and allow ourselves to eat others under certain conditions. We can even die of hunger on principle. Denny Barry and Andrew O'Sullivan, to take just two examples, perished in the early twentieth century on a hunger strike, protesting their continued detention by the Irish Free State. They didn't die because of a lack of food; they died because their concept of who they were as members of the Irish Republican Army trumped their animal nature. An extreme example, it's simply meant to demonstrate our rational nature, which, though it often allows us to meet our animal needs more effectively through the development of technology, in some ways takes us beyond mere animality.

With the transition to humanity the value that was miraculously born with the first reproducing cell reaches new heights. Things can get really good and really bad. For now life not only feels but understands itself. We can explicitly proclaim something superior or inferior, good or bad, moral or wicked. As animals we're subject to the suffering of desire, but we're also prone to the suffering of despair. It's possible for us to regard the deaths of Barry and O'Sullivan—the life and death of any human, the life and death of anything, in fact—as a full-fledged tragedy.

Another way of expressing the transition to humanity is to say that it's the beginning of freedom. All animals are free to pursue this prey over that prey. But as the existence of vegetarians demonstrates, humans are free to choose not to pursue prey at all. We have the power to develop very different ways of life that sustain (or don't sustain!) our animal needs. With this power of freedom comes our concept of morality, the idea that some uses of our freedom are good and others bad. As value reaches its pinnacle in humankind, a new thing appears in the universe: evil.

*

There's a Latin expression, much beloved by Thomas Hobbes, *homo homini lupus*: man is a wolf to man. It's always been taken to mean that humans can be as vicious as wolves to each other. But it's based on a profound misconception of wolves, which are anything but wicked. Even by our most humane standards, wolves shine as models of virtue. They form close-knit communities; they mate for life and are family oriented. Perhaps more to the point, they never use lethal violence except to satisfy their need for food, and when they do so, they kill quickly and efficiently. Yes, they sometimes eat one of our sheep, but they can hardly be blamed for not understanding human property law. Unlike wolves, we torture and kill our own kind, torture and kill other animals for fun, and often betray our packs. We steal our neighbor's sheep, knowing property law full well. Would that man were wolf to man!

If anything, we're more like certain birds who, if put in close quarters, will slowly peck each other to death, for birds and humans, weak as we are, haven't evolved powerful biological checks against the use of violence. If wolves were to use violence indiscriminately, they wouldn't survive to adulthood. But for us, at least without technology, killing is a tedious business. Nature, so to speak, has given us a little cruelty to get the job done.

But unlike birds and our other fellow animals, we do have the power to create technologies that make killing easy as pushing a button or pulling a trigger. Moreover, we have the capacity to reason, which means that we can kill and do other nasty stuff based on motivations beyond irritation or hunger. We are the animal of hate crimes. It's especially common in war for each side to demonize the other, to portray the enemy as a monster that needs to be exterminated. Hans Jonas's mother wasn't killed because of some biological imperative; she was killed because she was a Jew, and the Nazis had conceptualized the Jews as a plague on the world. Wolves are nice. Birds are nasty. Humans are downright evil.

*

How, then, are we to make sense of these profound leaps in the universe? How should we come to terms with the freedom and value that are shot through life and that come to such a risky pinnacle in humanity? We're free to say that it all "just" happened, that the value of life is accidental, that the adventures of freedom are cosmically meaningless. It's become passé to argue that it's meaningless to talk of God insofar as science offers no evidence of the divine. As Jonas points out, it's a viciously circular inference to define as meaningful only what can be described scientifically and then to dismiss everything nonscientific.

We're just as free to interpret the biological facts in the terms into which they move us to interpret them. For life, as Jonas points out, *seems* profoundly meaningful. The human spirit peeps of the divine—sometimes even cries out for it. Echoing Pascal and Kant, he says, "The fact that by cosmic scales man is but an atom is a quantitative irrelevancy: his inner width can make him an event of cosmic importance."[14] Our inner width is a window into the meaningfulness of being itself. We can refuse to believe what we see through that window, but it's hardly unreasonable to speculate on what appears, albeit darkly, on the other side.

For Jonas, as for my student Kathy, it's the experience of evil that most calls forth a religious interpretation of the raw biological data. As Jonas writes in a moment of ferocious eloquence,

> I am thinking of the gassed and burnt children of Auschwitz, of the defaced, dehumanized phantoms of the camps, and of all the other, numberless victims of the other man-made holocausts of our time. Among men, their sufferings will soon be forgotten, and their names even sooner. Another chance is not given them, and eternity

has no compensation for what has been missed in time. Are they, then, debarred from an immortality which even their tormentors and murderers obtain because they could act—abominably, yet accountably, thus leaving their sinister mark on eternity's face? This I refuse to believe. And this I like to believe: that there was weeping in the heights at the waste and despoilment of humanity; that a groan answered the rising shout of ignoble suffering, and wrath—the terrible wrong done to the reality and possibility of each life thus wantonly victimized, each one a thwarted attempt of God. 'The voice of thy brother's blood cries unto me from the ground': should we not believe that the immense chorus of such cries that has risen up in our lifetime now hangs over our world as a dark and accusing cloud? that eternity looks down upon us with a frown, wounded itself and perturbed in its depths?[15]

The problem of Auschwitz (to use Auschwitz as a metonymy for outrageous suffering) is a problem for all believers, but for Jews especially—not exactly because they were the ones who predominately suffered in the death camps, but because Judaism is a commitment to a unique covenant between God and His children. Christians, for instance, can say that God has given us freedom and thus the world is basically controlled by the devil; Auschwitz is simply a profound example of a common problem. But to the believing Jew, Auschwitz is an example of the profoundest kind of abandonment. Jews were executed not because they stood up for their faith, not because of any heroic commitment, but simply because of what Jonas calls "the fiction of race." Children, women, men, believers, nonbelievers, saints, sinners, and all the mediocre in-between were dehumanized, tortured, and destroyed simply because they were Jewish.

Confronting the problem of Auschwitz, and also considering his analysis of the development of life itself, Hans Jonas resorts to what Plato calls a "likely story," a myth that, as Jonas says, "I would like to believe 'true'—in the sense in which myth may happen to adumbrate a truth which of necessity is unknowable and even, in direct concepts, ineffable, yet which, by intimations to our deepest experience, lays claim upon our powers of giving indirect account of it in revocable, anthropomorphic images."[16] While some Jews understandably respond to the Holocaust by embracing with renewed vigor the faith that the Nazis almost extinguished, the problem of Auschwitz leads

Jonas to rethink the God of history, to imagine a new kind of Judaism as a universal faith.

Jonas conjectures that God, in creating this vast universe, spent all his energy and became very weak, essentially giving Himself over to the development of life itself. God's power is slowly reviving: first in the needy life that breaks out in plants, then in the desiring life that appears in animals, and so far at its highest in the rational life that comes on the scene with humanity. God's power is ultimately directed at the good. The differing levels of value that come onto the scene with the ascending life-forms are each moments where something good is born: first, life itself; then, pleasure; and finally, the understanding that life is good. To put it in biblical terms, God creates life and declares it to be good. Or, to put it in evolutionary terms, everything tries to survive. Or, to use the philosophical terms of Jonas, life says yes to itself.

But God's is a very fragile power, often incapable of fighting against the evil that also appears with our freedom. It's our task, Jonas speculates, to help out this weak, struggling God, whose success is far from guaranteed. The power of God is, to some extent, in our hands; and we should work to advance the cause of His goodness, even though the odds look insurmountable. In order to clarify his point, he quotes from the diary of Etty Hillesum, a young Dutch Jewess, who when the deportations in Holland began in 1942, volunteered for the Westerbork concentration camp, so she could help out at the hospital and share in the fate of her people. She was executed there in September of 1943. At one point she writes,

> I shall try to help you, God, to stop my strength ebbing away, though I cannot vouch for it in advance. But one thing is becoming increasingly clear to me: that You cannot help us, that we must help You help ourselves. . . . Alas, there does not seem to be much You Yourself can do about our circumstances, about our lives. Neither do I hold You responsible. You cannot help us, but we must help You and defend Your dwelling place in us to the last.[17]

*

One day, as Kathy and I were chewing over the problem of evil anew, our roles as teacher and student momentarily reversed: she said something that allowed me to see the problem in a bright new light. She wondered if our normal way of conceiving of power was wrong. We wonder why God didn't manifest His power by preventing some evil. But maybe, she ingeniously mused, power is in fact synonymous with love. We usually think that God's loving nature is part of His good nature, but perhaps it's part of His powerful nature. As a Christian who had experienced her religion at the mystical level, she had always felt Christ on the cross as the deepest expression of love. Though we're apt to see the crucifixion as God at His most humiliated, at His weakest, she speculated that it was God at His strongest.

With this idea, she was putting her finger on one of the central ideas of Christianity and also, for that matter, Daoism: what the world takes as weakness is in fact a path to maximal strength. In wrestling, as in Judo or chess, it's a commonplace that you must often give way in order to overmaster your opponent. Perhaps this is a cosmic principle. Perhaps God must give Himself completely over to suffering and death in order to be most triumphant. As Laozi in the *Daodejing* says, "Reversal is the movement of the way," and also,

> Those who are crooked will be perfected.
> Those who are bent will be straight.
> Those who are empty will be full.
> Those who are worn will be renewed.[18]

Or, as Jesus says in the Sermon on the Mount,

> Blessed are the poor in spirit: for theirs is the kingdom of heaven.
> Blessed are they that mourn: for they shall be comforted.
> Blessed are the meek: for they shall inherit the earth.
> Blessed are they which do hunger and thirst after righteousness:
>   for they shall be filled.[19]

There's a poem of W. H. Auden's that ends, "though truth and love / can never really differ, when they seem to, / the subaltern should be truth."[20] I think it would be humane to live by the following two principles: when truth and God seem to differ, go with truth; when truth and love seem to differ, go with love. But we should hope that in the end all those apparent differences prove illusory.

*

While extreme suffering generally can be seen as a movement of love's power, and certainly the Holocaust is an abuse of our gift of freedom, it's still difficult to reconcile an all-powerful God with Auschwitz. All sorts of good may flow from the death camps, but never ever enough in comparison with their undeniable, overwhelming evil. Why did God take the risk of humanity? If our wickedness can extend so far, how could our freedom be a gift? This, perhaps, takes us right back to Kathy's first conjecture and Jonas's conception of a weak God. Or else it takes us back to the book of Job, which in essence says that we must live with the paradox of God's power and goodness, the paradox of His inscrutability and the meaningfulness that He promises us. Either way, I'm not sure how well Kathy is going to sleep.

Atheists, of course, give up on God altogether.

Contrast their response with an event that haunted Elie Wiesel his whole life, an event that lurks behind almost everything he wrote. It seems that when Wiesel was a prisoner at Auschwitz he witnessed three forsaken scholars who formed a Rabbinic court of law, indicting and trying God for all the evils He had unleashed on the world, including the horrible risk of the sixth day of creation. The emaciated lawyers carefully laid out the arguments on each side. They deliberated for a long time. In the end, they found God guilty. After the verdict was delivered, a long silence ensued, which was finally broken by an old scholar of the Talmud, who declared, "It's time." Then they all said the evening prayer.

INTERLUDE ON ZOMBIES AND SUPERHEROES

Be a philosopher; but, amidst all your philosophy, be still a man.
DAVID HUME

Martin Kessler is a martial arts instructor, astrologer, hypnotist, fire twirler, escape artist, special investigator, Gnostic, inventor of "angel boxing," mentalist, poet, author under the pen name Simon Zealot, "of course"—he would say with a smile—"a rebel Djinn," and also a likely candidate for my most interesting student ever. He went to a top-notch liberal arts college and dropped out. For a while he wandered the country in a beat-up van. Once he settled down in a city to work at a shelter, enjoying the irony of working all day to help the homeless when he himself was homeless. When his long-time off-and-on-again girlfriend—a lovely, quietly self-assured, surprisingly sane woman—went to the famous Writer's Workshop at the University of Iowa, Martin found himself taking philosophy classes at the nearby community college.

Immediately we hit it off. Martin had read widely and knew about those things that interested him in considerable depth. So we'd argue good-naturedly about the validity of ancient heresies, or the will to power, or Daoism, or poetic meter—whatever one of us happened to be thinking about. Sometimes I'd have the upper hand; sometime he would. We learned from each other.

During his time in Iowa City, Martin made a living teaching gymnastics to children. My son, then five years old, signed up for his new class on parkour—the acrobatic art of getting from point A to point B as efficiently as possible—which Martin had discovered in the early period of its popularity. During the first day of training, he huddled up the squirrelly boys and whispered, "The course you're taking is officially called Basic Parkour, but really I'm going to teach you how to be superheroes." Naturally he had to be invited to our next birthday party, where in the darkness of early night he twirled around his entire body various good-sized spheres of fire to the gasps of wide-eyed kids and nervous parents. Then, after the children were in bed, he demonstrated to me and my wife his mastery of a hilarious martial art based on the movements of monkeys, and another based on the stumbling of drunkards.

Martin believes that when we free ourselves from shackling hang-ups and beliefs, we wield divine powers. His comment about superheroes to his young students was more than a rhetorical hook. He's attracted by Nietzsche's idea of the *Übermensh*, the superhuman. But Martin's real intellectual inspiration is Gnosticism, the age-old, perennially attractive belief system that holds that this world was created by an inept, if not evil, maker; that the real God completely transcends our universe; and that our true nature is a spark of divinity hidden away in a fleshy prison.

Though Martin is deeply absorbed in the arcane texts of this ancient heresy, he's just as deeply absorbed in our current age. When he'd speak in class, various otherwise disaffected students would perk up, much like the five-year-olds in superhero training, in part because Martin utilizes the mythology of our time to flesh out his vision of humanity. He believes that our age suffers from a zombie epidemic and that our true destiny is to become superheroes.

*

What is a zombie? According to a common etymology, the word is traceable back to the Kikongo word *nzambi*, which means god. Zombies are, in the popular imagination, the living dead, corpses animated by an outside magic. They usually have an insatiable leveling desire: zombies are always looking to make more zombies. According to Martin, zombies are a projection of human life numbed by distractions, hollowed out and remote-controlled by the magic we call consumerism. As Simon Zealot charmingly writes,

> Do you find that most of life's problems can be solved with a little creative shopping? Is television your primary form of entertainment? . . .

182 INTERLUDE ON ZOMBIES AND SUPERHEROES

Do you find that there's just not enough time in the day, especially for things like exercise? Are you tired right now? Despite this constant lack of energy, do you believe that everything will work out in the end? . . . If you answered "yes" to most or all of these questions then you might be suffering from an illness called phobosophitis, or, as it's known by its more common name, the zombie disease.[1]

And, in fine Nietzschean satirical style,

The basic ability to speak remains unaffected, and they appear to experience minor degrees of limited cognitive activity in response to many different kinds of external stimuli, but, in general, thoughts come with less and less frequency, and those that do come are of increasingly smaller orders of magnitude. Dreams are forgotten, all but the most animalistic passions fade, and the creative impulse, if it was ever present, dies. Things of an abstract nature, such as art, beauty, freedom, dignity, justice, or any sort of philosophical or spiritual speculations, will all gradually become more and more meaningless as the disease progresses, and such things will therefore elicit no authentic cognitive response, except perhaps for dismissal or hostility, from the infected.

The illness of phobosophitis, according to Martin, is related to a deadening materialism, nihilism really, the legacy of the non-Gnostic version of Christianity. Official religion numbed our spiritual longings with false visions of a comfortable heaven. Now that the plausibility of such visions has run its course, we're apt to become soulless bodies vegetating in front of bleeping screens. Some still cling to their outdated religions. Others reject religion altogether and philosophically embrace our deadening materialism, arguing that we're nothing more than animals with so many itches to be scratched. Either course, Martin believes, amounts to the same thing: "Culture is replaced by consumerism, education by certification, creation by industry."

He considers phobosophitis an epidemic. His spiritual intellect's great work is to develop a cure for the disease. Here is some of the doctor's advice: "Inoculate yourselves and those around you with your own art and self-awareness. Create wonders. Dance. Make love. Move at more than a shambling pace. Kiss in public. Climb something. Play. Disrupt misery and the viciousness of the miserable. Be alive. Welcome to the Zombie Resistance."

*

What is a superhero? The ancient Athenians had the goddess Athena whom they worshiped in the Parthenon. Americans have superheroes with names like Captain America whom we worship at the multiplex. Superheroes, of course, aren't gods: they're humans endowed by technology with godlike powers, either through mishap, like the detonation of the gamma bomb that turns Bruce Banner into the Hulk, or by design, like the manipulation of gadgets that empowers Bruce Wayne to be Batman. If asked why kids and increasingly adults read comics and go to superhero movies, most would say escapism. After all, what do superheroes wrestle with? They must use their powers responsibly to keep the whole world from being destroyed. We, in contrast, struggle with much more mundane problems, like nuclear weapons and global warming.

The Gnostic imagination is naturally attractive to our advanced technological age. For the Gnostics, our true selves are buried deep inside our gawky flesh, not unlike how Spider-Man hides beneath the dorky clothes of Peter Parker, or how Simon Zealot lurks beneath Martin's long black coat. Practically the definition of a human is one who dwells in mediated relationship to nature. But our age has taken that mediation to new heights, dizzyingly far from our bodies in many cases. Our cars, airplanes, phones, and screens allow us to transcend and float free of the limitations of foot, hand, eye, and ear. The video games that nourish immature imaginations couldn't be more Gnostic, with their avatars able to perform superhuman feats, not excluding dying innumerable deaths. As such marvels increasingly shape our minds, the boundaries of our native powers expand: these fleshy frames begin to seem coarse and plodding.

Our Gnostic imaginations are subject to an interesting paradox. Like most serious dualists, the Gnostics, while officially despising the body, often devote much time to it, either because its charms are hard to resist when you don't think they matter or, more seriously, because the Gnostics regard themselves as masters of body, who have an obligation, as long as they're tied to it, to whip it into shape. One telling image of our age is the row of humans on exercise bikes, all watching TV. This is what one might call practical dualism, though Simon Zealot would see it as advanced zombification.

Martin embodies our Gnostic paradox with considerably more panache than your standard jogger, spending countless hours perfecting his body's performance through gymnastics and martial arts in order to liberate his spiritual powers. His ongoing project is to construct an ideal educational system, one that disciplines the body and mind so that its dedicated practitioners emerge as knights of angelic chivalry, "fearless agents of compassionate and effective change," superheroes.

*

When I think on that old story of Adam and Eve in the garden, about how an almost inadvertent bite of an apple tragically endows us with divine knowledge, I often think about the director of the Manhattan Project, who awoke to the atom bomb's power and vowed to spend the rest of his days trying to control what he'd unleashed. "Now I am become Death, the destroyer of worlds," J. Robert Oppenheimer murmured on seeing the initial mushroom cloud, remembering the *Mahabharata*. But the truth is that we've been nibbling the fruit of good and evil throughout our history, at least as far back as the first flint that was flaked into a blade and sunk into flesh. The human matter out of which we imagine superheroes has always been available. In 442 BC, the Sophoclean chorus declares,

> Many the wonders but nothing walks stranger than man.
> This thing crosses the sea in the winter's storm,
> making his path through the roaring waves.
> And she, the greatest of gods, the earth—
> ageless she is, and unwearied—he wears her away
> as the ploughs go up and down from year to year
> and his mules turn up the soil.
> Gay nations of birds he snares and leads,
> wild beast tribes and the salty brood of the sea,
> with the twisted mesh of his nets, this clever man.
> He controls with craft the beasts of the open air, walkers on hills.
> The horse with his shaggy mane he holds and harnesses,
> yoked about the neck, and the strong bull of the mountain.

Language, and thought like the wind
and the feelings that make the town,
he has taught himself, and shelter against the cold,
refuge from rain. He can always help himself.
He faces no future helpless.[2]

But rather than encourage us to become yet more godlike, the Sophoclean chorus highlights the two crucial, sometimes irreconcilable
powers, Earth and Heaven, to which we ought to bow: "When he
honors the laws of the land and the gods' sworn right, high indeed
is his city."

The insight that we're godlike has always captured a portion of
our nature, but it's at best a quarter-truth. Yes, technology has given
us superhero powers; and yes, phobosophitis is a disease of our time.
But Simon Zealot exaggerates. We're neither *nzambi* nor *Übermen-
schen*. Same, by the way, for that other quarter-truth of our age, that
we're "just" animals, with goals that don't really extend beyond survival. Yes, we're animals with an evolutionary history, subject to all
the brute facts of the body; and yes, we can see the rudiments of humanity prefigured in our brother and sister vertebrates. But Martin is
surely right that we're more than simply carnivores stalking around
in the forest primeval.

We're human, all too human, thank God. We have serious limits
on us, not just an evolutionary history and all the brute facts of the
body, but our ignorance of the ultimate truths as well. We also have
the capacity to wield earth-shattering, heaven-opening powers; and
without some kind of harnessing of those energies into the goods of
spirit and mind, our days and nights are either wicked or drab affairs.
Philosophy is the story of humanely realizing our humanity, of making an honest living with both our transcendence and our ignorance,
of taking seriously those words engraved on the Temple of Apollo:
"gnothi seauton"—know thyself.

To fulfill our nature, we require a powerful dose of Martin's transcending energies, particularly in what can be a zombifying consumer
culture. I particularly like his advice about walking with a spring in
your step and occasionally climbing something. Yet we ought to conceptualize our true power in terms not of superhero expansion but
of pious recognition of our human condition. "Reversal is the movement of the way," the Old Master says. We must rise so we can fall

into place. Either that, or we fall down to learn how to get up. The problem with a movie like *The Matrix*, which basically expresses my issue with the Gnostic imagination, is that the whole thing is about transcending a phony, digital world, and yet the reality into which Neo and company awaken is even more like a video game than the matrix itself. At our best we're able to fuse in imagination, if not in life, superhero and zombie, god and beast, good and evil, into one believable human whole.

I'm grateful for the classics of our heritage that preserve such images of our humanity, particularly Plato's dialogues, which paint a picture of our energies wisely and fully deployed in the character of Socrates. But I'm not one to despair over the poverty of our age, at least not too much. Our society may be zombifying, but there are very few zombies. One doesn't have to scratch very deeply the madly texting teen or the Internet-glazed adult to find all the wonders and horrors and struggles of being human. Moreover, I'm lucky to have had teachers, students, and friends like Martin who have accomplished the central task of humane culture. They have made life worth living. When in the dank prison Socrates's companions despair of losing their wise friend, he says, "You must search for him in company with one another too, for perhaps you wouldn't find anyone more able to do this than yourselves."[3]

CONCLUSION: THE MOST BEAUTIFUL THING IN THE WORLD

Socrates said, "And if I have something good, I teach it to them and I introduce them to others who will be useful to them with respect to virtue. And together with my friends I go through the treasures of the wise men of old which they left behind written in books, and we peruse them. If we see something good, we pick it out and hold it to be a great profit, if we are able to prove useful to one another." When I heard this, I held Socrates to be really happy. XENOPHON

In his essay "The Sorcerer and His Magic," the anthropologist Claude Lévi-Strauss tells of a nineteenth-century Kwakiutl American Indian by the name of Quesalid who believed that the art practiced by his tribe's shamans was all a bunch of tricks. Becoming a double agent for the skeptics of the world, Quesalid infiltrated the shamanistic school with the purpose of learning, and eventually exposing, their hucksterism. Once inside, he did indeed learn of all sorts of shady tricks, like paying spies to gather information to be "gleaned" during the healing ceremony, or the art of hiding a bloody tuft of down in the mouth, which is then vomited up at a certain point in the ritual and presented to the sick person as the purged worm of illness.

Before Quesalid's training is over, he's summoned by a sick man who has just had a dream about him. Not knowing what else to do, Quesalid applies the trick of the "bloody worm." It works! The man gets almost immediately better. Baffled, the skeptical shaman figures that the recovery was due to how sincerely the patient believed in the dream.

Our hero continues his research, attending a healing ceremony of the neighboring Koskimo American Indians, whose shamans use a less dramatic form of the bloody-worm trick, simply spitting on the ground and claiming that their saliva is the patient's purged illness. In the case of one sick woman, the spit method doesn't work. Quesalid asks if he may practice on the woman. He applies the bloody-worm technique. The sick woman is healed.

Now Quesalid finds himself in mental tumult. If shamanism is just a trick, why is it working? More puzzling, how can one kind of trick work better than another? If one placebo is more effective than another, is it still a placebo? To make matters worse, he's deluged with questions by the discredited Koskimo shamans. How does Quesalid extract a bloody object from a patient? What relationship does the "worm" have to the sickness? He's even challenged by one of the shamans to a healing duel, which again Quesalid wins.

Although Quesalid, "rich in secrets," feels that most of his original skepticism is merited, he comes to believe that a kind of real magic is at work, even that shamanism can be fully authentic. "One shaman was seen by me," he writes in his autobiography, "who sucked at a sick man and I never found out whether he was a real shaman or only made up. Only for this reason I believe that he is a shaman; he does not allow those who are made well pay him. I truly never once saw him laugh."[1]

*

The story of Quesalid illustrates what I've been trying to define as philosophy. It begins in wonder, which launches the philosopher on a journey to discover the truth, to find a more satisfying relationship to reality. But rarely, if ever, do the philosopher's initial hypotheses pan out. Yes, Quesalid was right that certain techniques unknown to patients are employed by shamans. The skeptical-destructive side of philosophy goes a long ways. But there's always more to the story. In Quesalid's example, he finds that certain "tricks" really do work on the mind-body complex, and insofar as he seeks the truth, he must accommodate that awkward fact. One of the crucial moments of philosophy is the powerful confrontation with the mystery, which involves wrestling with the demon of doubt, and which eventually induces authentic piety. The final moment of philosophy involves finding how to live in relationship to the illumined mystery. As Kant says, "Skepticism is a resting-place for the human reason . . . but it is no dwelling place for permanent settlement."[2] We can try to puzzle out, as Lévi-Strauss ingeniously does in "The Sorcerer and His Magic," just how shamanism works. But Quesalid, as all true philosophers, must live the inquiry. He must find a style of existence able to navigate the strong currents and occasional storms of reality.

Not only does Quesalid's story handsomely illustrate my thesis about philosophy, it also helps to correct a common misconception about teaching. Our normal, lame view is that teachers possess some special knowledge—or, worse, some special craft of "facilitating learning." Students lack the knowledge, or the necessary learning environment, and teachers obligingly fill their need. Like everything, this view has its grain of truth. But this normal view of education fails miserably to account for all the moments teachers and students care most about: the moments of awakening and mental intimacy, the mutual illuminations, the freedom, the intellectual eroticism, the healing process of education itself, which could be reasonably called shamanistic.

The wicked epigram about teaching—those who can't do, teach—harbors a subversive truth. There's something missing in a good teacher, some ability or knowledge, sometimes unknown to the teacher, something that contact with a student can help to fill. The thing missing isn't what weakens the teacher; mysteriously, it's the source of the teacher's strength. The supreme example is Socrates, whose recognition of his ignorance empowers not just the dialogues but the entire history of Western thought as well. He's a successful midwife of ideas, precisely because of his restlessness in searching for the truth he lacks. But Quesalid's story teaches the same point. Part of what makes him an attractive figure, someone a tribesman might have a dream about, is his questing spirit, his invisible search for something real and true. It's his doubt as much as anything that makes him a powerful shaman.

Another way of getting at the true interior of the educational process is to see it through the lens of gift giving. Marcel Mauss identifies three obligations, which we've all felt, in the circulation of the gift: the obligation to give, the obligation to receive, and the obligation to reciprocate. Even though gifts involve exchange, the attitude of giving isn't immediately self-centered. Moreover, the dynamism of gift giving doesn't come to an end after a gift has been reciprocated. In fact, a gift is potentially infinite, unlike our regular economic exchanges, where as soon as the money changes hands, the purchased thing becomes ours, and whatever dynamism there was in the exchange is dead.

The logic of gift giving describes the true economy of education. The good teachers I've been lucky enough to have gave me an education. Of course, for schools to survive money must change hands and clear space for teaching and learning. As a teacher, I like to think that I teach for free but am paid for grading and attending meetings. Money provides for the possibility of education, but in only the most miserable teachers does money motivate their work. The education I received from my teachers came with the obligation to reciprocate—not to become teachers of my teachers, though one does desire to give back to them somehow, but to give an education to my students. This is the meaning of the word "tradition": a handing down of gifts through time—infinitely. Our word for "now" in its best sense is "the present." The obligation to teach arises in part from a surplus of knowledge. But, as I've suggested, it's much more than that. At least in philosophy, it's also linked to the lack of wisdom. As Kierkegaard puts it, "The disciple is the opportunity for the master to understand himself, as the master is the opportunity for the disciple to understand himself."[3]

*

I believe, as the epigraph to my book states, that "the deepest human life is everywhere." But I certainly don't mean to suggest that everybody is leading an admirable life. My time as a teacher—for that matter, my time with just about everybody—has convinced me of nothing so much as that we're completely confused. There's a legend (I've never actually encountered it in any text) that medieval theologians used to debate about how many angels could dance on a pin. Even if it's historically false, it captures an important truth about a lot of medieval theology: namely, that many of their most intense debates are built on so many highly implausible beliefs that both sides now seem totally absurd. But are our debates so much better that a future age won't look back on them with equal bafflement? Cromwell says (though this, too, is probably apocryphal), "I beseech you in the bowels of Christ, think it possible that you may be mistaken." I beseech you in the cortex of Socrates, think it possible that you may be mistaken. Most of what we still debate about is how many angels are dancing on the head of a pin. No doubt some of our present assumptions are a step in the right direction, particularly when measured against the medieval worldview. But I'd venture that at least a couple of the weird doctrines of medieval theology would be an improvement on our bizarre beliefs.

Despite our vertiginous confusion, I still hold to the idea—which I proudly admit is a little naive, a little Whitmaniacal—that the deepest human life is everywhere. First and foremost, I mean that within all of us are the very depths plumbed—and some still unplumbed—by Plato, Shakespeare, and company. Each human life reflects something important about who we are. Even a profound confusion is a profound confusion. Moreover, I believe that whatever holiness is within our reach can be found in a nursing student as well as in a personage with a glittering name, in a local chiropractor as well as in a world-historical metaphysician, in you and me as well as in Socrates and Confucius. The difference between my student Julia and Immanuel Kant, or my student Kathy and Hans Jonas, or you and any other illustrious or obscure name, pertains to our differing abilities to articulate the shape of a philosophical constellation; it has nothing to do with its inner substance. There's a story about how a band of travelers, looking for some pearls of wisdom, went to see the ancient sage Heraclitus. When they entered his abode, they found him warming his ass by the fire. This hunk of flesh was the great philosopher? Heraclitus just smiled, saying, "Come on in: the gods are here, too."

*

The pursuit of wisdom involves a confrontation with our ignorance, most famously embodied in the "I know I know nothing" of Socrates. But philosophy, as Plato shows, is more than that. It involves confronting the fact that our most stubborn attempts to think clearly come up short, but we nonetheless have to live as if we had answers to the more stubborn mysteries. Philosophy is everything that humanly follows from a real confrontation with our strange predicament. At its best it is a way of life. The division between the wise and the foolish is not between those with all the answers and those who are confused. The great dividing line is between our usual folly and an enlightened folly, by which I mean one that understands itself and has found a way of happily living in an impossible relationship. Philosophy, come to think of it, is a lot like marriage.

Because of something to do with language and something to do with being creatures of time, we'll never be able to answer my students' perennial question—"But what do you believe?"—in the satisfying way we can answer a question like, "How many moons does Saturn have?" There's a story about the Buddha that he took a bunch of autumn leaves in his hand and asked his disciple Ananda if these were the totality of red leaves. Ananda replied, "It's autumn: there are red leaves everywhere." The Buddha then delivered his lesson: "I've given you a few truths. There are thousands more."[4] Perhaps the worst attachment of all is the impatient desire to have the right answer. There's something beautiful about Socrates's "I know I know nothing," and the Buddha with the thousands of red leaves swirling about him. The Christian tradition, in which the search for the perfect dogma has often been central, has given us one of the most profound of all the philosophical traditions, and yet Thomas Aquinas, the master of the theologians, is said to have come down from his vision of God and declared his thousands of learned pages so much straw.

But, as Socrates and the other great ones teach us, we can't do without beliefs. They're a necessary part of being human. It's now a commonplace to think that all religions are equal, just different paths up a common mountain. It's just as much a half-truth as the commonplace it supplants, that only through the one right religion can a soul be saved. As G. K. Chesterton says with his characteristic charm,

> When he drops one doctrine after another in a refined skepticism, when he declines to tie himself to a system, when he says that he has outgrown definitions, when he says that he disbelieves in finality, when, in his own imagination, he sits as God, holding no form of creed but contemplating all, then he is by that very process sinking slowly backwards into the vagueness of the vagrant animals and the unconsciousness of the grass. Trees have no dogmas. Turnips are singularly broad-minded.[5]

Clearly, religions, like political regimes, are different and not equal on any number of scores. Part of transcending the turnip is taking a stand. However, at its best a belief is like a musical motif that organizes a much more complicated symphony. I believe that wisdom is compatible with any number of traditions, religious or otherwise. For wisdom is not so much the possession of right beliefs (though it involves dodging the worst of them) as finding a way to relate to our beliefs in such a way that the good parts of us are liberated. Wisdom isn't a doctrine: it's a style.

*

In his essay "What Makes a Life Significant," William James, one of my heroes as a writer and thinker, narrates a little journey of his own, which begins with a visit to the Assembly Grounds on the borders of Chautauqua Lake in New York. He planned on staying a day, but stayed a week, because the place was a gem of civilization: a town of several thousand inhabitants, in a lovely location, with a "first-class college in full blast," a gorgeous open-air auditorium with a chorus of seven hundred voices, lots of athletics, no crime, no poverty, no police, daily lectures by eminent thinkers, and "perpetually running soda-water fountains."

Strangely, when he left, James found himself thinking, "Ouf! what a relief! Now for something primordial and savage!" He suddenly disdained this community "so refined that ice-cream soda-water is the utmost offering it can make to the brute animal in man," reflecting that danger and courage, sweat and struggle, darkness and even death are what give the human world all its panache. Perhaps the romantics had seen things clearly: our civilization is overrun by the mediocrity of happiness. He sank into philosophical melancholy.

Then, on the train to Buffalo, James spied a laborer working high atop the construction of a skyscraper. In a flash of insight, he realized that he'd been locked in phony ways of seeing the world, thinking in terms of paradise and wasteland, which are paltry abstractions in comparison with a guy on the tiptop of towering scaffolding. In everyday people—day laborers, Viennese peasant women, soda jerks, even professors—he saw a real, unidealized heroism.

And there I rested on that day, with a sense of widening of vision, and with what it is surely fair to call an increase of religious insight into life. In God's eyes, the differences of social position, of intellect, of culture, of cleanliness, of dress, which different men exhibit, and all the other rarities and exceptions on which they so fantastically pin their pride, must be so small as, practically, quite to vanish; and all that should remain is the common fact that here we are, a countless multitude of vessels of life, each of us pent in to peculiar difficulties, with which we must severally struggle by using whatever of fortitude and goodness we can summon up. The exercise of the courage, patience, and kindness, must be the significant portion of the whole business; and the distinctions of position can only be a manner of diversifying the phenomenal surface upon which these underground virtues may manifest their effects. At this rate, the deepest human life is everywhere, is eternal.[6]

ACKNOWLEDGMENTS

Even a man who believes in nothing needs a good woman who believes in him.

Though I've never believed in nothing, I'm lucky enough to have been supported throughout the writing of this book by the irrepressible Helen Neumann, who believes in me, despite all the evidence to the contrary.

Without the generosity, insight, and encouragement of my friend Scott Newstok, these pages would be so much timber falling soundlessly in the *selva oscura*. I can't thank him enough.

It's obligatory to thank one's editor, but I thank mine, Elizabeth Branch Dyson, as heartily as I can. She's a real gem. Not only did she courageously pursue and defend my manuscript, she gracefully made it better.

I'm also deeply indebted to my friends in the Philosophical Breakfast Club—David Depew, Jim Throgmorton, Bob Sessions, and David Bullwinkle—for all their praise and criticisms over sausage, eggs, and coffee—or, if you're Bob, oatmeal. If there are still any mistakes, I put the blame squarely on them at this point.

Moving from morning coffee to late-night booze, I thank Michael Judge and Emiliano Battista; conversations with them over wine and whiskey have been inspirations to me. I also thank Sarah Kyle for an unforgettable insight.

My parents didn't bat an eye when I told them I was going into philosophy. I have to ask them, "What the hell were you thinking?"

I hope that my text itself has served as thanks to my students, with whom I've shared some of my most blessed moments. I wish that I could have included more of their stories. By the way, though I use the real names of some of the students whose stories I tell, I mask the identities of a few of them for various reasons.

Let me lavish a little time on thanking those teachers who gave me "a serious and orderly initiation into an intellectual, imaginative, moral, and emotional inheritance," to use Michael Oakeshott's description of what a real education is.

In my first class at Grinnell College, Professor Mary Lynn Broe, under orders to give us some necessary information about the campus, strode to the podium with her two Irish setters, Deirdre and Maud, and wove a speech about the color of sunsets in Sligo, what Djuna Barnes said to Hemingway, and how much she loved E. E. Cummings's willingness to write unabashedly about death, love, and springtime.

Professor Alan Schrift, my first philosophy instructor, a Nietzschean with the beard of Karl Marx, defended every philosopher he taught with the ferocious eloquence of a high-powered defense attorney. It makes a deep impression on a person to witness Nietzsche with Marx's beard pleading for Plato.

I remember a moment in Professor Johanna Meehan's Ethical Theory when she quoted Alexander Pope in the middle of her lecture on Kant—a simple moment, but the first time the word "civilization" had any real meaning for me.

Professor Ellen Mease read all of James Joyce's *Finnegans Wake* with me, because I asked her to. Anyone who's peered at even one sentence of the *Wake*'s 628 pages (here's one taken at random: "But Noodynaady's actual ingrate tootle is of come into the garner mauve and thy nice are stores of morning and buy me a bunch of iodines") will immediately understand the extent of her commitment to education.

I went to Emory University for graduate school in part because Jean-François Lyotard was there, one of the big shots of contemporary French philosophy. He was surprisingly scholarly and gentle, sometimes assigning us only two pages of Merleau-Ponty a week, which we would then work through in the seminar room word by word. But it turned out that the less famous philosophers at Emory were the ones who really taught me philosophy: Rudolf Makkreel, one of Kant's guardian angels; Ann Hartle, who was at the time completing a profound book on Montaigne with the perfect subtitle *Accidental Philosopher*; Donald Livingston, whose teachings about philosophy and common life, which can be found in his book *Philosophical Mel-*

ancholy and *Delirium*, have left a permanent mark on me; and most of all, Donald Phillip Verene, whose four authors (he believed everyone should be devoted to four authors) were Giambattista Vico, Georg Wilhelm Friedrich Hegel, Ernst Cassirer, and James Joyce.

When Verene found out that I'd read *Finnegans Wake*, he called me into his office—this was our first meeting—and poured me a glass of sherry. Scared to speak with this eminent scholar about an impenetrable book, I immediately qualified my achievement, "Dr. Verene, I can't really say that I've read *Finnegans Wake*. All I can boast is that my eyebeams have touched every word. I'm far from fluent in Joyce's 'jinglish janglage.'" He refilled my glass, which I had downed much too quickly, and told me there was only one way of reading *Finnegans Wake*: *his* way. Many years ago he went to Florence to write his great book *Vico's Science of the Imagination*. He worked on the manuscript every morning. After a large midday meal, he then lounged in the Italian sun and read a page or two of the *Wake* before taking a little nap, a *pisolino*. Only in the consciousness between waking and sleeping does the book make any sense. I should go to Florence, he said, if I was ever going to attempt *Finnegans Wake* again.

We found that we shared things beyond Joyce in common. We both were small-town Midwesterners (he was from Galesburg, Illinois), both were fond of cooking (he was a superb Italian cook, who had studied with Giuliano Bugialli), both loved the blues, and both were guilty of poetry. Though he directed my dissertation, we almost never spoke directly about philosophy. We talked of olives and Ezra Pound, small-town circuses, and Big Mama Thornton. I spent the nights of my prime on Vico, Joyce, and Hegel so we could discuss varieties of prosciutto over chilled glasses of his homemade limoncello. After puffing on a Dominican cigar, he'd say with a naughty twinkle, "God wanting to make the most beautiful thing in the world made the professor. Not to be outdone, the Devil created the colleague." Once, I got up the nerve to ask him if poetry or philosophy was the true expression of human nature. He looked me straight in the eye, "When they burned [the philosopher] Giordano Bruno in the Campo dei Fiori, they so feared his eloquence in the moment of death that they drove an iron spike through his tongue. There's a lovely café there now."

Finally, I'd like to put this book in the hands of Irene Rose and William James, my two kids. This is what your dad does.

RECOMMENDED FURTHER READING

PART 1: WHAT IS PHILOSOPHY?

Recent years have given us several reader-friendly, engaging intro-
ductions to philosophy as a way of life. Though I'd quarrel with most
of them at certain points (or maybe I should say, *Because* I'd quarrel
with most of them at certain points), I recommend Luc Ferry's *A Brief
History of Thought*, James Miller's *Examined Lives*, Sarah Bakewell's
How to Live, William Braxton Irvine's *On Desire*, Alain de Botton's *The
Consolations of Philosophy*, and anything by Leszek Kołakowski . Pierre
Hadot's *What Is Ancient Philosophy?* is a more scholarly account of the
idea of philosophy as a way of life. If you want something very short
and very simple about the basic questions of philosophy, I'd recommend Robert Solomon's *The Little Philosophy Book*. The best way of
finding out about Socrates is to read Plato's dialogues, especially
the four usually titled *The Last Days of Socrates*, though don't delay in
reading the *Symposium* and the *Republic*, too.

PART 2: WHAT IS HAPPINESS?

For further illumination about Epicureanism and Stoicism, I recommend Pierre Hadot again, *Philosophy as a Way of Life*. William Braxton
Irvine's *A Guide to the Good Life: The Ancient Art of Stoic Joy* is an excellent introduction to Stoicism as a modern option; I have drawn on
it in my own account of the Stoics. Stephen Greenblatt's *The Swerve:
How the World Became Modern*, which makes the dubious but charming
case that Epicureanism created modernity, is a splendid exploration
of the history and ideas of Epicureanism, with special emphasis on
Lucretius. As for original Stoic and Epicurean texts, the Axios Institute has a nice volume called *Epicureans and Stoics* that has many key
documents; I've drawn heavily on it. Thoreau's *Walden* is the great
American version of Epicureanism, with some twists.

PART 3: IS KNOWLEDGE OF GOD POSSIBLE?

Al-Ghazali's *Deliverance from Error*, which can be found in a good edition called *Al-Ghazali's Path to Sufism*, is not always easy going, but it's an excellent condensed document, as William James says, for "the purely literary student who would like to become acquainted with the inwardness of religions other than the Christian." Idries Shah's *The Sufis* is a good general introduction to Sufi history and wisdom. Descartes's *Discourse on Method* and *Meditations on First Philosophy*, two of the most well-known works in Western philosophy, are beautiful works of intellectual architecture. But it's Pascal's *Pensées* that really shouldn't be missed: exquisitely written, and always interesting. Idiosyncratically, I like Paul Valéry's essays on Descartes and T. S. Eliot's essay on Pascal. Walker Percy's *Lost in the Cosmos: The Last Self-Help Book* presents a contemporary version of Pascal's ideas; I've drawn on it consciously and unconsciously. The best scholarly work on al-Ghazali that I know of is Frank Griffel's *Al-Ghazali's Philosophical Theology*, where, among other things, he shows that the common Christian view that al-Ghazali destroyed philosophy in Islamic civilization is a straw man.

PART 4: WHAT IS THE NATURE OF GOOD AND EVIL?

Kant's meticulous, dry style is famously difficult. I'd start with some of his essays, particularly "What Is Enlightenment?" and "To Perpetual Peace." I highly recommend Susan Neiman's *Moral Clarity: A Guide for Grown-Up Idealists* as a clearly written, deep, contemporary application of Kantianism. Her scholarly book on Kant is also excellent. I've drawn on Neiman's work throughout this section. While I'm at it, let me also recommend her *Evil and Modern Thought*. Hannah Arendt's *Eichmann in Jerusalem: A Report on the Banality of Evil* is fascinating and philosophically exciting. The collection of essays by Hans Jonas called *Morality and Mortality* is not easy reading but well worth your time.

NOTES

PRELUDE ON LIGHT POLLUTION AND THE STARS

1.   Linda Hess, trans., *The Bijak of Kabir* (New York: Oxford University Press, 2002), 51.
2.   William James, *Writings: 1878–1899* (New York: Library of America, 1992), 867.
3.   Simone Weil, *Gravity and Grace*, trans. Emma Crawford and Mario von der Ruhr (New York: Routledge, 1952), 117.

PART 1: WHAT IS PHILOSOPHY?

1.   Plato, *Theaetetus*, trans. Benjamin Jowett (Fairford, Glouchestershire, UK: Echo Library, 2006), 155d.
2.   Samuel Taylor Coleridge, *Aids to Reflection* (London: Taylor and Hessy, 1825), 228.
3.   Marguerite Yourcenar, *That Mighty Sculptor Time*, trans. Walter Kaiser (New York: Farrar Straus and Giroux, 1992), 203.

CHAPTER 1

1.   Michel de Montaigne, *The Complete Essays of Montaigne*, trans. Donald Frame (Stanford, CA: Stanford University Press, 1965), 337.
2.   Herodotus, *The Histories*, trans. Aubrey de Sélincourt (London: Penguin, 1996), 3.38, p. 187.
3.   *Al-Ghazali's Path to Sufism and His Deliverance from Error*, trans. R. J. McCarthy (Louisville, KY: Fons Vitae, 2000), 19.
4.   Stanley Fish, "Does Philosophy Matter?" *Opinionator* (blog), *New York Times*, August 1, 2011, http://opinionator.blogs.nytimes.com/2011/08/01/does-philosophy-matter/.
5.   Chuang Tzu, *Wandering on the Way: Early Taoist Tales and Parables of Chuang Tzu*, trans. Victor H. Mair (Honolulu: University of Hawaii Press, 1998), 165. I've changed the Wade-Giles system of Romanization to the now more-accepted Pinyin system; thus, Chuang Tzu has become Zhuangzi, and Taoism has become Daoism.

6.   Quoted in Hans-Georg Moeller, *Daoism Explained* (Chicago: Open Court, 2004), 64.

7.   T. S. Eliot, "Little Gidding," in *The Complete Poems and Plays, 1909–1950* (Orlando, FL: Harcourt Brace Jovanovich, 1952), 145.

8.   Montaigne, *Complete Essays*, 611.

9.   Excerpt from "Ithaca" from *The Complete Poems of Cavafy*, trans. Rae Dalven. English translation ©1961, and renewed 1989 by Rae Dalven. Reprinted by permission of Houghton Mifflin Harcourt Publishing Company. All rights reserved.

CHAPTER 2

1.   Cicero, *On the Orator: Book Three*, trans. H. Rackham (Cambridge: Loeb Classical Library, 1942), 16.60.

2.   Montaigne, *Complete Essays*, 851–52.

3.   Cavafy, "Infidelity," in *Complete Poems*, 20.

4.   Bob Dylan, "Gotta Serve Somebody," *Slow Train Coming* (New York: Columbia Records, 1979).

5.   Immanuel Kant, *The Conflict of the Faculties*, trans. Mary Gregor (Lincoln: University of Nebraska Press, 1992), 115.

6.   Simone Weil, quoted in Carol A. Dingle, *Memorable Quotations: Jewish Writers of the Past* (Lincoln: iUniverse, 2003), 108.

7.   Plato, *The Last Days of Socrates*, trans. Hugh Tredennick and Harold Tarrant (London: Penguin, 1993), 15e–16a. Rather than the page numbers of my preferred editions I use the "Stephanus numbers" (e.g., 15e–16a), which are generally used to refer to Plato's works, because most editions of Plato's dialogues include these numbers in the margins of the text. These numbers are based on the pagination of a 1578 edition of Plato edited by Henricus Stephanus.

8.   Suetonius, *The Twelve Caesars*, trans. Robert Graves (London: Penguin Classics, 1957), 238.

9.   Plato, *Last Days of Socrates*, 22b–c.

10. Ibid., 38a.

11. Ibid., 22d.

12. Ibid., 114d.

13. Ibid., 64a.

14. Walt Whitman, "To One Shortly to Die" in *The Complete Poems* (London: Penguin Classics, 2004), 464.

15. Montaigne, *Complete Essays*, 29–30.

16. Plato, *Last Days of Socrates*, 40c–41b.

17. Alasdair MacIntyre, *After Virtue* (Notre Dame, IN: University of Notre Dame Press, 2007), 216.

18. Plato, *Last Days of Socrates*, 29d.

19. Ibid., 59b.

20. Hans Jonas, *Morality and Mortality* (Evanston, IL: Northwestern University Press, 1996), 84.

21. Lucretius, *On the Nature of the Universe*, trans. Ronald E. Latham (New York: Penguin Classics, 1994), 72 (bk. 3, lines 221–22).

22. Philip Larkin, "Aubade," in *Collected Poems* (New York: Farrar Straus and Giroux, 2001).

23. D. H. Lawrence, "Mystic," in *The Complete Poems of D. H. Lawrence*, ed. V. de Sola Pinto and F. W. Roberts, Reissue ed. (New York: Penguin Classics, 1994).

24. Plato, *Last Days of Socrates*, 107b.

25. Alexander Pope, "Essay on Man," in *The Major Works* (Oxford: Oxford University Press, 2008), 303 (lines 173–74).

26. Plato, *Last Days of Socrates*, 114d.

27. Ibid.

28. Ibid., 118a.

29. Quoted in Emily Wilson, *The Death of Socrates* (Cambridge, MA: Harvard University Press, 2007), 149.

INTERLUDE ON LAUGHTER AND TEARS

1. Arthur Schopenhauer, *Suffering, Suicide, and Immortality*, trans. T. Bailey Saunders (Mineola, NY: Dover, 2006), 2.

2. Montaigne, *Complete Essays*, 221.

3. Quoted in Søren Kierkegaard, *Parables of Kierkegaard*, ed. Thomas Oden (Princeton, NJ: Princeton University Press, 1978), 30.

CHAPTER 3

1. W. C. Handy, "Loveless Love," which can be heard on *Louis Armstrong Plays W. C. Handy* (Columbia Records, 1954). Originally the song was the famous "Careless Love," but Handy changed the lyrics as a response to the soul-numbing culture he saw growing up around him.

2. Quoted in *Epicureans and Stoics*, ed. Axios Institute (Mount Jackson, VA: Axios Press, 2008), 4.

3. Ibid., 36.

4. A. J. Liebling, *Between Meals* (New York: Modern Library, 1995), 6.

5. *Epicureans and Stoics*, 26.

6. William Blake, "The Marriage of Heaven and Hell" in *The Complete Poems* (New York: Anchor Books, 1988), 35.

7. *Epicureans and Stoics*, 33.

8. Ibid., 43.

9. Henry David Thoreau, *Walden: A Fully Annotated Edition* (New Haven: Yale University Press, 2004), 89 (chap. 2).

10. *Epicureans and Stoics*, 30.

11. Pierre Hadot, *Philosophy as a Way of Life*, trans. Michael Chase (Oxford: Blackwell, 1995), 235.

12. Carlo Petrini, quoted in Corby Kummer, "Doing Well by Eating Well," *Atlantic Monthly*, March 1999, http://www.theatlantic.com/past/docs/issues/99mar/eatwell.htm.

13. Wendell Berry, *A Continuous Harmony: Essays Cultural and Agricultural* (Washington, DC: Shoemaker and Hoard, 1972), 157.

14. *Epicureans and Stoics*, 20.

15. Ibid.

16. Ibid.

17. Ibid., 43.

18. Johann Wolfgang von Goethe, *Faust*, pt. 2, lines 1700–1701.

CHAPTER 4

1. Alfonso, quoted in Susan Neiman, *Evil in Modern Thought* (Princeton, NJ: Princeton University Press, 2004), 14.

2. Epictetus, *Handbook* 8.

3. Diogenes Laertius, *Lives of the Eminent Philosophers*, trans. R. D. Hicks, Loeb Classical Library (Cambridge, MA: Harvard University Press, 1942), 2:111–13.

4. Shakespeare, *Hamlet*, act 2, sc. 2, lines 250–51; Epictetus, *Handbook* 5.

5. Epictetus, *Handbook* 5.

6. Epictetus, *Handbook* 1.

7. Epictetus, *The Discourses of Epictetus*, trans. Robin Hard (New York: Everyman Paperbacks, 1995), 1.24.20; see also 1.25.7–21 and 2.16.37.

8. Victor Hugo, "Le comte de Buffon fut bonhomme," in *Selected Poems of Victor Hugo*, trans. E. H. Blackmore and A. M. Blackmore (Chicago: University of Chicago Press, 2001), 279.

9. *Epicureans and Stoics*, 51.

10. Epictetus, *Handbook* 14.

11. Seneca, *Dialogues and Letters*, trans. C. D. N. Costa (New York: Penguin, 1997), 58.

12. Marcus Aurelius, *Meditations*, trans. G. M. A. Grube (Indianapolis: Hackett, 1983), 2.1, 11.

13. Seneca, *To Polybius*, 17, quoted in William Braxton Irvine, *A Guide to the Good Life: The Ancient Art of Stoic Joy* (Oxford: Oxford University Press, 2009), 153.

14. Marcus Aurelius, *Meditations*, 7, 54.

15. Epictetus, *Handbook*, 48.

16. Seneca, *Dialogues and Letters*, 54.

17. Seneca, *Moral and Political Essays*, trans. John Cooper (Cambridge: Cambridge University Press, 1995), 3.36, 110.

18. Reinhold Niebuhr, *The Essential Reinhold Niebuhr: Selected Essays and Addresses* (New Haven, CT: Yale University Press, 1987), 251.

19. Epictetus, *Handbook* 52.

20. Aristotle, *Rhetoric* 2.2 1377b31.

21. Edward Gibbon, *The History of the Decline and Fall of the Roman Empire* (London: Penguin 2000), 83.

22. Marcus Aurelius, *Meditations* 7.61 and *Meditations*, 3.4.

23. Epictetus, *The Discourses of Epictetus*, 1:24.1–2.

24. Quoted in James Stockdale, *Courage under Fire: Testing Epictetus's Doctrines in a Laboratory of Human Behavior* (Stanford, CA: Hoover Institution, 1993), 8.

25. Ibid.

26. Ibid., 14.

27. Ibid., 15.

28. Nazim Hikmet, *Poems of Nazim Hikmet*, trans. Randy Blasing and Mutlu Konuk (New York: Persea Books, 1994), 101.

INTERLUDE ON WINE AND BICYCLES

1. Alfred North Whitehead, *Adventures in Ideas* (New York: The Free Press, 1967), 244.

PART 3: IS KNOWLEDGE OF GOD POSSIBLE?

1. Czesław Miłosz, "Either-Or," in New and Collected Poems: 1931–2001 (New York: Ecco, 2001).

CHAPTER 5

1.   Ovid, *Tristia* 5.10.

2.   Marquis Beccaria of Milan, *An Essay on Crimes and Punishments*, with commentary by M. de Voltaire, new corrected ed. (Albany: W. C. Little & Co., 1872), chap. 8.

3.   *Al-Ghazali's Path to Sufism*, 19.

4.   Marquis Beccaria of Milan, *Essay on Crimes and Punishments*, chap. 8.

5.   *Al-Ghazali's Path to Sufism*, 18

6.   Ibid., 20.

7.   Ibid., 23.

8.   Ibid., 24.

9.   Al-Ghazali, *The Ninety-Nine Beautiful Names of God*, trans. David B. Burrell and Nazih Daher (Cambridge: Islamic Texts Society, 1992), 38.

10. *Al-Ghazali's Path to Sufism*, 53.

11. Ibid., 57.

12.   Ted Hughes, *Winter Pollen* (New York: Picador, 1994), 150.

13.   *Al-Ghazali's Path to Sufism*, 57.

14.   John Donne, *Devotions upon Emergent Occasions and Death's Duel* (New York: Vintage, 1999), 119.

15.   Simone Weil, *Waiting for God*, trans. Emma Craufurd (New York: Harper Collins, 1973), 59.

16.   Al-Ghazali, *The Niche of Lights*, trans. David Buchman (Provo, UT: Brigham Young University Press, 1998), 22.

17.   Al-Ghazali, *Niche of Lights*, 18.

18.   John Milton, *Paradise Lost*, bk. 4, line 639; Alfred, Lord Tennyson, *Tithonus*, lines 55–63; William Shakespeare, *Romeo and Juliet*, act 2, sc. 2; Emily Dickinson, "Wild Nights."

19.   *Koran*, 24.35.

20.   T. S. Eliot, "The 'Pensées' of Pascal," in *Selected Essays* (London: Faber and Faber, 1934), 405.

21.   Emily Dickinson, "There's a certain slant of light."

22.   Hugo von Hofmansthal, *The Lord Chandos Letter and Other Writings*, trans. Joel Rotenberg (New York: New York Review Books, 2005), 47.

CHAPTER 6

1.   Jorge Luis Borges, "The Moon," in *Selected Poems*, ed. Alexander Coleman (New York: Penguin Books, 2000), 108.

2.   René Descartes, *The Philosophical Writings of Descartes*, 3 vols. trans. John Cottingham, Robert Stoothoff, Dugland Murdoch, and Anthony Kenney (Cambridge: Cambridge University Press, 1984–91), 2:116. (In the case of the *Meditations*, a widely read text, I've noted the Meditation number after the citation.)

3.   Ibid., 1:119.

4.   Ibid., 1:118.

5.   Ibid., 2:16; meditation 2.

6.   Ibid., 2:17, meditation 2.

7.   Paul Valéry, *Masters and Friends*, trans. M. Turnell (Princeton, NJ: Bollingen, 1968), 31.

8.   Descartes, *Philosophical Writings*, 1:127.

9.   Ibid., 3:309.

10.   Ibid., 2:20, meditation 2.

11.   Ibid., 2:19, meditation 2.

12.   Ibid., 2:28, meditation 3.

13.   Ibid., 3:23.

14.   Ibid., 2:37, meditation 4.

15.   René Descartes, *Principles of Philosophy*, trans. Valentine Rodger Miller and Reese P. Miller (Dordrecht: Kluwer Academic Publishers, 1991), 20.

16.   Descartes, *Philosophical Writings*, 2:56, meditation 6.
17.   Ibid., 3:346–37.
18.   Ibid., 1:113.

CHAPTER 7

1.   C. S. Lewis, *The Discarded Image* (Cambridge: Cambridge University Press, 1994), 98–99.
2.   Blaise Pascal, *Pensées*, trans. A. J. Krailsheimer (London: Penguin, 1966), 66 (201). After the page number, in parentheses, is the standard numbering of Pascal's *Pensées* based on what's called the First Copy; so, if you have a different edition, the quotation should be easily findable—unless your edition isn't numbered—or has the numbers of the Second Copy!
3.   Ibid., 6 (24).
4.   Ibid., 13 (47).
5.   Ibid., 37 (136).
6.   Ibid., 37 (133).
7.   Sir Thomas Browne, *Selected Writings*, ed. Sir Geoffrey Keynes (Chicago: University of Chicago Press, 1968), 153.
8.   Pascal, *Pensées*, 7 (31).
9.   Ibid., 29 (113).
10.   Ibid., 29 (114).
11.   Ibid., 122 (418).
12.   Ibid., 127 (423).
13.   Ibid., 125 (419).
14.   Ibid., 34 (131)
15.   Ibid., 69 (211).
16.   Ibid., 29 (114).

INTERLUDE ON CAMPFIRES AND THE SUN

1.   Quoted in T. S. Eliot, "Lancelot Andrewes," in *Selected Essays* (New York: Houghton Mifflin Harcourt, 1950), 297.

PART 4: WHAT IS THE NATURE OF GOOD AND EVIL?

1.   Isa. 45:7.
2.   Luke 14:26–27.
3.   Job 41:7.
4.   Eccles. 3:20.
5.   Luke 2:19.
6.   Gen. 3:4–5.
7.   Gen. 3:22.

CHAPTER 8

1. Quoted in Susan Neiman, *Moral Clarity* (Orlando, FL: Harcourt Books, 2008), 128.
2. Quoted in ibid., 160.
3. Immanuel Kant, *Grounding for the Metaphysics of Morals*, trans. J. W. Ellington (Indianapolis: Hackett Publishing, 1993), 7.
4. Mark Twain, *The Adventures of Huckleberry Finn*, chap. 31.
5. Kant, *Grounding for the Metaphysics of Morals*, 30.
6. Ibid., 36.
7. Ibid., 38.
8. William James, *Writings: 1878–1899* (New York: Library of America, 1992), 613.
9. Immanuel Kant, *Critique of Practical Reason*, trans. Lewis White Beck (New York: Macmillan, 1956), 166.
10. Immanuel Kant, "Idea for a General History with a Cosmopolitan Purpose," in *Political Writings*, ed. H. S. Reiss and H. B. Nisbet (Cambridge: Cambridge University Press, 1991), 47.
11. Kant, *Grounding for the Metaphysics of Morals*, 20.
12. Ezra Pound, *The ABC of Reading* (New York: New Directions, 1960), 29; William Carlos Williams, "Asphodel, That Greeny Flower."
13. Marguerite Yourcenar, *Memoirs of Hadrian*, trans. Grace Fick (New York: Farrar, Straus and Giroux, 1963), 293.

CHAPTER 9

1. Matt. 5.45.
2. Plato, *The Republic of Plato*, trans. Allan Bloom (New York: Basic Books, 1968), 379c.
3. William Blake, "On Another's Sorrow."
4. Quoted in Leszek Kołakowski, *Is God Happy?* (New York: Basic Books, 2013), 171.
5. Charles Baudelaire, "The Generous Gambler," in *Paris Spleen*, trans. Keith Waldrop (Middletown, CT: Wesleyan University Press, 2009), 60.
6. Aleksandr Solzhenitsyn, *The Gulag Archipelago 1918–1956*, abridged ed., trans. Thomas P. Whitney and Harry Willets (New York: HarperCollins, 2002), 312.
7. Hannah Arendt, *Eichmann in Jerusalem* (New York: Penguin, 2006), 277.
8. Quoted in Neiman, *Evil in Modern Thought*, 336.
9. Ibid., 338.
10. Hans Jonas, *Memoirs*, trans. Krishna Winston (Waltham, MA: Brandeis University Press, 2008), xv.
11. Hans Jonas, *Philosophical Essays* (New York: Atropos Press, 2010), xiii.

12. Hans Jonas, *Mortality and Morality* (Evanston, IL: Northwestern University Press, 1996), 49.
13. Ibid.
14. Hans Jonas, *The Phenomenon of Life* (Evanston, IL: Northwestern University Press, 2001), 283.
15. Ibid., 280.
16. Ibid., 278.
17. Quoted in Jonas, *Morality and Mortality*, 208.
18. Philip J. Ivanhoe and Bryan W. Van Norden, eds., *Readings in Classical Chinese Philosophy* (Indianapolis: Hackett Publishing, 2001), 169. *Daodejing*, chap. 22.
19. Matt. 5:3–6.
20. W. H. Auden, "The Common Life," in *Collected Poems* (New York: Vintage, 1991), 716.

INTERLUDE ON ZOMBIES AND SUPERHEROES

1. This and the other quotations from Simon Zealot can be found at http://www.bottlesofdjinn.com/2010/06/psa-about-phobosophitis.html.
2. Sophocles, *Sophocles I: Antigone, Oedipus the King, Oedipus at Colonus*, trans. David Grene and Richard Lattimore (Chicago: University of Chicago Press, 2013), lines 332–70.
3. Plato, *Last Days of Socrates*, 78a.

CONCLUSION

1. Quoted in Claude Lévi-Strauss, "The Sorcerer and His Magic," in *Structural Anthropology*, trans. Claire Jacobson and Brooke Grundfest Schoepf (New York: Basic Books, 1963), 2:178.
2. Immanuel Kant, *The Critique of Pure Reason*, trans. Norman Kemp Smith (New York: St. Martin's Press, 1965), A761/B789.
3. Quoted in Pierre Hadot, *Philosophy as a Way of Life*, trans. Michael Chase (Malden, MA: Blackwell Publishing, 1995), 154.
4. I first encountered this story in Kenneth Rexroth's poem "The City of the Moon."
5. G. K. Chesterton, *Heretics* (New York: John Lane Company, 1905), 286.
6. William James, *Writings: 1878–1899* (New York: Library of America, 1992), 867.

INDEX